Serialization and Persistent Objects

Jiri Soukup • Petr Macháček

Serialization and Persistent Objects

Turning Data Structures into Efficient Databases

 Springer

Jiri Soukup
Code Farms Inc
Richmond, ON
Canada

Petr Macháček
Image Code
Brloh
Czech Republic

ISBN 978-3-662-50936-4   ISBN 978-3-642-39323-5 (eBook)
DOI 10.1007/978-3-642-39323-5
Springer Heidelberg New York Dordrecht London

Printed on acid-free paper

Springer is part of Springer Science+Business Media (www.springer.com)

Preface

This book takes new directions in several situations where the existing software has reached a dead end and, for this reason, <u>it should be of interest to programmers at all levels of experience</u>.

It does not matter in what language you program, but it will help if you have a basic knowledge of the C++ syntax because most examples are written in C++.

The book covers a wide range of subjects in great depth. It is quite concentrated and could scare a beginner if he/she attempted to read it front to cover. Using this guide, you may start with a few selected chapters, and even if you are an expert who has designed his/her own persistent system, you may return to it many times after the first reading.

The book tackles several major issues:

Issue 1: Persistency

We all have been preconditioned to the notion that, when we want to store data, especially a lot of data, it is best to use a database. In many cases this is not true, and using persistent objects greatly simplifies the code and can improve performance by an order of magnitude.

Note that *serialization* (or *archiving*) is only one of several ways to implement persistent objects, and the book will show you that its existing implementations in various languages have flaws and an unnecessarily complicated interface.

If you are a beginner you should be aware of the opportunities persistent objects provide; you will need them sooner than you think. If you are currently using serialization, this book will be an eye-opener for you. And if you have designed your own persistent data, you may find little tricks that will improve their performance.

We believe that an automatic persistence for Objective-C would greatly simplify the design of iPhone applications, and the book provides a special solution for this purpose.

Issue 2: Bi-directional and Intrusive Data Structures

Data structures and their libraries are closely related to persistence because both revolve around references (or pointers). Well-designed libraries simplify implementation and use of persistence, and, in order to make your data persistent, any library you use must be persistent.

Existing "standard" libraries are a major hindrance to progress in software engineering. They cannot store bi-directional associations such as graph or aggregate; yet about half of the relations in real-live applications are bi-directional. Also, these libraries ignore a multitude of pointer-based (intrusive) data structures developed over the past 2 decades.

The big advantage of intrusive data structures is that they can automatically catch many otherwise hard-to-find errors. They also are natural sets, and they can be sorted just as fast as array-based collections. Libraries of intrusive data structures can even store design patterns.

Issue 3: Pointers (or References) as Members of Application Classes

If you think about it, the only purpose of using references as class members[1] is to create data structures, and it is not good practice for your application to create its own data structures. All data structures should come from a well-tested library. Leaving raw references in your classes is an architectural error that increases code complexity, muddles the architecture, and creates the potential for nasty errors.

In the existing practice, raw pointers are mostly used as implicit one-to-one relations or as a complement to a collection when you need a bi-directional one-to-many relation (Aggregate) not available from the standard libraries.

Reference members may create a hard-to-manage network—a situation similar to the reasons for introducing structured programming[2], where networks of *goto* statements were removed from code as a potential hazard. For the same reason, we recommend that explicit references in the application classes are banned. All references should be managed transparently by class libraries, not by the application.

If we accept this design concept, the implementation of persistence also becomes much cleaner and simpler. Pointer management is now removed from the application and is handled by a library.

---

[1] Variables in Objective-C.

[2] Dijkstra (1976).

Issue 4: Visibility of the Relations

The essential part of the program architecture is the overall data organization or *framework*, which consists of classes and their relations. This is the information provided by the UML class diagram. The problem with the existing programming style and integrated environments is that they focus on classes, while relations are buried and spread through the classes, and are generally hard to find. Understanding a code written by someone else with 20+ classes and 30 relations is a nightmare.

When using our new libraries, you declare all the relations in a short block of statements, one line per relation. The concept is reversed. Instead of classes implementing the relations, relations connect classes, and they have the same visibility as the classes.

This, again, simplifies the implementation and use of persistence. Persistent objects replace a database, and this block of statements that declare relations becomes a database schema. We handle our data structures as if they were a database.

Issue 5: UML Class Diagram Driving the Code

Line by line, the block of statements that declare relations (the database schema) corresponds to the UML class diagram. That could greatly simplify code generators such as Rational Rose which generate a code skeleton implementing the frame-work. With our new style of libraries, all these generators would have to do would be to generate the appropriate block of statements that declare the relations.

However, we believe[3] that the process should be reversed. UML class diagram is a useful visual aid, but it is more practical to drive the architecture by the block of statements from within the code. This completely removes the problems with the synchronization between the diagram and the code, and a high quality UML class diagram can be automatically produced with each compilation.

Richmond, ON, Canada   Jiri Soukup
Brloh, Czech Republic   Petr Macháček

---

[3] This is discussed at length in Soukup (2007).

Suggested Reading Paths
(Based on Reader's Experience)

Level 1: Beginner Able to Use Basic Collections

Start with Chap. 1, but skip Sect. 1.5. Its purpose is to show how difficult it is to use the built-in serializations, and it would be over your head.

Chapters 2 and 3 are the essential parts of this book, so work through them bit-by-bit. It will be a steep learning curve, but it will be worth it. Conceptually, it may move you ahead of many already "experienced" programmers.

Download the examples from the website and play with them as you read. The critical concepts to understand are the pointer masks, how we collect all active objects, the bitmap for memory blasting, persistent pointer class, the QSP algorithm (Sect. 2.5) which is completely new, and the block of statements that declare the data structures like a database schema.

Browse through Chaps. 4 and 5, not dwelling long on parts you don't understand. You will return to these chapters later. Skip Chap. 6 unless you are programming in Objective-C, and even then this chapter is mostly about implementing persistence for Objective-C, not about using it. For an example of how to use the new Objective-C persistence, experiment with the source of the benchmark (under chap6 or iPhone). By the time this book is published there should be more information and documentation on the website, plus a book blog.

You may find Chap. 7 useful for your decision as to what existing software would be most appropriate for your future projects.

Skip Chap. 8, which is beyond your interest and knowledge.

Level 2: Practitioner Already Using Serialization

Start with Chap. 1. Don't attempt to understand all the details in Sect. 1.5. Just note all the work you have to do when using the built-in serialization, and how convoluted some internal formats are.

Chapters 2 and 3 are the essential parts of this book, and you should read them carefully. Many parts are completely new and have not been published before. Download the examples from the website and play with them as you read. The critical concepts to understand are the pointer mask, how we collect all active objects, the bitmap for memory blasting, persistent pointer class, the QSP algorithm (Sect. 2.5), and the block of statements that declare the data structures (the "database schema").

Browse through Chaps. 4 and 5; they provide additional considerations you may not be familiar with. Skip Chap. 6 unless you are programming in Objective-C, and even then this chapter is mostly about implementing persistence for Objective-C, not about using it. For an example of how to use the new Objective-C persistence, experiment with the source of the benchmark (under chap6 or iPhone). By the time this book is published there should be more information and documentation on the website, plus a book blog.

You may find Chap. 7 extremely interesting and useful.

Skip Chap. 8 which is beyond your interest and knowledge.

Level 3: Software Architect

This book is mostly about the implementation of persistence and about the new style of implementing (and using!) class libraries. You may not be interested in technical details, but the book describes many new concepts that relates to your work and thinking.

Start with Chap. 1, and without going into the details in Sect. 1.5, note all the work required for the built-in serialization, and how convoluted some internal formats are.

Chapters 2 and 3 are the essential parts of this book, and you may find them interesting because of the algorithms they describe. Many parts are completely new and have not been published before. The critical concepts are the pointer mask, how to collect all active objects, the bitmap for memory blasting, persistent pointer class, the QSP algorithm (Sect. 2.5), and the block of statements that declare the data structures (the *database schema*).

The new handling of data structures (Chap. 3) leads to a major improvement in the cooperation between architect and coders. By controlling the database schema, the architect controls the architecture. The coders cannot deviate from it, but the database schema becomes the key communication tool between the two parties.

Chapters 4 and 5 provide additional details you should consider. Unless you are programming in Objective-C, skip Chap. 6, but even when you use Objective-C, this chapter is more about implementing persistence than about using it. However, Sect. 6.4 is about the importance of NS classes and difficulties with their conversion and it may be of interest to you.

You may find the performance benchmarks of different persistent systems in Chap. 7 most interesting and useful.

Browse quickly through Chap. 8 just to acquaint yourself with this proposal.

Please join the book blog, especially if you have any comments to make about Chap. 9.

Level 4: Expert or Someone Building Class Libraries or Persistent Systems

Read the book from front to back, paying special attention to all *Useful Tricks* and Chaps. 2 and 3. Chapters 4 and 5 provide additional details. Chapter 6 is important if you are using Objective-C, otherwise you can skip it. Chapter 7 has a wealth of information about the performance of different styles of implementing persistence. Chapter 8 is important for designers of class libraries and compilers.

Please join the book blog, especially if you have any comments to make about Chap. 9.

Book Website

The book website is at **http://www.codefarms.com/book**, with a blog and other information. It also allows you to download a zip file with source of all the Listings that are longer than just a few lines—usually expanded so that you can compile and run them. We highly recommend that you play with these programs and modify and evolve them. Besides these programs, which are usually in a single file such as List2_3.cpp, multi-file examples are stored as subdirectories that may even include tt.bat which compiles them, and rr.bat which runs them. All this is organized by chapter, as you would expect.

When you extract this zip file, you get directory **bk** with all the examples organized by chapter. When we refer to directory bk anywhere in the text, for example recommending you to look at bk\chap1\javaSerialization\readme.txt, we refer to this directory.

The website also provides access to Code Farms libraries: DOL, PTL, PPF, InCode, ObjcLib, Layout. They are open source subject to a simple, no-nonsense license which allows commercial use.

Acknowledgements

This book is the result of a truly international cooperation. Authors Jiri Soukup and Petr Macháček are from Canada and the Czech Republic, respectively. The publisher is a global corporation, but the editor Ralf Gerstner works from Germany. James Noble, David Pearce, and Steve Nelson—all from New Zealand—helped us with J-Aspects, while Olaf Spinczyk from Norway wrote the C++ Aspect example. The help with Objective-C came from Sean Yixiang Lu[4] in Singapore, and Raj Lokanath from California became a co-author of two chapters. Cay Horstmann from California helped us with advanced features of both Java and C++, including the format of Java serialization. We owe a lot to our pre-release expert reviewers Mark Bales (California) and Naresh Bhatia (Massachusetts), and to our contact in ObjectStore (Don White, Massachusetts). The author of the BOOST persistence, Richard Ramey from California, helped us with the BOOST implementation of the benchmark.

Most of all, we want to thank our wives Hana and Vera, both engineers and programmers like us, for their support and patience. This project took much more time than we anticipated.

---

[4] Who in the meantime relocated to Seattle.

Contents

Introduction

1

Abstract

We start with the definition of persistent objects and, as an example, we show how they relate to data structures, class libraries, allocation and UML class diagrams. Everything revolves around pointers or references, depending on which language you use. After this, we discuss the flaws of serializations built into different languages.

Keywords

Persistent systems • Serialization format • Archiving format • C++ • Java • C# • Objective-C • Definitions • Persistent objects • Persistent data structures • UML generation • Pointerless programming • Pointers • References • Intrusive data structures • Persistent pointers • Built-in persistence • Smalltalk • Formatter • Serialize • BOOST serialization •

1.1 Starting with an Example

If you are reading this book, you must be a programmer. And there is no better way to tell a programmer what this book is about than to show an example.

This may be hard for you but, for a while, forget everything you know about class libraries, serialization, databases, SQL and UML, and imagine that you want to design software that would keep records of books in a library. It doesn't matter whether this is a home collection of your personal favourites or a public library with many thousands of books—with possible searches and records of customers and loans this could quickly turn into a major project.

J. Soukup and P. Macháček, *Serialization and Persistent Objects*, DOI 10.1007/978-3-642-39323-5_1, © Springer-Verlag Berlin Heidelberg 2014

You could start with the core of this problem and code classes Library, Book, Author and Publisher with the basic data that should be stored, but without any pointers or data structures, not even any attached strings. Something like this:

```
class Library {
    Persist(Library);
    int bookCount;
};
class Book {
    Persist(Book);
    int location; // rack, shelf, index
    int year;
};
class Author {
    Persist(Author);
};
class Publisher {
    Persist(Publisher);
    int bookCount;
};
```

Then, in a separate block of statements or in a special file, you would declare what data structures (associations) connect these classes. For example:

```
Association Hash<Library,Book> books;
Association Hash<Library,Author> authors;
Association LinkedList<Library,Publisher> publishers;
Association ManyToMany<Book,WrittenBy,Author> writtenBy;
Association SingleLink<Book,Publisher> publisher;
Association String<Book> title;
Association String<Author> authorName;
Association String<Publisher> publisherName;
```

ManyToMany requires one additional class for the relation, so you would add

```
class WrittenBy {
    Persist(WrittenBy);
};
```

SingleLink<Book,Publisher> is essentially a pointer from Book to Publisher.[1] Everything involving pointers is treated as a data organization.

---

[1] Transparently implemented as a member of class Book: Publisher *publisher.

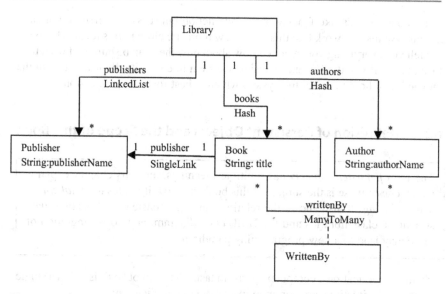

Fig. 1.1 With each compilation you would get an updated UML class diagram as an auxiliary diagram to guide you in debugging and evolving your program

This would automatically connect everything together and, after you add main(), you would have a program which would already compile and run:

```
int main(){
    Book *bk; Author *auth; Library *lib; WrittenBy *wb;
    ...
    bk=new Book(); // create new Book
    books.add(lib,bk); // add Book bk to Library lib²
    wb=new WrittenBy; // relational object needed for ManyToMany
    writtenBy.add(bk,wb,auth); // connect bk with Author auth
    ...
    auth=authors.next(auth); // move auth to the next author
    publisher.remove(bk); // remove link from bk to its publisher
    ...
    Persist::save(lib,"myfile"); // for root lib, save in "myfile"
    return 0;
}
```

At the end of the run, the call to Persist::save() would simply save all the data to disk, and if you called Persist::open() at the beginning of the next run, you would start running with the same data back in memory—no serialization, no SQL and no confusion about the data structures spread through the classes. The resulting program would also be as fast as you can possible achieve in a careful, hand-crafted design.

To top it all, each time you compile it you will automatically get a UML class diagram as shown in Fig. 1.1.

---

²On the 4th line of main(), note the different order of the parameters compared to the usual containers where you would have lib->books.add(bk); Reflecting the importance of the data structures which we place at the same visibility level as classes, our notation starts with the ID of the data structure.

This may sounds like fantasy or science fiction but it is not. There are already several systems that work like this, and a few more are close to this ideal. This book will tell you everything you need to know about how they can be built and what they do, and even if you don't want to design a system like this, it will arm you with the knowledge of how to select the system which is best for your application.

1.2   Definition of Persistent Objects and the Scope of this Book

The term *persistent objects* has multiple meanings, and this chapter explains which one of these is the subject of this book and how it relates to *serialization* and *archiving*. It also shows the relations among persistence, allocation, data structures, class libraries and the UML class diagram, and how integration of these may lead to a new programming paradigm.

In many applications, computers perform tasks that cannot be finished in a single session. Such situations are common in any type of application:

- We are typing this book using a text editor, and every so often we click on 'save'. Then, after a few hours, we save the result, exit and continue the next day.
- Any design which requires more than one session to complete is done in this way—think about designing an automobile or electronic circuit with millions of transistors.
- When biochemists analyze a sample of protein, be it fish liver or beer, a typical mass spectrometer gives them 2 GB of data. The software which crunches this data first eliminates noise, then calculates the spectrum of the substance, compares it with a library of known protein spectra and stores the results in a way that will allow additional evaluation later.
- Imagine a business system which collects news from the 12 major stock exchanges around the globe via high speed communication links. It runs continuously and builds sophisticated data structures that support fast queries 24 hours a day. The data collected over the past few days live in the virtual memory but are periodically saved to disk while the system is running.

You can find countless applications that save not only objects such as automobile parts with their dimensions and costs, but also the relations between them: their subparts (bolts, braces, gaskets and springs that form the given part), manufacturer, and compatibility with other car models.

In many applications, the performance of the data storage is critical.

- When editing text, you don't want to wait 2 min every time you hit 'save', and if the resulting file is too big you may have problems getting it sent through email.
- If you are not careful about the speed, traversing a VLSI design or even just displaying the chip layout on the screen may take minutes, even hours.
- The mass spectrometer produces new data every 3 min, and the data must be processed and stored before the next sample arrives.
- Most smartphone applications must be designed economically with high performance in mind.

- The conversion and transfer of data between the internal data structures and the database may require a significant amount of code and runtime—to the point where, in some applications such as in electronic CAD, using the traditional database is not acceptable.
- The additional code implies longer development time and more expensive maintenance.

It would be ideal if we had some magic which, in a single command, would move all the objects and data structures to the disk, and then again, in a single command, would load it all back to memory. Such magic could be considered to be the persistent objects which are the subject of this book.

Replacing a database by persistent objects is a good idea even on many small projects where performance is not important, simply because persistent objects are much simpler to use. This of course does not completely eliminate the use of the traditional databases, which are useful in situations where many users access the data simultaneously, or where the security of both access and storage is important.

If you Google 'what is persistent object' (or persistent data or persistent data structures), you get a variety of conflicting answers such as:

(A) *Persistent data denotes information that is infrequently accessed and not likely to be modified. The opposite of this is dynamic data (also known as transactional data) where information is asynchronously changed as further updates to the information become available.*

(B) *Persistent data exists from session to session. Persistent data are stored in a database on disk or tape.*

(C) *Persistent data structure is a data structure which always preserves the previous version of itself when it is modified; ... is not a data structure committed to persistent storage, such as a disk ...*

(D) *Object persistence and Java: Object durability, or persistence, is the term you often hear used in conjunction with the issue of storing objects in databases. Persistence is expected to operate with transactional integrity, and as such it is subject to strict conditions.*

Definition: PERSISTENT OBJECTS

Throughout this book, we define **persistent objects** as objects which, during the program run, work as if there was no persistency, but between program runs they are stored on disk. Their prime location can be in virtual memory or on disk, but their movement between these two locations is transparent and it does not involve a database. We also assume that this persistency is **automatic** in that the user does not have to write serialization/deserializaiton functions for every class.

Persistent data is synonymous with persistent objects, especially in computer languages which are not object oriented like C.

Persistent data structures are data structures which persist between program runs. They are synonymous with persistent objects.

Serialization is one of several possible approaches to implementing objects which are persistent but not fully automatic.

Writing serialization and deserialization functions for every class is tedious and error prone, especially for large projects and in changing environments, which is the reason why we eliminate this type of persistence from our consideration.[3]
Persistent objects discussed in this text are intended for massive use, and thus the main objectives are:
1. Performance (high speed and small data footprint)
2. Easy and elegant to use
3. Automatic and transparent to the user
If the computer language does not support features required for these objectives, we will not hesitate to use any dirty technique such as macros or code generators to achieve these objectives.

You don't have to be an expert programmer to appreciate this book. If you have a basic knowledge of C++, Java or Objective-C you will enjoy numerous algorithms and programming tricks that help to implement persistent objects. If you don't plan to implement your own persistent objects, this book will arm you with the knowledge of how it all works and why persistent objects are often better than a database.

This book also invites you to take part in an intellectual adventure. You will be exploring not only persistent objects but also how to build data-structure libraries which are far more general than the existing standard libraries. You will be writing your own allocation schemes, code generators and overloading operators. You will discover a new rapid yet reliable and high-performing software design style. Your data structures will automatically become a database, but you will manage them as a database and with every compilation your program you will generate its UML class diagram.

Wait a minute, you may say. Why are we going to talk about allocation, data structures and UML? Isn't this a book about Persistent Objects?!

Traditionally these four areas (persistence, data structures, allocation and UML) are considered orthogonal—in the sense that each of them can be (and should be) designed as an independent module.

In reality these areas are NOT independent. They have a common culprit—the pointers or references[4] connecting related objects. In persistence everything revolves around pointers because they change between the program runs. The values of the pointers depend on the allocation of the objects; the data structures are built with pointers and UML works with relations implemented with data structures. Thinking at the UML level, the sole purpose of pointers is to build relations, and therefore application classes should have no visible pointer/reference members. Only the data structures stored in a library should use pointers which are transparent to the application.

The key task of any persistent system is to find all the pointers—where they are and what their values are. This information is available inside the compiler which also controls how the objects will be allocated. One has to wonder: Why isn't the

---

[3] We had an opportunity to review a recognized business management system with a million lines of C++ code, which was impossible to maintain. Serialization and deserialization functions represented one-third of the entire code.

[4] Depending on which language you use.

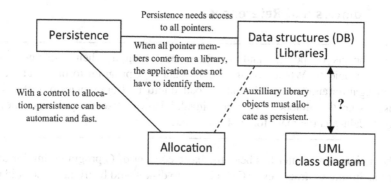

Fig. 1.2 Persistence, class libraries and allocation are generally considered to be independent (orthogonal) parts of software design. However, their cooperation can create a powerful design environment. We also question whether it is better to drive the architecture with the UML class diagram or to derive it from the code, thus demoting the UML class diagram to a passive visual aid

persistence a part of C++ language—it could be completely transparent and simple to implement? Why Objective-C uses Archiving with the cumbersome serialization functions that the user must provide? Why serializations in Java, C#, and Objective-C cannot handle long chains of objects as we will be discussed in this book?

Existing class libraries are mostly array-based and not pointer-list-based. They cannot support bi-directional associations and do not cover many useful pointer-based data structures. They were designed without any plan for persistence,[5] and converting them now would be a major programming task.[6]

This book will eventually lead you to Pointerless Programming[7]—see Fig. 1.2.[8]

Pointerless Programming (Integrated Approach as Described in This Book)
- Uses persistent objects instead of a database.
- Removes pointers/references from application classes.
- Manages data structures as if they were a database.
- With every compilation, creates the UML class diagram.
- Includes structural patterns in data structure libraries.

---

[5] Accepting STL as a standard without making a provision for persistency was a mistake. In 1993, persistency was a known concept, and early versions of Code Farms DOL library and of what is now called ObjectStore © PSE Pro for C++ were commercially available.

[6] When working on Chap. 7 we explored the possibility of making the Objective-C Foundation classes persistent. For a person not familiar with the library it would be an extremely difficult task. It is a big and complex library, pointers are often disguised through *typedef,* and all allocation calls should be located, analyzed and possibly replaced.

[7] This applies even to Java which claims to be "pointerless" but really isn't, because its references are only more intelligent pointers. In Java, this means no references are explicitly used as members of application classes.

[8] This may be considered a heresy, but this book takes a non-orthodox view on many subjects.

1.3   Pointers and References

> The concepts of pointer and reference are essential when implementing
> persistent objects. When storing internal data of a program to disk and then
> restoring it for another run, the data is loaded into a different place of memory,
> thus making all pointers or references invalid. How to reset the pointers to new
> correct values is the main topic of this book.

The notion of a pointer has been the basic concept of C programming for over
30 years. Storing C structures or C++ objects to disk would be trivial if they did not
include any pointers.

A pointer stores the address of some object in the virtual memory. A reference
not only stores the object address but also maintains, on the target object, a counter
of how many references point to it. When the counter on some object decreases to
0, it means that no reference leads to this object. In other words, the program does
not know about this object any more, and it can be destroyed.

This feature, which is often hailed as a great advantage of Java, can easily be
added to C++ as a smart pointer class, Reference<T>, which assumes that all
classes are derived from class RefCount<T>. Listing 1.2 shows the idea,[9] including
how to overload operators -> and =, which is something we will need later in
different situations. A similar class has been used by the Data Object Library[10]
since the mid-1990s.

Listing 1.1 Comparing pointers and references

```
// C++                          // JAVA
// next and ap are pointers     // has only references,
// a is an instance of A        // even a comes from heap

class A {                       class A {
    A *next;                        A next;
};                              }
int main() {                    int main() {
    A *ap, a;                       A ap, as; // a not allowed
    ap=new A;                       ap=new A;
    a.next=ap;                      as=new A;
    ap->next= &a; // footnote (1)   ap.next=as;
    ...                             ...
}                               }
```

---

[9] As with most listings in the book, the full source is available under directory bk, in this case as
bk/chap1/list1_2.cpp.

[10] http://www.codefarms.com/dolclasses

Listing 1.2 Generic Reference class in C++

```
template<class T> class Reference {
    T *ptr;
    void updCount (T* p1, T *p2) {
        if (p1==p2) return;
        if (p2) (p2->count) ++;
        if (p1) {
            (p1->count) --;
            if (p1->count==0) delete p1;
        }
    }
public:
    Reference () {ptr=NULL; }
    Reference& operator= (const Reference& rhs) {
            updCount (ptr,rhs.ptr); ptr=rhs.ptr; return *this; }
    Reference& operator= (T *rhs) {
            updCount (ptr,rhs); ptr=rhs; return *this; }
    T* operator-> () {return ptr; }
};

template<class T> class RefCount {
friend class Reference<T>;
    int count;
public:
    RefCount () {count=0; }
};

// Application program
class Car : public RefCount<Car> {
public:
    int seatNum;
    void prt () {...}
};

int main () {
    Reference<Car> ref1,ref2; //instead of: Car *ref1,*rf2;
    ref1=new Car;
    ref2=new Car;
    ref2->seatNum=4;
    ref1=ref2; // first Car automatically destructed
    ref2=NULL; // count for the second Car reduced to 1
    ref1->prt ();
    return (0); // when going out of scope, second Car is destructed
}
```

Figure 1.3 shows the memory representation of two objects such as car instances from Listing 1.2. They are not allocated right next to each other. The allocator keeps several values—usually 16 or 12 bytes—for each object. One of these values is usually the size of the object. In languages like Java or Objective-C this space also includes the reference counter. When using our Reference<T> template, the counter is inside the object. It seems like a minor difference but it makes a difference when allocating primitive objects such as text strings, which normally would not be derived from any base class.

Regardless of whether pointers or references are used, the fact that they store addresses is a major obstacle in making objects persistent. In each program run, objects are loaded into different memory locations, making the original pointers invalid. How to convert (or *swizzle*) these pointers is the main topic of Chap. 2.

Reference<T>:

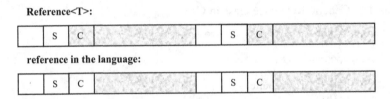

reference in the language:

Fig. 1.3 Comparing memory representation of objects when using Reference<T> with objects in languages with built-in reference counting. White space is managed by the allocator, C is the reference counter and S stores the size of the object

Note that only pointers used as class *members* (in C++ jargon) or references used as class *fields* (in Java jargon) need such a conversion—not the temporary pointers declared in your methods.[11] For example, in class A from Listing 1.1, `ptr` must be converted for every A object (every instance of class A), but `ap` from main() there does not require any conversion.

Another interesting fact is that we have all been taught—and are accustomed—to the notion that chains of objects should end with a NULL pointer:

```
for(p=start; p; p=p->next){...}
```

It may come as a shock that using a ring is much better.[12] The functionality is the same, but the ring allows a simple integrity check which prevents nasty runtime errors against which even Java is not protected. When using a ring, a NULL pointer may flag a disconnected object, while a pointer which is not NULL indicates that the object is already connected in some chain. Figure 1.4 shows what may happen with NULL-ending chains.

Example: Ring of Books, with method append() which prevents the corruption

```
class Book {
  Book *next;
public:
  Book(){next=NULL;}:w
};
class Ring {
  // append b2 after b1 in the ring of Books
  // returns the new tail
  static Book* append(Book *tail,Book *b1,Book *b2){
    if(b2->next){
      printf("cannot append Book which is already in a ring\n");
      return tail;
    }
    b2->next=b1->next;
    b1->next=b2;
    if(b1==tail)tail=b2;
    return tail;
  }
}
```

---

[11] In other words, only pointers from the heap must be converted, not pointers from the stack.

[12] Since the mid-1980s, Mikael Palczewski convinced Jiri about this (he had a hard time), Jiri is using rings and not NULL-ending lists.

Two NULL- ending chains:

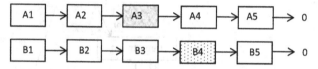

If you insert A3 after B3 without first disconnecting it from chain A, chains are mixed up, and Java destroys A4and A5:

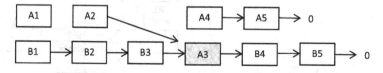

When you insert B4 after B1 without disconnecting it first, B5 is lost and an attempt to traverse the chain ends in an infinite loop.

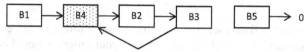

Rings never use NULL pointers:

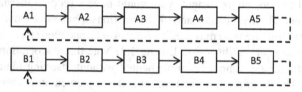

Fig. 1.4 Rings are better than NULL-ending chains, both in C++ and in Java. When using a ring (*dashed arrow*), method `append()` can check for `next!=NULL` and avert the disaster—see example

1.4 Persistent Objects as a Light-Weight Database

> Instead of connecting your program to an external database, it is often more practical to make your data structures (or framework) persistent and use them as a fast internal database.

Let us assume that you are designing software which will keep a record of university departments, lecturers, the courses they give, and the students who enrol in those courses. You may start with an UML class diagram such as shown in Fig. 1.5, where symbols on connecting lines express multiplicity (* means *many*) and directionality. Lines without arrows represent bi-directional associations.

Fig. 1.5 UML class diagram
for the Faculty problem

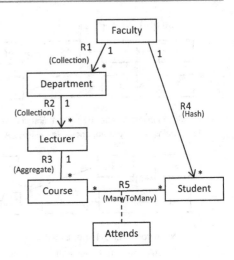

If you decide to use a database, this diagram would allow you to generate, automatically or manually, the database schema, and your program would consist mostly of the user interface and the database interface. However, if you had a utility that would make all the objects persistent, you would have a second alternative. You could implement all the objects and their relations (=associations) as a memory resident data structure (you may call it a *framework*), and then store/restore it from disk by this magical[13] utility—see Listing 1.3. Note that Associations R3 and R5 are bi-directional and cannot be implemented without inserting members into several classes. The description in the bracket is the implementation choice.[14]

---

[13] You will have to wait until Chap. 2 to see how this really works.

[14] This is only a hypothetical implementation. The listing is on the website, but it would not run without converting it to a specific collection library.

Because the collection library does not have bi-directional associations, adding Course crs to Lecturer lect requires two steps:

```
courses.add(lect,crs);
crs->taughtBy=lect;
```

Leaving them like that would be error prone; they should be encapsulated under a single function which we may call addCourseToLecturer(), but where would you place it and other similar functions? It would spread the association to even more places.

Listing 1.3 Implementing Faculty framework with collections

```
class Faculty {
     Collection<Department> depts; // R1
     HashTable<Student> students;  // R4
};
class Department {
     Collection<Lecturer> lecturers; // R2
};
class Lecturer {
     Collection<Course> courses; // R3
};
class Course {
     Lecturer *taughtBy; // R3
     Collection<Attends> atts; // R5
};
class Student {
     Collection<Attends> atts; // R5
};
class Attends {
     Course *toCourse;    // R5
     Student *toStudent; // R5
     int mark;
     int attendance;
};

int main(int argc, char *v[]) { // call with c to create, with o to open
     Faculty *f;
     if(argv[1][0]=='c'){
          f=new Faculty;
          d=new Department;
          f->depts.add(d);
          .. generate initial data
     }

     if(argv[1][0]=='o'){
          f=utility.open("facultyFile");
     }
     .. add, remove, modify data

     utility.save("facultyFile",f);
     return 0;
}
```

Instead of spreading the data structures through the individual classes as we did in Listing 1.3, it would be much nicer to code the same problem as shown in Listing 1.4, which assumes that all the required data structures are available from a library which is, however, different from the container libraries used today. Chapter 3 will show how such new libraries can be built.

In Listing 1.4, relations (data structures) have the same importance and visibility as classes; we say they are *first class entities*. The block of DataStructure statements is equivalent to the database schema, but is used to declare data

structures. <u>Note that all pointers have disappeared from the application classes; they</u>
<u>are transparently managed by the library.</u>

The only difference between Fig. 1.5 and Listing 1.4 is that the listing uses the specific implementation. The notion of general association is lost. This can be corrected in two ways:

(a) Data structures that implement the same association may know each other, and allow an easy exchange when required.

(b) In addition to the individual data structures, the library may have a general association which automatically uses one of the implementations as a default.

Listing 1.4 Hypothetical (ideal) implementation of the Faculty problem, with relations defined separately and given meaningful names: R1=depts, R2=lecturers, R3=courses, R4=students, R5=atts

```
class Faculty {
};
class Department {
};
class Lecturer {
};
class Course {
};
class Student {
};
class Attends {
      int mark, attendance;
};

// Definition of data structures = database schema
DataStructure Collection<Faculty,Department> depts;
DataStructure Collection<Department,Lecturer> lecturers;
DataStructure Aggregate<Lecturer,Course> courses;
DataStructure Hash<Faculty,Student> students;
DataStructure ManyToMany<Course,Attends,Student> atts;

int main(int argc,char *v[])
      ... // same as in Listing 1.2
}
```

<u>Existing standard libraries,</u>[15] <u>both in all the C languages and in Java, conceptually</u>
<u>cannot support important data structures such as *Aggregate, ManyToMany, Graphs,*</u>
<u>*or the Finite State Machine*</u>. They support only uni-directional Collections, Vectors, Trees and Lists, and cannot represent data structures which require adding members (usually pointers) to more than one class. They cannot support bi-directional relationships, and they do not treat relations as first class entities.

---

[15] Boost library is an extension of the STL library, and will soon become the C++ standard. It supports graphs and has tuplets which are the heart of many-to-many associations, but the interface is less elegant and less user friendly than the intrusive implementation; there is also a performance hit both in speed and required space. This will be discussed in Chap. 3.

Fig. 1.6 Comparing implementation of the standard *Collection* and *List* with *Intrusive List*. D stands for Department, L for Lecturer. *Collection* uses an array of pointers, *List* uses auxiliary link objects and *Intrusive List* links directly the Lecturers

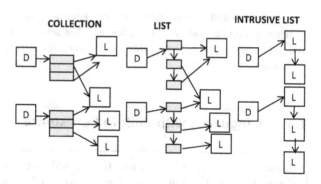

If you attempt to implement the Faculty problem (Fig. 1.5) with existing standard libraries, you will run into the following problems:

(a) Standard collections allow the same object to be several times in the same collection, and implementing a *set* with these collections is costly. On the other hand, intrusive list which is a natural *set* is not supported—see Fig. 1.6.

(b) Aggregate is bi-directional, thus not supported by standard libraries.

(c) Bi-directional ManyToMany is not supported by standard libraries.

We will discuss this in more detail in Chap. 3.

The requirement of inserting members into multiple classes resembles Aspects (Laddad 2003) which will be briefly discussed in Sect. 4.5.

There is yet another, completely different approach to managing pointers. Instead of allocating objects in virtual memory, we can allocate them on disk. Then, when the program needs to access the data, the sections of disk are paged to virtual memory, and pointers are swizzled any time they are dereferenced (invoked). In order to make this smooth and transparent, all pointers in the applications code must be replaced by a *smart pointer* which does all of this automatically. This approach is used by the Persistent Pointer Factory (PPF) and is described in Sect. 2.4.

Listing 1.5 Replacing pointers with a PersistPtr<T>. All pointer declarations must change, but operator -> is overloaded

```
// original code                      // using persistent pointers
class Book {                          class Book {
public:                               public:
    int ISBN;                             int ISBN;
};                                    };
class Author {                        class Author {
  Book *book;                             PersistPtr<Book> book;
  void prtISBN(){                         void prtISBN(){
    printf("%d",book->ISBN);                printf("%d",book->ISBN);
  }                                       }
};                                    };
```

Swizzling pointers whenever accessing them may seem like a major performance overhead, but the benchmark results in Chap. 8 show it is not significant, as long as we set up the parameters of the paging in such a way that all the active pages remain in memory simultaneously. The method also has several advantages including unlimited data space and good performance when accessing small subsets of data (transactions).

1.5   Languages with Built-In Persistence

Before discussing persistence which we could add to existing languages, we should look at the built-in serialization some of them provide. We do not recommend any of these solutions, but you have to see the complexity of their user interface and of their file format in order to appreciate what's coming in Chap. 2.

In this chapter we will look at how to use the built-in persistence in some languages, and what format they use to store the objects. The purpose is not to teach you how to use these different implementations of serialization. We only want you to get a gut feeling for how easy/difficult they are to use, and what representation (format) they use for disk storage.

We will not discuss individual internal implementations because they are proprietary and are continuously changing. Nevertheless, from the disk record and overall behaviour we can sometimes deduce what they are likely to hide under the hood.

Regarding the format of the disk storage, again, we do not expect you to analyze or understand all the gory details. Just look for the overall concept and how verbose these files can be.

1.5.1   Persistence in Early Smalltalk

In an early version of Smalltalk it took a relatively long time to start or close a program, but when you re-started it you were exactly at the point where you stopped before. The internal data (its heap) was automatically persistent. However, at odd, unexpected moments, the program would pause for a long time, sometimes for minutes,[16] before continuing to run. From this behaviour, one could guess what was happening inside:

---

[16] In those days computers were much slower than today.

Fig. 1.7 Example of
converting references in early
Smalltalk

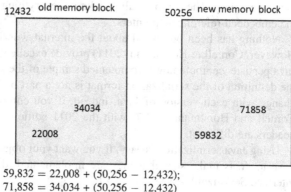

$$59,832 = 22,008 + (50,256 - 12,432);$$
$$71,858 = 34,034 + (50,256 - 12,432)$$

Smalltalk reserved a block of memory for the heap, and then allocated all objects from it. When you allocated more objects than the size of the block, Smalltalk paused the application, allocated a bigger block and copied the old block into this new heap.

We don't know whether, internally, references stored offsets within the heap and not the addresses as pointers usually do. If it stored offsets, then swizzling of references was not required, and the pause was caused just by copying a large block of virtual memory.

If the references stored addresses, it would work as follows. On exit, the raw image of the heap was copied to disk. On re-entry, the heap was read to memory and references swizzled. When the block was not large enough and the program increased the heap, references were also swizzled. Swizzling references was simple because Smalltalk knew where they were, and they had to be swizzled by the same increment—see Fig. 1.7.

1.5.2 Java Serialization[17]

It was a wise decision to add serialization to Java language. Java is much more protected (and thus more restricted) than C++. As you will see later, many programming features and tricks that help us to implement persistent objects in C++ do not work in Java. Without providing its own serialization, Java would be significantly disadvantaged. Also, as we said earlier, adding persistence directly to the

---

[17] With the permission of the authors, most of this chapter is based on examples from Cornell & Horstmann (2011), pp 39–51.

language is easy. The compiler already knows everything about classes, objects and the embedded references (pointers).

Nothing has been published about the internal workings of Java serialization. However, Cornell & Horstmann (2011) provide excellent instruction on how to use Java persistence, including a commented sample of the serialization file. Note that the definition of the serialization format is not a part of Java language, and it may change with each version of Java. Indeed, if you compare the second edition of Cornell and Horstmann (1997) with the 2011 edition, all the internal codes and headers are different.

Using Java serialization is easy. If you want your objects to be persistent, all you have to do is make sure that they are implemented, directly or indirectly, with interface Serializable—see Listing 1.6.

Listing 1.6 Example of making classes persistent

```
class Employee implements Serializable {
     private String name;
     private double salary;
     private Date birthday;
}
class Manager extends Employee {
     private Employee secretary; // reference
     public Employee getSecretary(){return secretary;}
     public void setSecretary(Employee e){secretary = e;}
}
```

References, such as member *secretary*, form a graph connecting objects. When you invoke serialization on an object, it saves not only the object itself but, recursively, also all the objects it can reach via references.

Real-life problems usually have one object that represents the entire problem—we call it *root object*, from which all other objects can be reached. Listing 1.7 shows a simple problem of two managers, Carl and Tony, who share the same secretary, Harry. In this case, there isn't a single root; you have to give Java the two managers in order to reach all objects.

Listing 1.7 Example storing the data space reachable from the root objects[18] (for full running example, see bk\chap1\javaSerialization\readme.txt)

```
import java.io.ObjectInputStream;
import java.io.ObjectOutputStream;

Employee harry = new Employee();
Manager carl= new Manager();
carl.setSecretary(harry);
Manager tony = new Manager();
tony.setSecretary(harry);

// serialization to file store.dat
Manager[] staff = new Manager[2];
staff[0] = carl;
staff[1] = tony;
ObjectOutputStream out = new ObjectOutputStream(
                      new FileOutputStream("employee.dat"));
out.writeObject(staff);
out.close();

// retrieve the data including harry
ObjectInputStream in = new ObjectInputStream(
                      new FileInputStream("employee.dat"));
Manager []newStaff = (Manager[]) in.readObject();
in.close();

// newStaff[] now has the two new roots
carl=newStaff[0];
tony=newStaff[1];
 harry=carl.getSecretary();
```

If we change Listing 1.7 so that Carl has secretary Harry, Harry has secretary Tony, and Tony has secretary Carl, the objects are connected into a loop. It does not make a meaningful example, but it allows us to test that Java serialization can handle such loops, and it does. To run this example, go to bk\chap1\javaSerialization\src and copy ObjectStreamTest.4 to ObjectStreamTest.java.

Nevertheless, there are situations when Java serialization may crash with stack overflow.

Situation 1: A long chain of references may cause stack overflow, but not always. If the LinkedList in Listing 1.8 is a Java container, everything works fine. However, for LinkedList from another library, for more than just a few books Java serialization will crash. The online example[19] crashes for more than 1,000 books.

---

[18] For full running example, see bk\chap1\javaSerialization\readme.txt.

[19] Look at custom coded linked list of Books in bk/chap1/javaSerialization/stackOverflow1, where build.bat compiles it, and run.bat runs it. In order to run it for 2000 books, type: `run 2000`.

Listing 1.8 Example where, for 50,000 Books, serialization ends in stack overflow. The behaviour depends on the origin of LinkedList

```
import java.util;
class Book implements Serializable {
}
class Library implements Serializable {
    // when LinkedList is from Java library, serialization runs fine
    // For a custom LinkedList, serialization triggers stack overflow
    LinkedList<Book> books;
}
```

Situation 2: When two classes have containers holding objects of the other class, Java serialization may crash even when Java containers are used; see Listing 1.9, first. This happens even if these are Java containers. The online example[20] runs fine up to 1,000 books, but for more books it crashes with stack overflow.

Listing 1.9 Examples of implementing ManyToMany with two containers; some may cause stack overflow

```
import java.util;

// (1) Implementation which causes a stack overflow
class Book implements Serializable {
    NotJavaContainer<Author> authors;
}
class Author implements Serializable {
    NotJavaContainer<Book> books;
}

// (2) Java container which causes a stack overflow //
class Book implements Serializable {
    ArrayList<Author> authors;
}
class Author implements Serializable {
    ArrayList<Book> books;
}

// (3) Desperate man's ManyToMany does not crash,
//      but is neither clean nor efficient
class Book implements Serializable {
}

class Author implements Serializable {
}

class Library implements Serializable {
    HashMap<Book,Container<Author>> booksToAuthors;
    HashMap<Author,Container<Book>> authorsToBooks;
}
```

It is interesting to compare cases (2) and (3) in Listing 1.9. In case (2) there is just a reference between Book and Container<Author>. In case (3) the

---

[20] If you want to experiment with this example, go to bk/chap1/javaSerialization/stackOverflow2, where build.bat compiles it, and run.bat runs it. In order to run it for 2000 books, type: run 2000.

Fig. 1.8 The concept of Java serialization

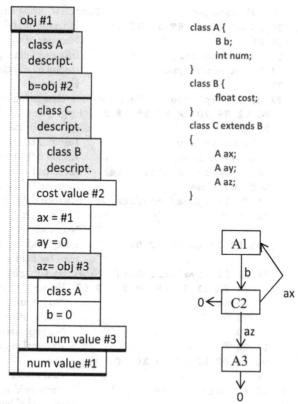

reference is replaced by index search in a hash table, which certainly takes more time to execute, and requires additional internal data space.

It works because there are fewer references and the networks splits into smaller pieces. We call it a *desperate man's implementation* because Java serialization crashes in case (2), which is the only proper, logical, simple and efficient solution in this case.

Useful Trick No.1.
When replacing references by hash tables, we can build bi-directional associations without inserting references into the participating objects. That can be useful in some situations, but it obscures the true purpose of what we are building, and requires more memory space and time to traverse.

As a result of the recursive process in which Java traverses the data, the disk data have a hierarchical nature, which isn't easy to read visually. The concept is explained in Fig. 1.8.

In addition to the individual objects, the disk record must also include a description of all participating classes. Some persistent systems store the description of the classes at the beginning of the file, but Java stores it when encountering the first object of that particular type.

72 00 07 Manager	New class, string length, class name (serial #2)
36 06 AE 13 63 8F 59 B7 02	Fingerprint and flags
00 01	Number of data fields
L 00 09 secretary	Instance field type and name
74 00 0A LEmployee;	Instance field class name-String (serial #3)
78	End marker
72 00 08 Employee	Superclass-new class,string length,class name (serial #4)
E6 D2 86 7D AE AC 18 18 02	Fingerprint and flags
00 03	Number of instance fields
D 00 06 salary	Instance field type and name
L 00 07 hireDay	Instance field type and name
74 00 10 Ljava/util/Date;	Instance field class name-String (serial #5)
L 00 04 name	Instance field type and name
74 00 12 Ljava/lang/String;	Instance field class name-String (serial #6)
78	End marker
70	No superclass
40 F3 88 00 00 00 00 00	salary field value-double
73	hireDay field value-new object (serial #9)
72 00 0E java.util.Date	New class, string length, class name (serial #8)
68 6A 81 01 4B 59 74 19 03	Fingerprint and flags
00 00	No instance variables
78	End marker
70	No superclass
77 08	External storage, number of bytes
00 00 00 83 E9 39 E0 00	Date
78	End marker
74 00 0C Carl Cracker	name field value-String (serial #10)
73	secretary field value-new object (serial #11)
71 00 7E 00 04	existing class (use serial #4)
40 E8 6A 00 00 00 00 00	salary field value-double
73	hireDay field value-new object (serial #12)
71 00 7E 09 08	Existing class (use serial #8)
77 08	External storage, number of bytes
00 00 00 91 1B 4E B1 80	Date
78	End marker
74 00 0C HarryHacker	name filed value-String (serial #13)

Fig. 1.9 Section of the Manager-Employee serialization file from Cornell and Horstmann (2011); *shaded area* describes classes. With the permission of the authors

In C-based languages, object address can be used as its unique ID. In Java we don't have access to addresses, so the serialization uses the order of the objects in the file as their IDs when recording references.

The serialization file is byte-encoded, and Fig. 1.9[21] shows the serialization file for Manager Carl Cracker and his secretary Harry Hacker annotated by Horstmann C. The record is full of cryptic headers and special codes[22] which are not a part of Java language; they may and often change from one version of Java to another.

---

[21] We had to re-type the original in order to make it readable here.

[22] For the description of these codes, look at pp 39–59, Vol. II of Cornell & Horstmann (2011).

Figure 1.8 is from the 2011 version of Core Java. A similar listing is in the 2012 version (Horstmann and Cornell 2012) starting on p. 49.

With wide industry participation, the JAXB[23] project is developing and evolving Java serialization with XML output, including the specification, reference implementation and the Technology Compatibility Kit (TCK). The goal is a production-quality implementation that is used directly in a number of products by Oracle and other vendors.

1.5.3 C# Serialization

C# and Java are similar languages. They use references and not pointers, do not support multiple inheritance and both have reflection. One would expect that the serialization in both languages would be similar but it is not. Only the user interface is similar—see Listing 1.10.

Listing 1.10 Invoking serialization in C#, binary output format[24]

```
[Serializable] class Employee {
    private string name;
    private double salary;
    private DateTime birthday;
}
[Serializable] class Manager : Employee {
    private Employee secretary;
    public void setSecretary(Employee e){secretary = e;}
    public Employee getSecretary(){return secretary;}
}
static void Main(string[] args) {
    Manager m = new Manager();
    Employee s = new Employee(); // s for secretary
    m.setSecretary(s);

    // for root m, write all data to file manager.bin
    Stream fileOut = new FileStream("manager.bin", FileMode.Create);
    BinaryFormatter formatter = new BinaryFormatter();
    formatter.Serialize(fileOut, m);
    fileOut.Close();

    // read the data from the file, nm will be the new manager
    fileIn = new FileStream(filename, FileMode.Open);
    m = (Manager)formatter.Deserialize(fileIn, null);
    fileIn.Close();
    return 0;
}
```

C# serialization with the binary format is equivalent to Java serialization. However, C# serialization also supports several XML formats.

The advantage of the XML format is that it can read the stored data even if the structure of the serialized classes has changed, for example if we add or remove

---

[23] http://jaxb.java.net

[24] Full code which also generates Figs. 1.10 and 1.11 is in bk/chap1/CSharpSerialization/SerializeToBin/Program.cs bk/chap1/CSharpSerialization/SerializeToXml/Program.cs.

Fig. 1.10 C# binary
serialization: (**a**) basic record,
(**b**) overall file organization,
(**c**) class info record, (**d**)
instance record

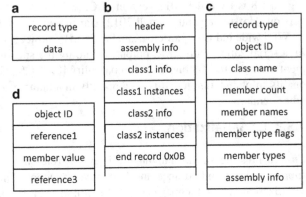

members. The disadvantage of the XML format is a larger data file and longer time to
save/restore the data. In Listing 1.10 the format is selected by the choice of the formatter:

BinaryFormatter generates binary format as shown in Fig. 1.10. Binary serialization is typically used for .NET Remoting,[25] and is unsuitable for long-term storage. The
disk format may depend on the version of .NET Framework. We have no explanation
for the binary serialization being slower[26] than the XML serialization, especially for
large data sets—it defies any logic and could be a result of poor implementation. We
have not seen any problems with circular references or large reference chains.

XmlSerializer can serialize only public classes and public members. It must
have a default constructor, and if several references point to the same object,
multiple copies of the object appear on the file. It also cannot handle circular
references and objects of type `ArrayList` or `List<T>`.

SoapFormatter uses the SOAP format, which makes XML hard to read visually. It handles correctly circular references and multiple references to the same
object. Objects and members can be serialized even if they are not public. However,
it cannot serialize generic classes such as `Dictionary<T>`.

DataContractSerializer is the most sophisticated formatter. It does everything
that SoapFormatter does, but it also handles generic classes. When using this
formatter, every serialized class must be decorated with the attribute
`DataContract`, and every serialized member must have the attribute
`DataMemeber`. In order to handle circular and multiple references, all classes
with at least one instance referred more than once must be decorated not only with
`DataContact` but also with `DataContract(IsReference=true)`.

Figure 1.10 provides clues to the organization of the binary file, such as shown in
Fig. 1.11:

In Fig. 1.10b, assembly info describes dll or exe files where the serialized objects
are stored.

---

[25] For more information on .NET Remoting, see MSDN.

[26] For experimental results, see the benchmark in Chap. 8.

Bytes	Data
Header	
00	Record type (Serialized stream header)
01 00 00 00 FF FF FF FF 01 00 00 00 00 00 00 00	Header bytes - format version..etc
Assembly info	
0C	Record type (Binary library)
02 00 00 00	Assembly ID (2)
45	String length (69 characters)
53 65 72 69 61 6C 69 7A 65 54 6F 42 69 6E 2C 20 56 65 72 73 69 6F 6E 3D 31 2E 30 2E 30 2E 30 2C 20 43 75 6C 74 75 72 65 3D 6E 65 75 74 72 61 6C 2C 20 50 75 62 6C 69 63 4B 65 79 54 6F 6B 65 6E 3D 6E 75 6C 6C	Assembly name ("SerializeToBin, Version=1.0.0.0, Culture=neutral, PublicKeyToken=null")
Class info (Manager)	
05	Record type (ClassWithMembersAndTypes)
01 00 00 00	Object ID (1)
16	String length (22 characters)
53 65 72 69 61 6C 69 7A 65 54 6F 42 69 6E 2E 4D 61 6E 61 67 65 72	Class name ("SerializeToBin.Manager")
04 00 00 00	Member count of Manager (4)
09	String length (9 characters)
73 65 63 72 65 74 61 72 79	Field name ("secretary")
0D	String length (13 characters)
45 6D 70 6C 6F 79 65 65 2B 6E 61 6D 65	Member name("Employee+name")
0F	String length (15 characters)
45 6D 70 6C 6F 79 65 65 2B 73 61 6C 61 72 79	Member name ("Employee+salary")

Fig. 1.11 (continued)

11	String length (17 characters)
45 6D 70 6C 6F 79 65 65 2B 62 69 72 74 68 64 61 79	Member name ("Employee+birthday")
04 01 00 00	Member info - types (4,1,0,0 = Class, String, Primitive, Primitive)
17	String length (17 characters)
53 65 72 69 61 6C 69 7A 65 54 6F 42 69 6E 2E 45 6D 70 6C 6F 79 65 65	Class of the "secretary" member ("SerializeToBin.Employee")
02 00 00 00	Assembly ID of class of the "secretary" member (2)
06	Data type of the "salary" member (Double)
0D	Data type of the "birthday" member (DateTime)
02 00 00 00	Assembly ID of this object (2)
Instances (Manager)	
09	Record type (Member reference)
03 00 00 00	Object ID of referenced object (3)
06	Record type (String object)
04 00 00 00	Object ID of the string instance (4)
09	String length (9 characters)
48 75 67 6F 20 42 6F 73 73	String value ("Hugo Boss")
00 00 00 00 00 4C FD 40	Field value (salary = 120000.0)
00 00 F1 A8 25 28 97 08	Field value (birthday in ticks=619007616000000000=24.07.1962)
Class info (Employee)	
05	Record type (ClassWithMembersAndTypes)
03 00 00 00	Object ID (3)
17	String length (17 characters)
53 65 72 69 61 6C 69 7A 65 54 6F 42 69 6E 2E 45 6D 70 6C 6F 79 65 65	Class name ("SerializeToBin.Employee")
03 00 00 00	Member count of Employee
04	String length (4 characters)

Fig. 1.11 (continued)

6E 61 6D 65	Field name ("name")
06	String length (6 characters)
73 61 6C 61 72 79	Field name ("salary")
08	String length (8 characters)
62 69 72 74 68 64 61 79	Field name ("birthday")
01 00 00	Member info - types (1,0,0 = String, Primitive, Primitive)
06	Data type of the "salary" member (Double)
0D	Data type of the "birthday" member (DateTime)
02 00 00 00	Assembly ID of this object (2)
Instances (Employee)	
06	Record type (String object)
05 00 00 00	Object ID of the string instance (5)
04	String length (4 characters)
4A 75 64 79	String value ("Judy")
00 00 00 00 00 7C D5 40	Field value (salary = 22000.0)
00 40 D5 57 46 9C B6 08	Field value (birthday in ticks = 627861024000000000 = 13.8.1990)
Footer	
0B	End mark

Fig. 1.11 C# binary format as generated by Listing 1.10. For more details see MSDN pages (http://msdn.microsoft.com/en-us/library/cc236844(v=prot.10).aspx), or Lluis Sanchez Goal's web pages (http://primates.ximian.com/~lluis/dist/binary_serialization_format.htm) for the older format

In Fig. 1.10c, class ID is identical with the ID of its first instance. Names of inherited members include the base class name, e.g. baseName+memberName.

One byte flags identify basic types such as *int* or *char* in MSDN,[27] and assembly info provides basic metadata about the assembly—full name, version, etc.

In Fig. 1.10d, the record of the first object does not include any ID—its ID is the same as the class ID. References and member values must be in the same order as listed under (c).

Observations:

The comparison of the three XML serializer formats in Fig. 1.12 is interesting: You can see that XmlSerializer format is similar to Java—it is the result of a recursive function call, and is also the reason why this serializer cannot handle long reference chains and circular references—Java serialization also runs into this problem.

The organizations of the other XML files and of the binary file are more linear, easier to read visually and clearly results of a better algorithm which we will describe in Chap. 2.

XML files do not store types of individual members. Serializer gets them from the assembly (dll) through reflection. For this reason, it is essential that the program which reads the data from the disk uses exactly the same application classes. To change the type of a member while keeping its name will likely crash your program.

The binary serialization stores the type for each member, even though it could get around it in the same way as the XML serialization does. We can only guess the reason: Binary serialization is designed for .NET Remoting where applications send serialized data over the network, and the stored types can be used for checking that the classes are identical.

1.5.4 Objective-C Archiving

Objective-C has two mechanisms to make objects persistent: Core Data[28] framework and Archiving. Core Data is a layer that manages entity-relationships and stores all the objects either in the SQLite database or in a file. This is a more complex environment than the simple and fast storage which is the subject of this book.

Archiving is the Objective-C term for *serialization*. In Objective-C lingo, *serialization* is used for the process of recording a single object, while *archiving* means storing the entire object graph. This may confuse someone used to serialization in other languages.

From observing limitations of Archiving and its behaviour and interface, we can guess that it traverses through the object graph using a recursive function just like Java does. It requires the user to write functions that identify members and provide instruction how to reach the adjacent objects—see Listing 1.11. This clearly is not the automatic persistence we are seeking in this book. It requires a lot of manual work to make application classes persistent. Nevertheless, we show it here for comparison with the new, more efficient, and easier to use persistence which we will develop in Chap. 6.

Depending on which Coder is used, Archiving can produce either a binary or an XML file. The XML output for the Manager/Employee pair is in Listing 1.12, and the

---

[27] http://msdn.microsoft.com/en-us/library/cc236866(v=prot.10).aspx

[28] See (Core Data 2013).

XmlSerializer:

```
<?xml version="1.0"?>
<Manager xmlns:xsi="http://www.w3.org/2001/XMLSchema-instance"
xmlns:xsd="http://www.w3.org/2001/XMLSchema">
  <name>Hugo Boss</name>
  <salary>120000</salary>
  <birthday>1962-07-24T00:00:00</birthday>
  <secretary>
    <name>Judy</name>
    <salary>22000</salary>
    <birthday>1990-08-13T00:00:00</birthday>
  </secretary>
</Manager>
```

SoapFormatter:

```
<SOAP-ENV:Envelope xmlns:xsi="http://www.w3.org/2001/XMLSchema
-instance" xmlns:xsd="http://www.w3.org/2001/XMLSchema"
xmlns:SOAP-ENC="http://schemas.xmlsoap.org/soap/encoding/"
xmlns:SOAP-ENV="http://schemas.xmlsoap.org/soap/envelope/"
xmlns:clr="http://schemas.microsoft.com/soap/encoding/clr/1.0"
SOAPENV:encodingStyle="http://schemas.xmlsoap.org/soap/encoding/">
<SOAP-ENV:Body>
        <a1:Manager id="ref-1" xmlns:a1 =
"http://schemas.microsoft.com/clr/nsassem/SerializeToXml/...">
                <secretary href="#ref-3"/>
                <name id="ref-4">Hugo Boss</name>
                <salary>120000</salary>
                <birthday>1962-07-
        24T00:00:00.0000000+02:00</birthday>
        </a1:Manager>
        <a1:Employee id="ref-3" mlns:a1 =
"http://schemas.microsoft.com/clr/nsassem/SerializeToXml/...">
        <name id="ref-5">Judy</name>
        <salary>22000</salary>
        <birthday>1990-08-13T00:00:00.0000000+02:00</birthday>
        </a1:Employee>
</SOAP-ENV:Body>
</SOAP-ENV:Envelope>
```

DataContractSerializer:

```
<Manager z:Id="i1"
xmlns="http://schemas.datacontract.org/2004/07/SerializeToXml"
xmlns:i="http://www.w3.org/2001/XMLSchema-instance"
xmlns:z="http://schemas.microsoft.com/2003/10/Serialization/">
        <birthday>1962-07-24T00:00:00</birthday>
        <name>Hugo Boss</name>
        <salary>120000</salary>
        <secretary z:Id="i2">
                <birthday>1990-08-13T00:00:00</birthday>
                <name>Judy</name>
                <salary>22000</salary>
        </secretary>
</Manager>
```

Fig. 1.12 Comparing outputs of the three serializers

binary file for the same problem is in bk/chap1/objcArchiving/boss.plist and has
380 bytes.[29]

Listing 1.11 Archiving Manager-Employee objects in Objective-C. Compared to
other languages, using this serialization is a programer's nightmare. [Most readers may
not be familiar with the Objective-C syntax, so we reduced this listing to comments
which explain the logic.] [For full running code see bk/hap1/objcArchiving/list1_11.m]

```
// The class definitions similar to C++, C# or Java,
// each class must have two custom coded methods.
// coder is the object which controls XML or binary recording
@interface Employee : NSObject<NSCoding>
{
    NSString* name; // pointer to a separate object
    double salary;
    NSDate* birthday; // pointer to a separate object
}
-(id)initWithCoder:(NSCoder*)coder;
-(void)encodeWithCoder:(NSCoder*)coder;
@end

@interface Manager : Employee<NSCoding>
{
    Employee* secretary;
}
-(id)initWithCoder:(NSCoder*)coder;
-(void)encodeWithCoder:(NSCoder*)coder;
@end

// lets look inside one of these methods
@implementation Employee
-(void)encodeWithCoder:(NSCoder*)coder {
    [coder encodeObject:name]; // encode another object
    // instruction to encode 'salary' value
    [coder encodeValueOfObjCType:@encode(double) at:&salary];
    [coder encodeObject:birthday]; // encode another object
}    @end

// User also has to supply another C-style function for each class.
// This function is simple for binary storage, for example
void archiveBossToBinaryPlist(Manager* boss, NSString* filename) {
        [NSKeyedArchiver archiveRootObject:boss toFile:filename];
}

// but for XML storage, it again gets quite involved
void archiveBossToXmlPlist(Manager* boss, NSString* filename) {
    NSMutableData *data = [NSMutableData data];
    NSKeyedArchiver *archiver =
        [[NSKeyedArchiver alloc] initForWritingWithMutableData:data];
    [archiver setOutputFormat:NSPropertyListXMLFormat_v1_0];
    [archiver encodeObject:boss];
    [archiver finishEncoding];
    [data writeToFile:filename atomically:YES];
    [archiver release];
}
```

---

[29] All this for two simple objects is ridiculous. The file has about five times as many lines as XML
files produced by C# serializer.

Listing 1.12 XML file for the Manager-Employee pair, produced by objC archiving. [See also bk/chap1/objcArchiving/boss.xml]

```
<?xml version="1.0" encoding="UTF-8"?>
<!DOCTYPE plist PUBLIC "-//GNUstep//DTD plist 0.9//EN"
"http://www.gnustep.org/plist-0_9.xml">
<plist version="0.9">
<dict>
     <key>$archiver</key>
     <string>NSKeyedArchiver</string>
     <key>$objects</key>
     <array>
        <string>$null</string>
        <dict>
            <key>$0</key>
            <dict>
                <key>CF$UID</key>
                <integer>2</integer>
            </dict>
            <key>$1</key>
            <real>120000</real>
            <key>$2</key>
            <dict>
                <key>CF$UID</key>
                <integer>3</integer>
            </dict>
            <key>$3</key>
            <dict>
                <key>CF$UID</key>
                <integer>4</integer>
            </dict>
            <key>$class</key>
            <dict>
                <key>CF$UID</key>
                <integer>8</integer>
            </dict>
        </dict>
        <string>Hugo Boss</string>
        <date>1962-07-24T16:00:00Z</date>
        <dict>
            <key>$0</key>
            <dict>
                <key>CF$UID</key>
                <integer>5</integer>
            </dict>
            <key>$1</key>
            <real>22000</real>
            <key>$2</key>
            <dict>
                <key>CF$UID</key>
                <integer>6</integer>
            </dict>
```

```xml
        <key>$class</key>
        <dict>
            <key>CF$UID</key>
            <integer>7</integer>
        </dict>
    </dict>
    <string>Judy</string>
    <date>1980-07-01T16:00:00Z</date>
    <dict>
        <key>$classes</key>
        <array>
            <string>Employee</string>
            <string>NSObject</string>
        </array>
        <key>$classname</key>
        <string>Employee</string>
    </dict>
    <dict>
        <key>$classes</key>
        <array>
            <string>Manager</string>
            <string>Employee</string>
            <string>NSObject</string>
        </array>
        <key>$classname</key>
        <string>Manager</string>
    </dict>
    </array>
    <key>$top</key>
    <dict>
        <key>$0</key>
        <dict>
            <key>CF$UID</key>
            <integer>1</integer>
        </dict>
    </dict>
    <key>$version</key>
    <integer>100000</integer>
</dict>
</plist>
```

1.5.5 BOOST Serialization in C++

Boost.org provides free peer-reviewed portable C++ source libraries. These libraries are used worldwide, and were included in several reports of the C++ Standards Committee. The BOOST serialization[30] was designed by Richard Ramey between 2002 and 2004, and has been recently proposed as the serialization standard for C++. Ramey is still the key person on this project.

---

[30] http://www.boost.org/doc/libs/1_52_0/libs/serialization/doc/index.html (BOOST library serialization 2013).

TEXT (85 bytes):

```
22 serialization::archive 9 0 0 1 0
0 9 Hugo Boss 120000 1
1 11 Carol Able 22000
```

BINARY (100 bytes)

XML (516 bytes):

```
<?xml version="1.0" encoding="UTF-8" standalone="yes" ?>
<!DOCTYPE boost_serialization>
<boost_serialization signature="serialization::archive" version="9">
<m class_id="0" tracking_level="1" version="0" object_id="_0">
    <Employee class_id="1" tracking_level="1" version="0" object_id="_1">
            <name>Hugo Boss</name>
            <salary>120000</salary>
    </Employee>
    <secretary class_id_reference="1" object_id="_2">
            <name>Carol Able</name>
            <salary>22000</salary>
    </secretary>
</m>
</boost_serialization>
```

Fig. 1.13 BOOST serialization: comparing output files for the different styles of archiving

Because C++ does not have reflection, the user interface must help the serialization to identify pointer members in all the application classes—either by listing their names or locations. Boost serialization requires more. The user must provide function `serialize()`, which not only lists the members to be stored (usually all the members again), but must also invoke `serialize()` for the base class—see Listing 1.13.

BOOST documentation uses the term *serialization* for what we call *persistence*, and unlike in Objective-C, *archiving* in the BOOST terminology means the *format* of the disk data. Thus BOOST has three archiving styles:

(a) Binary

(b) ASCII text

(c) XML

Compared to the built-in serialization of other languages, the disk file is very compact—see Fig. 1.13. The penalty is that the serialization does not check whether the classes and the data model of the programs that read and write the data are identical.[31]

---

[31] Code in bk/chap1/boostSerialize also has options for other styles of archiving.

Listing 1.13 BOOST serialization applied to the Manager/Employee (secretary) problem using the binary archiving style. Code added for serialization is in bold

```
class Employee {
private:
      friend class boost::serialization::access;
      template<class Archive>
      void serialize(Archive & ar, const unsigned int version) {
            ar & name;
            ar & salary;

   }
public:
    string name;
    double salary;
};

class Manager : public Employee {
private:
      friend class boost::serialization::access;
      template<class Archive>
      void serialize(Archive & ar, const unsigned int version) {
            // serialize base class
            ar & boost::serialization::base_object<Employee>(*this);
            // serialize own members
            if(secretary != NULL) { ar & secretary; }
      }
    Employee *secretary;
public:
    Employee *getSecretary(){return secretary;}
    void setSecretary(Employee *s){secretary = s;}
};

int main() {
    Manager *m = new Manager();
    Employee *s = new Employee();
    m->addSecretary(s);

    //save to file
    std::ofstream ofs("manager.bin",
       std::ios_base::out|std::ios_base::trunc|std::ios_base::binary);
    boost::archive::binary_oarchive oa(ofs);
    ofs.close();

    //load from file
    std::ifstream ifs("data.bin",
                            std::ios_base::in|std::ios_base::binary);
    boost::archive::binary_iarchive ia(ifs);
    ifs.close();
    m = new Manager();
    s = m->getSecretary();
    return 0;
}
```

The XML file and the program that generates it are available from bk\chap1 \boostXML.

An interesting feature of Boost serialization is that it allows an alternative—a non-intrusive interface which makes the class persistent. Instead of adding method serialize() to class Employee as we did above, we can leave class Employee completely unchanged and only add a separate template:

```
// intrusive version, as above
class Employee {
        template<class Archive>
        void serialize(Archive & ar, const unsigned int version) {
            ar & name;
            ar & salary;
        }
    ... // as before adding persistence
};

// non-intrusive version
class Employee {
    ... // as before adding persistence
};
template<class Archive>
void serialize(Archive & ar, Employee & e, const unsigned int version)
{
    ar & e.name;
    ar & e.salary;
}
```

This looks like a silver-bullet solution to the problem of making existing libraries persistent. However, there is a catch: If the members to be serialized are not public, and they usually are not, then this does not work.

We do not recommend this method, and we agree with Mark Bales who observed that separating persistence from the base class leads to potential problems when classes change. One of his engineers implemented this approach when Mark wasn't looking, and it's been a performance and maintenance nightmare.

Fundamentals of Persistence

2

Abstract

This chapter is the heart of the book. It explains algorithms, technical details and programming tricks of various approaches to implementation of persistent data—binary and ASCII serialization, memory paging, disk paging and smart pointers. The last section presents QSP (Quasi-Single-Page), a new design of persistent data which, besides other languages, also works in Objective-C and with iPhone applications.

Keywords

Algorithm • Hidden pointer • Object graph • Pointer mask • Regular pointer • Reference • Smart pointer • Swizzling pointers • Traversing objects

This chapter describes several different approaches to the implementation of persistent objects, including algorithms and implementation techniques some of which may not have been published. We start with the concept of pointer mask which, for each class, stores the information about the location of its pointers.

Some algorithms and implementation techniques presented in this chapter have never been published. All the examples in this Chapter are coded in C++, yet many of these ideas are also applicable to other languages. We'll start with the concept of the pointer mask which, for each class, stores the information about the location of its pointers.

Pointer Mask is an object that is used to capture the structure of a class, focusing specifically on where its pointer members are located. You can think of it as a singleton instance of the class which is first filled out with zeros and then all its pointers are set to small positive integers, either 1 (just to identify the pointer location) or to a number specifying the pointer type.

J. Soukup and P. Macháček, *Serialization and Persistent Objects*,
DOI 10.1007/978-3-642-39323-5_2, © Springer-Verlag Berlin Heidelberg 2014

Pointer masks have many uses and advantages:
– They tell us instantly (both in code and visually) where we have all the pointers.
– They make it easier to code and debug algorithms.
– They are easy to generate automatically.
– Other representation such as the list of pointers and their offsets within the object can be easily derived from the mask.
– By comparing the masks, we can see whether the old/new classes are different.

Another way of looking at the pointer mask is to start with the fact that, within any object, pointers always start on a 4-byte boundary.[1] Imagine any object broken down into 4-byte sections of potential pointer locations. Instead of some valid pointer, the mask stores an integer in each of these four bytes, so naturally it has the same size as any instance of this class. These integers are 0 for those object members that represent just numbers or text, and are set to non-zero value for pointers.

When constructing a pointer mask, it is important to know that, at the setup time, just before the program starts to run, the persistent system assigns to each class an integer index. It is the same code as if you wanted to find out how many application classes are involved:

```
class Utill {
        static int classesCount;
};
class Library {
        static int classIndex;
};
class Book {
        static classIndex;
);
class Author {
        static classIndex;
};

int Util::classCount=0;
int Library:classIndex=classCount++;
int Book:classIndex=classCount++;
int Author:classIndex=classCount++;
```

---

[1] On a 64-bit architecture, it is 8-bytes.

POINTER MASK (Example)

```
class Book {                          class Author {
    int numPages;                         ...
    char *title;                          ...
    char category                         static int classIndex;
    Author *authors;                  };
    Book *next;
    static int classIndex;
};
```

The compiler may keep internal table that looks like this

```
Book  [ int  char*  char  Author*  Book* ]
```

where each of these members takes 4 bytes of the object, 8 bytes on a 64-bit architecture. Pointers, integers and floats all start on a 4-byte boundary, and even the single character takes 4 bytes including the 3 bytes of padding the compiler inserts. Note that the static members (here classIndex) are not stored inside these objects.

In the persistence systems which store pages of objects as blocks of bytes, we are interested only in the locations of pointers, but if we want to traverse the object graph - as in a typical serialization, we need to know the pointer types.

For this purpose, we create a mask, specific for each class, which has exactly the same number of bytes as one instance of that class. Each 4-byte location which is a potential location of a pointer is treated as an integer, which is 0 for locations that do not store pointers. For pointer locations, it stores the pointer type as the classIndex of its target object. Pointers to built-in types have fixed numbers, for example char* may be recorded as -1. If we assign Book::classIndex=17 and to Author::classIndex=18, then the masks are:

Book **mask** with types	0	-1	0	18	17

Book **mask** without types	0	-1	0	1	1

Pointer masks will get more interesting when we will discuss composite objects involving structure-members, inheritance (especially multiple inheritance) and hidden pointers inserted by the compiler.

2.1   Algorithms and Techniques

This chapter describes how to add, automatically and transparently, members and methods to a class. It discusses regular pointers, hidden pointers inserted by the compiler, smart pointers, references, and pointer swizzling. discusses two algorithms (recursive and stack based) which traverse the pointer network and collect all active objects – the critical step in every serialization.

2.1.1   Adding Members and Methods to a Class

Both when making objects persistent and when building intrusive data structures (see Chap. 3), we need to add capabilities to the existing classes. That implies additional methods and members to support these capabilities. There are four ways to do it: from below, from above, inserting them inside, and using a linked storage. Examples in this book mostly *inside* the required methods and members, but keep in mind that this is not the only way. In some situations one of the other options may be a better solution.

2.1.1.1 Adding from Below
If we want to add certain methods and members to every allocated object, we can derive all application classes (and all library classes) from the same base class. For example

```
class PersistBase {
    int counter;
    int mySize();    // ??? see Note1
    static int mode; // ??? see Note2
};
class Employee : public PersistBase {
    int ID;
    Employee *next;
};
```

Note1: Unless mySize() could reach into the allocation record, which may depend on the compiler and OS, or unless counter keeps the size from the time the object was allocated, this would not work.

Note2: This value would be the same for all classes and all objects, an interesting implementation of "global" variable—see bk\chap2\fromBelow.cpp.

2.1.1.2 Inserting Inside

If we want to add more than one member or method to a class,[2] we can insert them with a macro. In the following example each class has an index, and even from the base class we can determine the size of the allocated object. The program prints size=16 which is the size of Manager.[3]

```
#define Persist(T)                                    \
public:                                               \
    virtual int mySize(){ return sizeof(T); } \
    static int classIndex

class Employee {
    Persist(Employee);
    int ID;
    Employee *next;
};
class Manager : public Employee {
    Persist(Manager);
    Employee *secretary;
};
int main(){
    Manager *m=new Manager;
    Employee *e=m;
    printf("size=%d\n",e->mySize());
```

Useful Trick No. 2

Macros, especially long ones, complicate debugging, because compilers and debuggers treat each macro as a single line, but sometimes there is no other choice. The way to minimize the negative impact of a long macro is to insert, with a macro, a short function which calls another function outside of the class.[4] For example, in Listing 2.9 - far below, p.60, macro INH_REC(T) inserts a line with a call to Util::iRep(). This does two things: (1) it allows us to insert the function yet code it, or most of it, as normal code, not as a macro and (2) it allows the outside function to use class parameters which are private and normally not available outside.

---

[2] The difference from adding to an object *from below* becomes apparent when inheritance is involved.

[3] Two 4-byte members in Employee, one in Manager plus one hidden pointer as will be explained in Sect. 2.1.2.

[4] This coding style was recommended by Sean Yixiang when coding the Objective-C persistence in Chap. 7.

Here is a simpler example, where we are adding a long function foo() to class Book. The function needs the value of member ISDN, which is private. We can do it with a long macro, which is not nice and is difficult to debug:

```
#define FOO \
void foo(){ \
        .. long code using value of ISDN \
}

class Book {
private:
        int ISBN;
public:
        FOO
};
```

Instead of using a long macro, we can code the main part of foo() outside of Book, either as a plain C function, or as a static function of some utility class:

```
class Utility {
friend class Book;
    static void foox(int isbn){
        ...bulk of the function, using the private Book::ISDN
    }
}

#define FOO \
    void foo(){Book::foox(ISBN);}

class Book {
private:
    int ISBN;
public:
    FOO
};
```

2.1.1.3 Adding from Above

As *from below*, this method allows one to expand object, not class. We derive a special class from the class we want to expand and add the members and methods there. The disadvantage is that in calls to new() and possibly other methods you have to cast to the expanded class (starting with Exp_...). For example:

```
class Employee {
    int ID;
    Employee *next;
};

class Exp_Employee : public Employee {
public:
    Exp_Employee *nextFreeList;
    static Exp_Employee *freeListStart;
    static void addFreeList(Employee *e) {
        Exp_Employee *ee=(Exp_Employee*)e;
        ee->nextFreeList=freeListStart;
        freeListStart=ee;
    }
    static void delFreeList(Exp_Employee *e) {...}
};
Exp_Employee* Exp_Employee::freeListStart=NULL;

int main() {
    Employee* e=new Exp_Employee;
    Exp_Employee::addFreeList(e);
```

2.1.2 Hidden Pointers

The first step to implementing any style of persistence is to understand the internal representation of objects. In the early years of C++ there was a multitude of compilers, each with its own quirks and representation of objects. Writing portable C++ persistence used to be a pain.[5]

The C++ standard does not specify the internal implementation of objects, but most compilers today use the model shown in Fig. 2.1.[6] If neither the class itself nor the classes from which it inherits have virtual functions, the memory image consists of all the members (fields) in the same order as they are hierarchically listed in the class definition.[7] If there are virtual functions, then there is a *hidden pointer* at the beginning of the object.[8] In the case of multiple inheritances, there are additional hidden pointers inside the object. Hidden pointers point into the internal table of virtual functions, and are identical for all instances[9] of the same class. Application programmers have no access to these hidden pointers and tables, and often are not even aware of their existence.

---

[5] The code of DOL library (Data Object Library 2013) still has ifdef statements for Borland, Watcom, Microsoft, Mac, Linux, Zortec, DEC, VMS, Sun, Lucid, GNU, IBM, Solaris, Liant, Amdahl, Coherent, Apollo, Saber and HP compilers.

[6] For the program which generates this information, go online to bk/chap2/dispPtrs

[7] As in plain C.

[8] In most OO languages including Java and C# the internal object representation is probably similar.

[9] Terms *object of classA, A-object,* or *instance of A* mean the same thing.

```
class C {...};
class B : public C {...};
class D : public C {...};
class A : public B, public D {…};
class E : public B {…};
```

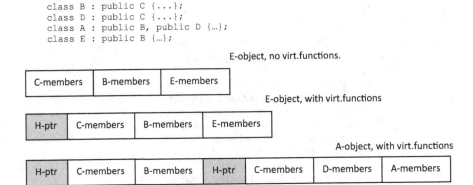

Fig. 2.1 Examples of hidden pointers in C++ objects (Visual Studio 2010). Note that an A-object includes two different instances of the C-class

On a 32-bit architecture, pointers and 4-byte numbers always start on a 4-byte boundary. On 64-bit architecture, pointers and 8-byte numbers usually start on an 8-byte boundary.[10] The sizeof() function returns the true size of the object, including the hidden pointers.

A convenient tool for detecting and manipulating these pointers is operator new () which can be controlled by an outside variable, static pointer objBuf, to do three things[11]:

(1) When objBuf=NULL, new() allocates a new object as usual.
(2) When objBuf points to a block of memory, new() adds hidden pointers to it, thus turning it into a valid object.
(3) When objBuf=(char *)(1), new() allocates a 0-filled object, then sets the hidden pointers to

Case (1) is used for allocation of objects during the program run.
Case (2) is useful when retrieving persistent objects from the disk.
Case (3) creates a mask similar to Fig. 2.1.
The algorithm recognizes a valid pointer by having a value which is a multiple of 4.

---

[10] The lowest two bits of any pointer are always 0 and, temporarily, they may store flags or other information during some algorithms.
[11] See Listing 2.1.

Listing 2.1 Overloaded operator new() which works in three different modes: normal, updating hidden pointers, and generating a mask. [For the explanation of how this relates to so called "placement new", see the Note after the listing.]

```
class A {
        ...private members, no pointers
public:
    static void *objBuf; // controls what new() does
    static void *mask;    // for
    void* operator new(size_t size){
        unsigned long u=(unsigned long)objBuf;
        if(u==0) return malloc(size); // normal operation
        else if(u&3) return mask=calloc(1,size); // create mask
        else return(objBuf); // insert hidden pointers
    }
};
void* A::objBuf=NULL;
```

Note:

Placement new gets a section of memory and turns it into a valid object by filling in the hidden pointers. For example for class Book,

```
            void *v=calloc(sizeof(Book),1);
            Book *bp=new Book(v);
```

or on one line

```
     Book *bp=new Book( calloc(sizeof(Book),1) );
```

If we wanted to control the allocation of objects by calloc or some custom allocation function the application would have to change all the calls to new() to this ugly and potentially error-prone syntax.[12]

Overloading new() as we did in Listing 2.1 hides all this, and the application can create objects as usual. No change of calls to new() is required:

```
            Book *bp=new Book();
```

However, the last line of operator new in Listing 2.1

```
        else return(objBuf); // insert hidden pointers
```

is really nothing else than placement new, which we use in a special case when we just want to set or update hidden pointers. The difference from the normal placement new is that the memory is not supplied as the function parameter, but as the static class member objBuf.

---

[12] Note that this is similar to what you have to do when using ObjectStore (c) PSE Pro for C++.

Fig. 2.2 Mask for the Manager class from Listing 2.2. Each box corresponds to a potential pointer location (4B or 8B depending on the system architecture). Pointer locations are marked by the index of the target class, here 2 = text string, 10 = Employee

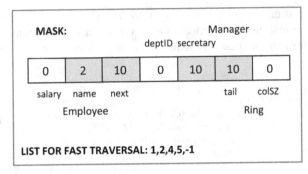

2.1.3 Regular Pointers

Regular pointers are the pointers the application inserts into classes. After you write objects to disk and then read them back to memory, the new objects are in different locations, and all the regular pointers must be replaced (*swizzled*) to the new addresses of their target objects. If you read the object back within the same program run, hidden pointers are the same, but for a different run even hidden pointers usually change.

How to detect all these pointers is one of the key tasks every persistent system must tackle.

For example, if a company hierarchy is described by classes Manager and Employee, we can represent the internal structure of each class by a mask—see Listing 2.2 and Fig. 2.2. Such masks are useful when planning algorithms or debugging code, and we will use them extensively throughout this book.

Note that it is reasonably fast to traverse a mask when swizzling pointers. However, a small performance improvement can be achieved by keeping, in addition to the mask, a list of non-zero entries in the mask. Note that mask in Fig. 2.2 does not have any hidden pointers because the two classes have no virtual functions.

Listing 2.2 Another version of Manager/Employee classes (online listed only as list2_2.txt)

```
template< class T> class Ring {
    T *tail;
    int colSZ;
};
class Employee {
    float salary;
    char *name;
    Employee *next;
};
class Manager : public Employee {
    int deptID;
    Employee *secretary;
    Ring<Employee> myPeople;
};
```

2.1.3.1 Detecting Pointers with Reflection

When reflection is available, we don't need a mask. And even if we had one it would not help much. Languages with reflection usually work with references, and objects and their parts cannot be accessed by their memory addresses.

When we need to traverse references of an object, the reflection allows us to traverse members and, for each member, it tells us whether the member is a reference and what is the type of its target. Listing 2.3 shows how this is done in Java, and Listing 2.4 shows the C# implementation.

It may not be obvious from this code, but it traverses pointers all through the inheritance hierarchy, e.g. for the Manager object from Listing 2.2, the code visits

```
Employee::name,
Employee::next,
Ring::tail,
Manager::secretary.
```

Listing 2.3 Using Java reflection to traverse references[13]

```java
import java.lang.*;
import java.lang.reflect.*;

Field[] fields = cls.getDeclaredFields();
Object val; Class targetClass;

for(Field field : fields ) {
    if(field.getType().isPrimitive())continue;
    val=field.get(this);
    if(field.getType() == String.class){
        ... // create or find new val
        field.set(this,val);
    }
    else {
        targetClass=field.getType();
        ... // create or find new val
        field.set(this,val);
    }
}
```

---

[13] For full source, see bk/chap2/reflectJava.

Listing 2.4 Using C# reflection to traverse references[14]

```
//flags: which members we want to enumerate
System.Reflection.BindingFlags flags =
    System.Reflection.BindingFlags.Public |
    System.Reflection.BindingFlags.NonPublic |
    System.Reflection.BindingFlags.Instance;

Object val; Type targetClass;
foreach (System.Reflection.FieldInfo field in
                    this.GetType().GetFields(flags)){

    if(!field.FieldType.IsClass)continue; // not a reference
    val=field.GetValue(this);
    if(val==null)continue; // no conversion for null references
    if(field.FieldType == typeof(string)){   // string
        ...// create or find new val
      field.SetValue(this,val);
    }
    else {
        targetClass=field.FieldType;
        ...// create or find new val
        field.SetValue(this,val);
    }
}
```

2.1.3.2 References Registered for Each Class

All C++ and Objective-C persistent systems must get the information about pointers externally, and one possibility is to assume that the user registers all persistent classes by listing their pointers.

In C++, our favourite method is to use macros PTR and STR[15] in the default constructor. It has the advantage that it automatically traverses the inheritance hierarchy, and the result is a mask which is a flat view of even highly composite object. Here is an example of how to use these macros:

```
class Employee {
    static void **mask; // not persistent
    float salary;
    char *name;
    Employee *next;
public:
    Employee(){
        salary=0.0;
        STR(name); PTR(next,Employee);
    }
};
```

Listing 2.5 shows how this syntax can generate the mask. The listing may appear long, but note that there is a lot of repetition: the same functions and static variables are added to all three classes.

---

[14] For full source, see bk/chap2/reflectCs.

[15] A similar method to register pointers is also used by POST++.

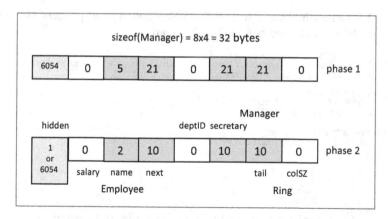

Fig. 2.3 Generating mask for the Manager class. Listing 2.5 produces directly the phase2 mask with true value of the hidden pointer (6054). The online version at bk/chap2/list2_5.cpp generates first the phase1 mask and then converts it to phase2 with 1 marking positions of hidden pointers. Mask codes: 0 = invariable members, 1 = hidden pointer, 2 = char*, 10 = Employee*

At the setup time, before the program starts to run, each class gets its unique index. Automatic assignment of class indexes happens at the setup time, before the application program even starts to run—look at the last line just before main().

Inside createMask(), the call to new() with objBuf=1 creates a 0-filled instance of Manager and inserts hidden pointers. Then, through PTR() and STR(), the default constructor Manager() marks the pointer locations in the mask.

Figure 2.3 has two numbers in the box for the hidden pointer: 1 or 6054. In most environments, hidden pointers are large numbers which are easy to distinguish from the class index stored for regular pointers. In environments, where the system stores index(!) into the virtual function table, we mark hidden pointers by using 1 in the mask, and storing the value of the hidden pointer in a separate, additional mask.

objBuf must be either a global variable or a static variable of a special Utility class.

Listing 2.5 Generating mask with both hidden and regular pointers (for full, slightly modified source, see bk/chap2/list2_5.cpp)

```
#define PTR_SZ sizeof(char*)
int totIndex=9; // index of application classes will start from 10
void *objBuf=NULL; // global allocation control

#define PTR(P,T)                                          \
if(objBuff==NULL || objBuf==(void*)1)P=NULL; \
else P=(T*)(T::getIndex())

#define STR(P)                                            \
if(objBuff==NULL || objBuf==(void*)1)P=NULL; \
else P=(char*)(2)

class Employee {
    float salary;
    char *name;
    Employee *next;
public:
    // ... static members and methods, new()as for Manager
    Employee(){STR(name); PTR(next,Employee);}
    int virtual trueClass(){return classIndex;}
};
// ... initialize static members as for Manager

class Ring {
    Employee *tail;
    int colSZ;
public:
    // ... static members and methods, new()as for Manager
    Ring(){PTR(tail,Employee);}
    int virtual trueClass(){return classIndex;}
};
// ... initialize static members as for Manager

class Manager : public Employee {
    static void *mask;
    static int classIndex; // app.classes start from 10
    static int mySize;
    int deptID;
    Employee *secretary;
public:
    Ring myGroup;
    static int getIndex(){return classIndex;}
    void* operator new(size_t size){
        unsigned long u=(unsigned long)objBuf;
        if(u==0) return malloc(size); // normal operation
        else if(u&3){ return mask=calloc(1,size); } // mask
        else return(objBuf); // insert hidden pointers
    }
    static void createMask(){
        int i; char *s; int *ip;
        objBuf=(void*)1;
        new Manager; // phase one of setting the mask
    }
    static void prtMask(){ ... }
    Manager(){PTR(secretary,Employee);}
    int virtual trueClass(){return classIndex;}
};
void* Manager::mask=NULL;
int Manager::mySize=sizeof(Manager);
int Manager::classIndex=totIndex=totIndex+1;

int main() {
    Manager::createMask();
    Manager::prtMask();
```

When we replace the statements that repeat for every class by macro
PERSIST(T), this complex code turns into nice and crisp Listing 2.6.

Macro INIT_STAT(T) initializes static variables for each class, and macros PTR
(P,T) and STR(P) are as before. The parameters of all these macros are types; they
are just like templates/generics except that they represent a block of code—not a
class or a function.

Listing 2.6 Code from Listing 2.5, where generic-like macros replace code that
repeats for every class

```
class Employee {
    PERSIST(Employee);
public:
    float salary;
    char *name;
    Employee *next;
    Employee(){ STR(name); PTR(next,Employee); }
};
INIT_STAT(Employee);

class Ring {
    PERSIST(Ring);
public:
    Employee *tail;
    int colSZ;
    Ring(){ PTR(tail,Employee); }
};
INIT_STAT(Ring);

class Manager : public Employee {
    PERSIST(Manager);
public:
    int deptID;
    Employee *secretary;
    Ring myGroup;
    Manager(){ PTR(secretary,Employee); }
};
INIT_STAT(Manager);

int main() {
    Manager::createMask();
    Manager::prtMask();
    printf(
      "classIndex: Employee=%d Ring=%d Manager=%d\n",
       Employee::getIndex(),Ring::getIndex(),
       Manager::getIndex());
    return 0;
}
```

Useful Trick No. 3
Macro PTR(P,T) can set member pointer to 1, or generate the pointer name
and type as text strings.

```
#define PTR(P,T) \
    (P)=(T *)1; \
    printf("pointer name=%s targetType-%s\n", #P, #T);
```

For the strings the macro could be replaced by a method, possibly static method of the class; setting the pointer to a value must be through a macro if you want it that simple.

For the strings, the macro could be replaced by a method, possibly static method of the class; setting the pointer to a value must be through a macro if you want this simple interface.

2.1.3.3 Smart Pointer that Registers Itself

Another way to generate the mask is to replace pointer members that we want to be persistent by an instance of a special smart-pointer class, see Listing 2.7. Such a smart pointer does not take more space than a normal pointer and is used just as a normal pointer, but it can record itself in the mask.

Listing 2.7 Mask generation with smart pointer (code sketch only, no program online)

```
template<class T> PersistPtr {
    T *ptr;
public:
    PersistPtr(){
        ptr=NULL;
        ... // mark the mask at the position of 'this'
    }
    T* operator->() const{ return ptr; }
    ... // other operators
};

class Employee {
    PERSIST(Employee);
public:
    float salary;
    PersistPtr<char> name;            // <<<<<<
    PersistPtr<Employee> next;        // <<<<<<
    Employee(){}
};
INIT_STAT(Employee);

/* similar syntax for classes Ring and Manager */

int main() {     // remaing exactly as before
    Manager::createMask();
    Manager::prtMask();
    return 0;
}
```

So far we have been working with pointers leading to a single object or to a single text string. However, there can also be pointers to various types of arrays:

```
class B;
class C {
      B *bArr; // to array of B objects
      B **bpArr; // to array of (B*)
      int *iArr; // to array of int
      char *cArr; // to array of characters
      char **cpArr; // to array of (char*)
      int aSize; // assume all arrays have this size
};
```

To register all these situations, calls to PTR() and STR() are not sufficient. We also need to register the size of the array which in most cases is already a member of the class which stores the pointer. If it is not, we always can set up special macros for such situations: ARR() for an array of objects and ARP() for an array of pointers are handy to register such situations. For example, the pointers used by class C in the last example can be registered by the following default constructor:

```
class C(){ARR(bArr,A,aSize); ARP(bpArr,B,aSize); ARR(iArr,int,aSize);
          ARR(cArr,char,aSize); ARP(cpArr,char,aSize);
}
```

Note that aSize is the name of the member, not a numerical value!

2.1.3.4 Smart Library Registering Pointers

The problem with registering pointers is that if you miss even a single one, it will not be swizzled,[16] and your program will crash on loading the data from disk. Also, as will be explained in Sect. 2.1.6, if a pointer is missing in the mask, the object to which it leads and perhaps many other objects may be missing on the disk file. Registering pointers is not something application programmers should do in their everyday work.

The idea of registering pointers opens another Pandora's box. What is the true purpose of these dangerous pointers inhabiting our classes, and why are they allowed to live there with all the mischief they can cause? And could we hide and isolate them in some place where they would be under better control?

That goes far beyond persistence, but the problem with registration of pointers only adds to the many reasons why we should avoid raw-pointer members in application classes.

The purpose of pointers is to implement data structures and relations. For example, instead of using raw pointers tail and next in Listing 2.6, it is better to replace these pointers by a generic data structure consisting of classes Ring<T> and RingPart<T> that comes from a library which takes complete care of these pointers including their registrations, and these pointers are transparent to the application code.

---

[16] As introduced in Chap. 1, *swizzle* is a commonly used term for the process of updating pointers when the objects move to a different memory location.

When following this strategy, we end up with no pointer-members in our application classes. However, the necessary condition for all this is that the library must support bi-directional data structures, which also is the prime reason we always use DOL or InCode libraries and not the standard containers.

Compare the following three implementation of the same class:

```
class Project {      //   Code with raw pointers
    char *name;    //   bad choice, raw pointer
    Manager *mgr; //   bad choice, raw pointer
};

class Project : public OneToOne<Manager>,
                public String { // better code, Style 1
};
class Project { // best code, Style 2
    String name; // better choice, pointer handled by library
    OneToOne<Manager> mgr; // library class, better choice
};
```

Styles 1 and 2 remove pointers from the application code but, in more complex situations, Style 2 ends up using multiple inheritance and, in our experience, it is more difficult to manage.

The format in which we record pointers in the library classes does not have to be particularly efficient or easy to use, because you register the class when you add it to the library, and, from that moment on, many people use it but nobody is even aware that there is any registration.

For example, Data Object Library (Data Object Library 2013) is a C++ library of bi-directional intrusive data structures which are also persistent. Each data structure is represented by a class which does not have any attributes, and its methods (operations of the association) have access to pointers and other attributes of the application classes that participate in the data structure. For an example, see Doubly Linked Aggregate in Fig. 2.4. When you want to set up an aggregate between classes Room and Students, you declare

```
Association Doubly_Linked_Aggregate <Room, Student> students;
```

The pointers are registered in a library files *registry* and *zzmaster* which essentially contain this record[17]:

```
Doubly_Linked_Aggregate 2
    1: child 2
    2: next 2, prev 2, parent 1
```

which means that in our Room/Student example we will have

---

[17] Line1: two participating classes, Line2: pointers in the first class with the index of their target class, Line3: pointers in the second class with the index of their target class.

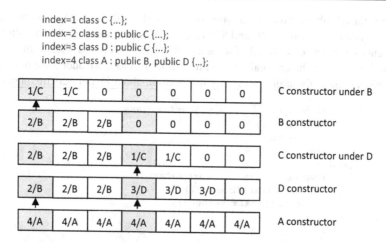

Fig. 2.4 Evolution of tMask when allocating a new A-object. This is a dynamic process which takes the advantage of default constructors for all the classes being called bottom up. Any time a non-zero location or a hidden pointer is overwritten, it is an indication of inheritance—see the *arrows*

```
class Room {
    Student *child;
    ...
}:
class Student {
    Student *next;
    Student *prev;
    Room *parent;
    ...
};
```

Pointers can come only from the library, so the library can determine what the mask of the two classes will be. All this is transparent and the user does not have to worry about registration of pointers.

2.1.3.5 Detecting Pointers with a Code Generator

Until now we have assumed that the persistence would be added to the application program as additional source or library. However, applying a code generator to some of the tasks, such as detecting pointers, can significantly simplify the user interface. It is not considered a "pure" programming technique, because it may complicate debugging, use of debuggers and IDE, and using software designed in this way as a part of a larger system, but it leads to a more elegant interface.

We can think of many ways to detect pointers with a code generator. Let's explore one possible approach which we have never used on a real application, but which would be fairly simple to implement. Assume that for every class in the application source, e.g. class Employee, we create a twin, Twin_Employee, which has the same members and thus the same mask. We discard all its methods, but add a default constructor with PTR() and STR() statements as in Listing 2.6. This allows us to generate simple code which, for each of the Twin-... classes, finds it mask. If we can link together the original class with its twin, it is as if we added the mask to the original class without providing any information about its pointers members.

```
class Employee {     // application class
     float salary;
     char *name;
     Employee *next;
public:
     float getSalary(){return salary;}
     void setSalary(float sal);
     Employee(){salary=10000;}
};


class Twin_Employee {           // twin class
     float salary;
     char *name;
     Employee *next;
public:
     Employee(){STR(name); PTR(next,Employee);}
};
```

What we proposed includes some logical leaps, and we have to explore the idea step by step in order to verify that it will really work. We do not have to make a complete syntax analysis.

Let's assume that, as the first pass, we convert the code to a stream of tokens while implementing all the name substitutions encoded by typedef or #define statements and removing comments and access indicators.[18] We get

```
class Employee { float salary ; char * name ; Employee * next ;
float getSalary ( ) { return salary ; } void setSalary ( float sal )
; Employee ( ) { salary = 10000 ; } } ;
```

In the second pass, we add the twin underscore (__) prefix to the class name and monitor the depths of { }, (), [] and <> brackets (each separately) as we traverse the tokens. We throw away any token for which the depth of { } is not 1 or the depth of any other bracket is more than 0. That gives us

```
float salary ; char * name ; Employee * next ; float getSalary ( ) {
 } void setSalary ( ) ; Employee ( ) { }
```

This allows us to identify statements which end with one of three ways:
```
     { } or ( ) or; or just  ;
```

---

[18] Public, private or protected.

Eliminate statements that do not end just with ";" and we have the list of members

```
float salary;
char * name ;
Employee * next ;
```

This allows the code generator to create the twin class

```
class Twin_Employee {   // added Twin_
     // next part is the list of members after pass 3
     float salary ;
     char * name ;
     Employee * next ;
     // remaining part is all generated, using members with *
public:
     Employee(){STR(name); PTR(next,Employee);}
};
```

This allows us to generate mask for class Twin_Employee as described in Sect. 2.1.3.2. The last missing piece of this puzzle is how, for an object of class Employee, we could quickly find the mask of Twin_Employee.

Let's assume that the code generator also creates class derived from class Employee, which adds methods and possibly members.[19] We will use prefix Exp_ for this class in order to show that it is an expansion of the original class. If we do not add any non-static members, the class will have the same original size.

```
class Exp_Employee : public Employee {
     void *getMask(){ return Twin_Employee::mask; }
};
```

The result is elegant. If you want to make any application code or library persistent you run the code generator on their classes and the only change you have to make in the code is to replace all calls to the new() operator:

```
int main() {
     Employee *e12, *e2; void *mask;
     e1=new Exp_Employee;
     e2=new Exp_Employee;
     mask=(Exp_Employee*)e1->getMask();
     // otherwise use e1 and e2 as if there is no persistence
```

This is not necessarily better than using PTR() and STR() in your application classes. You may have many new() statements spread through your code, while PTR () and STR() statements are localized in the class definitions and may be much fewer. However, making an existing class library persistent with a code generator may be easier, since a typical container library may not have many, if any, new() statements.

---

[19] This is the method of adding *from above* as described in Sect. 2.1.1.3. It adds to each allocated object, not to the class.

All this works even when some application classes inherit from other classes, assuming that the code generator converts all the classes to their twin classes. For example, if we have

```
class Employee {
    ...
};
class Manager : public Employee {
    ...
};
```

it converts it to

```
class Twin_Employee {
    ...
};
class Twin_Manager : public Twin_Employee {
    ...
};
```

2.1.4 Arrays

When you come across a pointer while reading C++ code, you cannot tell whether it leads to a single object or to an array of objects. And even if you know that it leads to an array, you have no clue about its size. That can lead to nasty surprises. The program in Listing 2.8 writes outside of its memory space, and that results in strange behaviour. It compiles on our laptops,[20] but then it we attempt crashes when we attempt to run. However, when we uncomment the printf() statements, it compiles and runs without crash. Yet there is nothing wrong with the printf() statement.

---

[20] Using Visual Studio 2010.

Listing 2.8 A pointer can lead to a single object or to an array, which is a potential source of errors

```
class A {
public:
    int weight;
};
class B {
    A *ap;
    A arr[8];
public:
    void foo(){
        ap=new A;
        ap->weight=123;
        ap[0].weight=234; // OK even though ap is not an array
// printf(" before the first potential problem\n");
        ap[2].weight=567; // wrong, possible crash
        ap=new A[60];
// printf(" before the second potential problem\n");
        ap[60].weight=789; // possible crash, index overflow
        ap->weight=999; // OK, really gets ap[0].weight
// printf(" before the third potential problem\n");
        arr[62].weight=789; // possible crash, index overflow
    }
};
```

In order to save an array properly to disk, we need to know when the pointer represents an array, and the size of that array. This is the reason why all persistent systems and languages with built-in persistence assume that pointer members always point to a single object, and that arrays are implemented through a special Array class, which stores the pointer, the size of the array, and the number of used entries. This class is usually one of the special types, and has a pre-assigned internal index just like char, int, or float.

2.1.5 Extracting Inheritance

An interesting feature of what we have done so far is that we have achieved persistency without extracting any information about inheritance among application classes. Virtual function PersistObj::trueClass() does everything we need.

However, there are situations when the information about inheritance may be useful or even essential, for example when generating UML class diagram.[21] In languages with reflection this information is readily available. In C++, there are two ways to extract this information, and both are simple and straightforward.

METHOD 1: Partial syntax analysis (using a code generator).

---

[21] We will discuss this in more detail in Sect. 4.4.

- Concatenate all the source with definitions of all application classes into one file. This usually means all the *.h files; for small programs it may be just one *.cpp file with the entire program.
- Make pass eliminating comments and lines starting with #. At the same time, break the source into tokens separated by one space. Monitor the depths of { }, (), [] and <> brackets (each separately) and throw away any token for which at least one of these depths is not 0. After you do this, Listing 2.6 is reduced to

```
class Employee { } ; INIT_STAT ( ) ; class Ring { } ; INIT_STAT ( ) ;
class Manager : public Employee { } ; INIT_STAT ( ) ; int main ( ) {
}
```

- Make another pass searching for token `class`. When you find it, look for two possible patterns:

`class A {`   A does not inherit from another class
`class A :`   A inherits from one or more classes In the second case, the continuation must be

$$X \; B \, , \, \ldots \, , \; X \, D \, \{$$

where X is anything or missing, and B . . . D are names of the classes from which A inherits.

METHOD 2: Evolving tMask (no code generator).

Let's write a program which watches how default constructors visit their parts of the object. The algorithm is similar to how we created the pointer mask in Sect. 2.1.3.2, but instead of recording pointers we will let all default constructors to write in it the index of the class to which they belong. The constructors are invoked bottom up, and when the areas overlap it implies inheritance—see Fig. 2.4.

Listing 2.9 shows the implementation of the algorithm which is a bit tricky to debug. It produces the following output:

```
A=4      Inheritance of A:
B=2      ----- 2 inherits from 1
C=1      ----- 3 inherits from 1
D=3      ----- 4 inherits from 2
E=5      ----- 4 inherits from 3
```

How does it work:

`Utility::tMask` stores the mask as it is built, and because it is static and public, it is essentially a global variable.

Operator `new()` which is under `Persist(T)` catches the initial mask before the constructors start to add to it, but only when `inhFlg=1`. For `inhFlg=0`, operator `new()` allocates normal objects as expected.

Under `INH_REC(T)`, a call to `Utility::iRep()` is inserted to every default constructor. This function fills the appropriate section of the mask with the class signature.

Listing 2.9 Extracting inheritance without using code generator (Fig. 2.5)[22]

```
typedef unsigned long UL; // unsigned integer as long as a pointer
#define HP_LIMIT 1000; // lower limit on hidden pointers
class Utility {
public:
    static int totIndex;
    static int inhFlg; // 0=normal, 1=detecting inheritance
    static UL *tMask;
    static void reportInheritance(int a, int b) {
        printf("----- %d inherits from %d\n", a, b);
    }
    static void iRep(int sz, UL *localMask, int cIndex) {
        int i, report;
        sz=sz/sizeof(char*);
        for(i=0; i<sz; i++) {
        if(localMask[i]>0 && localMask[i]<1000) {
            if(i+1>=sz) report=1;
            else if(localMask[i+1]!=localMask[i]) report=1;
            else report=0;
            if(report) reportInheritance(cIndex, (int)localMask[i]);
        }
            localMask[i]=cIndex;
        }
    }
};
int Utility::totIndex=1; // we want it to strat from 1, not from 0
UL* Utility::tMask=NULL; // allocated by new()
int Utility::inhFlg=0;

#define PERSIST(T)                                            \
public:                                                       \
static int classIndex;                                        \
static int inhFlg; /* 1 when searching for inheritance */ \
void* operator new(size_t size) {                             \
    void *r=malloc(size); /* normal operation */          \
    if(Utility::inhFlg) Utility::tMask=(UL*)r;             \
    return r;                                                 \
}                                                             \
static void reportInheritance() {                             \
    Utility::inhFlg=1;                                     \
    Utility::tMask=(UL*)(new T);                           \
    delete Utility::tMask;                                 \
    Utility::tMask=NULL;                                  \
    Utility::inhFlg=0;                                     \
}

#define INH_REC(T) if(Utility::inhFlg) \
  Utility::iRep(sizeof(T), (UL*)((T*)this), classIndex)

#define INIT_STAT(T) \
int T::classIndex=Utility::totIndex=Utility::totIndex++

class C {
PERSIST(C);
    int c;
public:
    C() {INH_REC(C);}
};
INIT_STAT(C);

... other classes coded in the same style

class A : public B, public D{
PERSIST(A);
  int a;
public:
    A() {INH_REC(A);}
};
INIT_STAT(A);

int main() {
    A::reportInheritance();
```

---

[22] Running source is in bk\chap2\list2_9.cpp

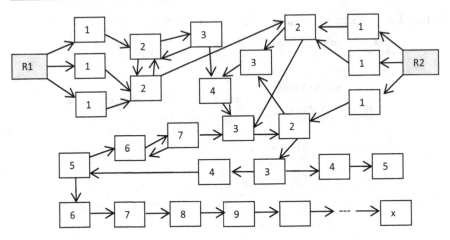

Fig. 2.5 Visiting objects by traversing pointers from roots R1 and R2. Nodes marked 1 are direct neighbours of the roots, nodes marked 2 are their direct neighbours, and so on until there are no unvisited neighbours. The numbers express the depth from the roots

2.1.6 Collecting All Active Objects

In serialization, and only in serialization,[23] we have to find all objects in our data space and save them to disk. There are three possible approaches:

(A) If the data structures are simple, the application can include a function which traverses all the objects and writes them to disk. That is efficient, but difficult to manage for complex projects, and certainly not automatic.

(B) For each class we can maintain a list of its active objects. Operator `new()` adds an entry to this list, and destructor moves it to the free list. Both lists use the same two[24] references per object. This is fast, efficient, the list of active objects is ready when we need it and, as a bonus, we get the free lists for the reuse of discarded objects. The price is the space of two references per object, and the potential problem with objects that were not properly destroyed remaining on the active list.

(C) Objects and references form a directed graph — see Fig. 2.5. Usually, in this graph, there is one or a few root objects from which we can reach all the other objects by traversing the references. If there isn't such a root or roots, you can always add a class that will serve this purpose. This is the method used by most existing serializations, and it deserves more discussion. There are two basic approaches to its implementation, and if you are not careful there may be unpleasant side effects.

---

[23] When the persistence is built on memory pages we do not need to do this.

[24] When using a doubly-linked list, removing an object is instant; removing it from a singly-linked list requires a search.

When traversing a general graph like this, we can proceed in two ways—depth first or breadth first. The depth-first search is usually coded as a recursive function which we call with obj=root. This is a pseudo-code:

```
void depthSearch(void *obj){
        for(all references ref of obj){
            if(ref not stored yet){
                depthSearch(ref);
            }
            store(obj);
        }
    }
```

The breadth-first search is best implemented with a FIFO[25] queue, and the implementation is not recursive:

```
void breadthSearch(void *obj){
        queue.in(obj); // add obj to the queue;
        while(queue not empty){
            obj=queue.out(); // get next object from the queue
            save(obj);
            for(all references ref of obj){
                if(ref has not been in queue yet){
                    queue.in(ref);
                }
            }
        }
    }
```

Both implementations need one bit on every object, in order to mark whether the object has been stored (depth-first) or whether it has entered the queue (breadth-first).

Both implementations need additional storage, stack or queue, which may grow to the size proportional to the number of objects. There is an important difference though: the system stack used by the recursive function usually has a fixed limit, but you can code the FIFO queue so that it increases its size when needed. If you have many objects the implementation with the fixed-sized queue may crash. That is the reason why Java serializations and some C# serializations crash for long chains of references.[26]

In order to traverse the graph of references, regardless which algorithm we use, we need three things:

(a) Location of all the pointers embedded in each object; this information is in the mask we described in Sect. 2.1.3.
(b) Type (and size) of the target object as allocated. When inheritance is used, this type may not agree with the type of the pointer.
(c) Additional bit or some other way to mark objects that have been recorded; otherwise the traversal may end up in an infinite loop.

---

[25] First In First Out.

[26] DOL and QSP persistence for Objective-C in Chap. 7 use the breadth-first implementation.

The standard way of solving item 2 is to have a virtual function which returns the type of the allocated object, either directly or through class Reflect—see online listing list2_9x.cpp.

There are three ways to provide the additional bit needed under item 3:

1. We can add a member *from below* or *from above* (Sects. 2.1.1.1 and 2.1.1.3).
2. We can keep a dictionary, for example a hash table, of references to all objects that have been stored (depth-first) or were admitted to the queue (breadth-first). This requires both additional storage and processor cycles at the part of code which repeats many times.
3. If you aim for ultimate performance, you can use the following, a rather dirty trick to store the required bit.

Useful Trick No. 4

All references and object sizes are multiples of four, with two lower bits never used.

One of these bits can record whether an object was already visited. If you have any control over the allocation, the obvious candidate is the field storing the size of the object. This field usually precedes the memory image of the object.[27]

Example of how this could be applied to a member[28]:

```
#define flagMask (size_T)3;
#define sizeMask ~(size_T)3;

class Book {
        size_t size; // always multiple of 4
        void setFlag(int flg){
            size=size&sizeMask;
            if(flg)size=size | 1;
        }
        int getFlag(){ return size&flagMask; }
        void setsize(int flg){
            size=size&sizeMask;
            if(flg)size=size | 1;
        }
        size_t getFlag(){ return size&flagMask; }
```

Now we have everything ready for the algorithm which collects all objects—see Listing 2.10. Function getAllObj() lives under the Utility class, and it builds a chain of UtilLink objects that point to recorded active objects.

Functions setBit(), clearBit(), and getBit() provide access to the special bit. The mask of regular pointers has been converted into a more convenient format—a table where each entry gives the offset of the next regular pointer.

---

[27] For more details see Chap. 6 where this trick is used in the QSP persistence for Objective-C.

[28] size_t is the same as unsigned int for 32-bit compiler, but 64-bit compiler it is unsigned long long, which is 8 byte long.

For example, if the mask is [H, int, R, R, float, R, int], where H is the hidden pointer, and R is the regular pointers, then tab[]={8,12,20,−1}.

Listing 2.10 The heart of the algorithm that expands, breadth-first, from the root to all other objects via their pointers. This sample program works only with pointers to single objects. It handles neither strings nor arrays

```
class PersistObj {
public:
        virtual Reflect *trueClass(){return NULL;};
        virtual void createMask(){};
};
// when we remember head and tail, this list works as a queue
class UtilLink {
public:
        PersistObj *obj;
        UtilLink *next;
        UtilLink(PersistObj *rt,UtilLink *last){
                        obj=rt; if(last)last->next=this;
                        next=NULL;}
};

UtilLink* Utility::getAllObj(PersistObj *root){
        UtilLink *u,*unew,*tail; PersistObj *p,*regPtr;
        int i,*tab,*code; Reflect *ref; void **locRegPtr; char *msk;
        createAllMasks(); // until this time they may not be needed
            ref=root->trueClass(); // get reflection for the target object
            root=ref->trueObj; // replace root by the true object
            allObj=new UtilLink(root,NULL); // root is first on the list
            for(u=tail=allObj; u; u=u->next){
                p=u->obj; // object to expand, it is a true object
                already
                Utility::clearBit(p); // before reflection, clear the
                 bit
                ref=p->trueClass(); // reflection on the target object
                tab=ref->ptrOff; // offsets for pointers on p
                for(i=0; tab[i]>=0; i++){ // walk through regular pointers
                    locRegPtr=(void**)((char*)p+tab[i]); //location of
                    regPtr
                    regPtr=(PersistObj *)(*locRegPtr);
                    if(regPtr==NULL)continue; // do not follow, NULL
                    pointer
                    // skip when target on the list or when p==target
                    if(Utility::getBit(regPtr) || p==regPtr)continue;
                    ref=regPtr->trueClass(); // reflection on the target
                    regPtr=ref->trueObj; // replace regPtr by true object
                    unew=new UtilLink(regPtr,tail); // add to the chain
                    tail=unew; // remember the new tail of the chain
                    Utility::setBit(regPtr); // mark new object as expanded
                }
                Utility::setBit(p); // give p the "used" status again
        }
        // make all objects valid again by removing the bit
        for(u=allObj; u; u=u->next){
                p=u->obj;
                Utility::clearBit(p);
        }
        return allObj; // beginning of the chain
}
```

Note that in C and C++ (but not in C#. Objective-C or in Java) pointers can lead into the middle of an object. This can be result of multiple inheritance or of an improper use of an embedded object as shown in Listing 2.11, where d spans over 56 bytes, between addresses 6044696 and 6044751, and pointers a, b, c, and x point to various locations inside this span.

The objects that we want to save should include only full, allocated objects, not their parts possibly overlapping or incomplete. In Listing 2.11 the virtual function trueObj() takes care of pointers such as a and b (it replaces them by d), but unfortunately it cannot correct pointers such as c or x. However, if such a pointer exists anywhere in your design,[29] there must also be a pointer to the entire D object which contains the small part.

Such duplications are easy to eliminate. Before writing the object to disk, do this:

ALGORITHM 2.1: Eliminate Embedded Objects from the List

1. Sort the objects by two keys:
    Priority 1: Increasing starting address
    Priority 2: Decreasing address of the last byte
2. Traverse the list while dropping embedded objects.
    Assuming we have an array of pointers to the objects, arr[], we do it like this:

```
for(i=0,k=1; k<numObj; k++){
    if(arr[k]->start[k] <= arr[k]->end[i])continue;
//remove k
    else {i++; arr[i]=arr[k];}
    }
```

Listing 2.11 In C++, there are three situations when a pointer can lead inside an object—in case of multiple inheritance, when pointing to an embedded object or pointing inside an array of objects

```
class A {int a; };
class B { int b; };
class C {int c; };
class D : public A, public B {
public:
    int d;
    C cObj;
    C arr[10];
};
int main(){
    D* d=new D;
    A* a=(A*)d;
    B* b=(B*)d;
    C* c= &(d->cObj);      // bad practice, but it can happen
    C* x=(&(d->arr[7]));  // bad practice, but it can happen
printf("sizeD=%d d=%d a=%d b=%d c=%d x=%d\n",sizeof(D),d,a,b,c,x);
// PRINTS sizeD=56 d=6044696 a=6044696 b=6044700 c=6044708 x=6044740
```

---

[29] It should not – it would be a poor design.

2.1.7 Java-Style Collecting Objects

As we can deduce from the output of Java serialization in Fig. 1.6, Java uses the depth-first algorithm which calls recursive function `serializeObj(root)`—this is a pseudo code[30]:

```
void serializeObject(Object obj){
        if(class.myClass is not serialized)writeClass(obj.myClass);
        mark obj as serialized;
        for all members m of obj do {
            if(m is a reference){
                if(object m already serialized){write reference;}
                else {serializeObject(m)};
            }
            else write m;
        }
    writeObject(obj);
}
```

where `serializeObject()` recursively traverses inheritance hierarchy.

As we explained before, besides the performance penalty for calling a recursive function, this approach is vulnerable to stack overflow. For example, if you have a linked list of 100,000 objects, you may need 100,000 stack frames, and your program will crash with *StackOverflowError*.

2.1.8 Binary Serialization

We use the term *binary* for the serialization in which the byte images of the objects are written to the disk as they are. This is quite different from the binary Java serialization or the binary serialization in C# which creates and expands the description of each object and stores this description in a binary format.

Of all the approaches to persistence described in this book, only the binary option of the DOL library has used[31] this method. Yet it is simple, and as the benchmark in Chap. 8 shows, it is highly efficient.

DOL is based on the idea of integrating a library of data structures with persistence.[32] The application classes are not allowed to use members which are raw, plain pointers. All pointers are pre-registered in the library, so there is no need to detect them in the application classes.

When collecting active objects, the breadth-first approach is used, and when writing objects to disk, each object or array or objects is written in two records:

---

[30] The underlined functions are pseudo code. There are no functions with these names in Java.

[31] Since 1989.

[32] The idea was introduced in Chap. 1 and is discussed more in Sect. 2.1.3.4.

1. Header, as a block of bytes:

```
struct ObjectHeader {
    unsigned long objAddress; // starting address
    int objSize; // size of single object
    int numObjects; // 1 if single object
    int typeCode;
};
```

2. The object as the block of bytes.

Note that there are no generated object IDs. The original object address is used as its ID.

The pointers are swizzled when reading the data from the disk. Pairs (oldAddress, newAddress) are stored in a hash table, with the oldAddress used as the key. The table is used both as a container of all objects that were read from the disk and also for the conversion of the pointers to these objects.

With buffered IO, the disk access is reasonably fast. Figure 2.6 shows the typical format of the output file.

2.1.9 ASCII Serialization

The serialization which stores objects as blocks of bytes is highly efficient in both speed and data footprint. However, when transferring data from one operating system to another, for example between MS Windows and UNIX or Apple, binary data is meaningless unless you provide an automatic format translation. However, an ASCII text file usually works without a special conversion. This is one of the reasons why C# and Java provide XML serialization. ASCII format also allows visual reading of the file, which helps debugging.

The problem with generating ASCII representation of objects is that, especially in C languages, some types may need a different representation depending on the context. A byte can be a true ASCII character or a small integer; representing characters as numbers is inefficient and misleading when debugging, and if the character represents a number, some values will be unprintable characters. With float numbers there may be a question of accuracy. My experience is that pointers can be safely stored as (unsigned int) or hex, but that for other fields it is better to let the application programmer decide about their storage format.

That brings us to the problem we encountered with a large business system where serialization and deserialization functions represented one-third of the code—see footnote 3 in Chap. 1. Maintaining separate serialization functions for writing/reading is dangerous. If the two functions do not match, everything breaks down.

ASCII serialization in DOL[33] (Data Object Library 2013) has complete control of both hidden and regular pointers, and it stores/restores them transparently and

---

[33] In DOL, some macros have different names, but for the sake of clarity we use macros that we have been using so far.

```
+++++++++++++++ GENERAL INFO   (block of 28 bytes )
style = style of persistence
time = time stamp (8 bytes)
numClasses = number of classes
+++++++++++++++ NEXT CLASS ++++++++++++++++++++++
ClassHeader (block of 12 bytes)
mask1 = mask of pointers (objSize bytes)
mask2 = mask of inheritance (objSize bytes)
nameString  (size defined in the header)
+++++++++++++++ NEXT CLASS ++++++++++++++++++++++
ClassHeader (block of 12 bytes)
mask1 = mask of pointers (objSize bytes)
mask2 = mask of inheritance (objSize bytes)
nameString  (size defined in the header)
+++++++++++++++ NEXT CLASS  ++++++++++++++++++++++
      ..... repeats numClasses -times
+++++++++++++++ NEXT OBJECT +++++++++++++++++++++
ObjectHeader (block of 12 bytes);
Object ... raw block of bytes
+++++++++++++++ NEXT OBJECT +++++++++++++++++++++
ObjectHeader (block of 12 byte s);
Object ... raw block of bytes
+++++++++++++++ NEXT OBJECT +++++++++++++++++++++
        ..... repeats until the end of file
```

Fig. 2.6 Format of the DOL binary serialization file. All records are binary

automatically. The user supplies only the format for the remaining fields such as characters, floats, and signed/unsigned integers, and a simple code generator creates pairs of serialization functions that are guaranteed to match. Here is how Employee and Manager objects are managed in the application code, and what is the resulting disk image:

```
// PERSIST(T) manage pointers such as next,tail,secretary
class Employee {
    PERSIST(Employee);
    float salary;
    int phone;
};
FORMAT(Employee,"%6.2f %d",salary,phone);

class Manager : public Employee {
    PERSIST(Manager);
    char deptID[4]; // string of up to 3 characters
};
FORMAT(Manager,"%3s",deptID);

// Invocations of the data structures from a library
RELATION_RING(Manager,Employee) myEmployees;
RELATION_ONE_TO_ONE(Manager,Employee) toSecretary;
```

Image of a Manager object on the disk file:
Line 1 (address, class, how many): 6044696 13 1
Line 2 (automatic pointers—next, tail, secretary): 6045012 6044540 6045084
Line 3 (user controlled—salary, phone, deptID): 10450.50 6133885211 A23

2.1.10 Deallocation and Garbage Collection

The great advantage of serialization is that it does not require any garbage collection or special deallocation techniques. During the program run, objects are dynamically allocated and deallocated through calls to `malloc()` and `free()` which are hidden under the operator `new()` and `delete()`. And because only active objects are written to the disk, the serialization itself works as a space-cleaning mechanism.

2.2 Memory Paging

Persistence based on memory paging is a good alternative to serialization. We allocate objects from pages of memory, and when storing the data we move entire pages between the memory and the disk, without looking at individual objects. This method is fast and space efficient, but it must take over both allocation and reuse of the free space including arrays. Since we are not saving individual objects, we need a different mechanism to identify pointers and, for this purpose, a special bitmap can be handy.

2.2.1 Bitmap

The mask which we used in serialization clearly identified pointers inside any object, without paying attention to inheritance and embedded objects. It gave us a flat view with positions of the pointers clearly visible.

Perhaps we can apply a similar idea to the entire data space, and instead of saving individual objects, we could save the entire data space, in one shot, as a large block of bytes. The only thing we would need would be a mask that would show us where are the pointers that we have to swizzle. If that mask uses one bit for each potential location of a pointer with addresses divisible by 4 (or 8), the mask would add the overhead of only 1/32 (or 1/64) of the data space—a quite reasonable price to pay for the service we'll get—see Fig. 2.7.

For example, assume that we have an address space of 65536 bytes, from 52004 to 117539 and at address 70104 we allocate a 20-byte object with 3 pointers offsets

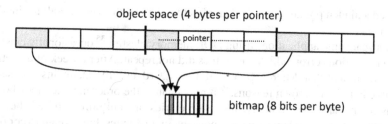

Fig. 2.7 Mapping potential pointer locations from the object space into the bitmap

{0,8,16}. The address space has 65536/4 = 16384 potential pointer locations, so the bitmap needs 16384 bits = 16384/8 = 2048 bytes.

When allocating the new object at address 70104, the pointer locations are 70104, 70112 and 70120, and the following bits must be set: (70104 − 52004)/4 = 4525, (70112 − 52004)/4 = 4527, and (70120 − 52004)/4 = 4529.

We have to mark both the hidden and the regular pointers because both must be swizzled, each using a different algorithm.

Note that when using smart pointer PersistPtr<T> explained in Sect. 2.1.2, updating of the bitmap is especially efficient. The default constructor of this pointer can automatically set the appropriate bit in the bitmap.

```
template<class T> PersistPtr {
    T *ptr;
public:
    PersistPtr(){
        ptr=NULL;
        ... // mark the bitmap at the position of 'this'
    }
    T* operator->() const{ return ptr; }
    ... // other operators
};
```

When swizzling pointers during serialization, we had to swizzle only regular pointers. We knew the type of each object, so we could just copy[34] hidden pointers from the mask of its class.

When we work with a block of memory, swizzling is more difficult. We have to distinguish between hidden and regular pointers, and we cannot copy hidden pointers from the mask because we have no clue which mask would apply.

A hidden pointer can be recognized by its value—it must be in a narrow address range of the virtual function table for the old data.

Since the introduction of C++ in the early 1990s, all C++compilers used the same convention. If two programs shared the same *.h files and listed them in the same order, the virtual function tables were identical, except for usually being in a different memory location. The conversion of hidden pointers was easy: after we

---

[34] This was done by a special operator new().

detected a hidden pointer, we added an offset which was the same for all the hidden pointers.

This year some applications using DOL memory blasting[35] occasionally crashed with a mysterious error, which sometimes did not repeat. After a week of detective work we found that Microsoft Visual C++ 2010 usually maintains the same v.f. table but, for unknown reasons,[36] it may change the order in which the classes are listed in that table. Usually, the table entries are uniformly spaced, but we encountered one case when they were not—by mere 4 bytes, but enough to confuse our original, simple algorithm. Replacing it was not trivial, because swizzling of hidden pointers is typically performed for every active object, so the performance matters.

The new DOL algorithm first checks whether all the old/new pairs fit the uniform-offset pattern. If they do, it uses the offset. If they do not, it uses an algorithm which is easiest to explain by an example:

Let's assume that we have four classes and that we know the values of their hidden pointers—both the old ones (before saving to disk) and the new ones (when reading the data from disk).[37] Assume that the old values are sorted[38]:

i	class	olddif		new
0	Publication	3359488		8799040
1	Journal	3359504	16	8799008
2	Book	3359536	32	8799056
3	Report	3359572	36	8799024

In this case, the range of the original pointers is $335572 - 3359488 = 84$, which is different from the new pointers $8799008 - 8799060 = 48$. Also, the old pointers are not uniformly spaced.

We make a sparse table sTab[] with $(3359572 - 3359488)/16 + 1 = 6$ entries, where 16 is the smallest value in the dif column. Then for each i we set sTab[old [i]-old[0])/16]=new[i], which gives us the following table:

k	sTab
0	8799040
1	8799008
2	0
3	8799056
4	0
5	8799024

The conversion is instant. For example, when converting old hidden pointer 3359536, we calculate $k = (3359536 - 3359488)/16 = 3$, and the new value is

---

[35] DOL binary and DOL ascii do not use bitmap.

[36] This could be because of the incremental compilation in VS2010.

[37] These values can be found from masks derived in Sects. 2.1.1 and 2.1.2.

[38] In order to demonstrate the algorithm, we disturbed the numbers more than when we encountered them in real situations.

`sTab[3]=8799056`. In real applications, we have not encountered a case where `sTab[i]=0` for more than one `i`.

2.2.2 Pages of Memory

The bitmap allows us to build simple yet highly efficient persistent data. We can allocate a large block of memory, and we set aside an additional, 32-times smaller block, for the bitmap. We modify the new() operator so that it allocates new objects from this block, and we make sure that all default constructors mark the bitmap for all the pointer members. When saving objects to disk, we simply dump the entire block to disk, together with the old address and type of the root object and the table of old hidden pointers.

When reading the data from the disk we allocate the same amount of memory, copy the disk content in it and swizzle all the pointers recorded in the bitmap. If there is only one block, all pointers are swizzled by the same increment. The bitmap is persistent—no swizzling is required.

This is so simple and efficient that you must be wondering why anybody would bother to use serialization. The weakness of this approach is the fixed size of the block. In real life applications, you rarely know how much space your data might require, and allocating a bigger block of memory, copying the old image in it and swizzling all the pointers may pause your program for long enough to make this approach prohibitive. After all, this is essentially the early-Smalltalk model from Chap. 1, only improved by the bitmap.

What we need is an arrangement which would use not one block of data but pages of virtual memory, with system pages still working behind the scene as usual.

The following scheme was proposed by Mark Kraemer from Zycad Corp. in 1993, was implemented as *memory blasting* in DOL, and was first published on pp. 379–386 in Soukup (1994).

The DOL implementation assumes that the size of these pages is a power of 2. This is only a minor performance improvement which allows frequently used division to be replaced by logical shift, and modulus operation by logical AND. The following description assumes that the page size, `pgSz`, can have any size which is A multiple of 4 bytes (or 8 bytes on 64-bit hardware).

The problem with this entire approach is that, for a given pointer, we need fast access to the page in which its target object is located. For this purpose, we keep array `pageStart[]`, where `pageStart[i]` stores the starting address of the page which starts anywhere between `i*pgSz` and `(i+1)*pgSz-1>`. In other words, page starting on address `p` is recorded in `pageStart[p/pgSz]`, using integer division. For any allocated page there is only one corresponding entry in `pageStart[]`, and some `pageStart[]` entries may be 0; see Fig. 2.8. The best way to learn how this works is to go step by step through a simple example.

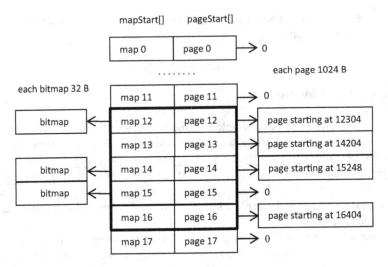

Fig. 2.8 Persistent memory consisting of pages pgSz=1024

Example[39]:

As shown in Fig. 2.8, assume we allocated four pages that start at 12304, 13584, 15248, and 16404, and we record them by dividing their starting address by the page size, for example $13584/1024 = 13$.

Question: Where is pointer 15372?

Answer: $15372/1024 = 15$, pageStart[15]=0, it is on page 14 (one step down). Address inside page $= 15372 - 15248 = 124$, bit number $124/4 = 31$

Question: Where is pointer 15260?

Answer: $15260/1024 = 14$, pageStart[14]<=15260, it is on page 14. Address inside page $= 15260 - 15248 = 12$, bit number $12/4 = 3$

Question: Where is pointer 15208?

Answer: $15208/1024 = 14$, pageStart[14]>1508, it is on page 13 (step down). Address inside page $= 15208 - 14204 = 1004$, bit number $1004/4 = 251$

Example[40]:

Assume that data from Fig. 2.8 was stored on disk, and we are restoring the data. Typically, the pages are allocated to completely different locations—they may not be in the same order. Let's see how we swizzle regular pointers if the new pages are as shown in Fig. 2.9.

Question: Convert old pointer value 14228.

Answer: $14338/1024 = 13$, $14228 > 14202$, old page is 13. Address within the page is $14228 - 14204 = 24$

From Fig. 2.9, old page 13 corresponds to new page 52

New address is $53748 + 24 = 53772$

---

[39] This is the same example as used in Soukup (1994) on pp. 381–382.

[40] This example is *not* in Soukup (1994).

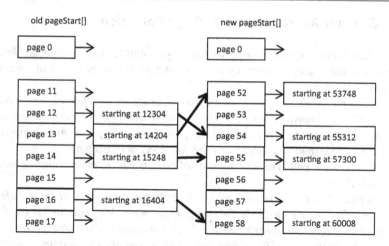

Fig. 2.9 Assignment of pages when reading data from disk can be random (example)—see *heavy arrows*. Page size must remain the same, here 1024 bytes

Potential improvements and interesting details

1. The beginning of arrays pageStart[] and mapStart[] is usually unused, for example entries 0–11 in Fig. 2.9, and entries 0–51 for the new pageStart[] in Fig. 2.9. The idea is to start the array from the index corresponding to the first page, and be ready to shift the assignment if some page has a lower address.

2. There is no need to store on disk the unused entries –those with pageStart[i]=0. You can either store the used section (heavy frame in Fig. 2.8) as it is, or store the array as a sparse array.

3. Bitmaps are persistent; they do not need any swizzling.

4. The size of arrays mapStart[] and pageStart[] depends on the original estimate of the total expected data space. If this estimate is exceeded, we do not have to reallocate the existing pages, only these arrays. In order to make this fast, we recommend to select the page size close to the realistic estimate of the required space—without any safety. That way you end up with one or a few pages, and even if the arrays have to be re-allocated, it is fast.

Useful Trick No. 5

If your objects have many non-structural members, detecting pointers by traversing the bitmap is not efficient, because the algorithm walks through many 0s before it hits a pointer. We can speed up this search significantly by treating the bitmap as an array of integers. Only if an integer is not 0 do we examine its bytes, and only if a byte is 0 do we examine its bits.

2.2.3 Dynamic Allocation and Garbage Collection

Any of these techniques work quite well until you start to destroy objects. Unless you manage free space, the memory and disk footprints may grow out of control.

Real life story

One of our consulting appointments was to examine the core of a telephone switch and try to improve its speed. Telephone switch is a computer which processes human voices converted to a stream of numbers, multiplexed and transferred in packages. The system was written in a special object-oriented language (not C++), and each telephone call created hundreds of objects which, often within seconds, were again deleted.

We suspected that the creation and especially destruction of all these objects took a long time, so we made the following experiment. We requested a block of memory at the beginning of each phone call, and allocated all the objects from it.[41] *Instead of the destruction of individual objects at the end of call, we simply freed the entire block of memory. It made the switch 30 % faster!*

Then we tried a different strategy. For each class, we kept a linked list of free objects. Instead of allocating new objects, we picked the ready-made objects from this list and, instead of destroying them, we hooked them to the list by resetting two pointers. It was even faster!

We learned two lessons: (a) When looking for high performance, do not underestimate the time needed for creation and destruction of objects. (b) Keeping free lists of objects by class is very efficient.

The problem with building persistence on pages of memory is that you must take over memory management including the disposal and reuse of objects. And this memory management must be persistent. For example, the disk file must record the beginning of each list, and the pointers connecting the free list must be marked in the bitmap.

A highly effective and simple to implement method of reusing objects is to keep, for each class, a list of discarded objects. If the list is empty, operator new() allocates the next object from the last, not completely used page. When it is not empty, it just picks up an object from the beginning of the list. Operator delete() always attaches the unwanted object to the list.

If you want to be able to mix non-persistent objects with persistent ones, you need new() and delete() for persistent objects, and a set of different functions, say npNew() and npDelete(), for non-persistent objects which are managed outside your memory pages, directly from the heap.[42]

---

[41] This is sometimes called *arena allocation*.

[42] You can override delete() but you cannot overload it with different parameters.

When an object is discarded, we believe it is not a dirty technique to use its first 4 bytes for the pointer that forms the free list. When the object is being reused, we only have to correct the first 4 bytes if there is a hidden pointer. The free list works like this:

```
class Book {
    Book *freeList;
    void addFree(Book *b){
        *((Book**)b)=freeList;
        freeList=b;
    }
    Book *getFree(){
        Book* b=freeList;
        if(b) freeList=(*((Book**)b));
        return b;
    }
}
```

There are several ways to make free lists persistent, but only the following method is both conceptually correct and has the ultimate runtime performance. When moving an object to the free list, we reflect the change of its status by changing its fingerprint in the bitmap to 100...00, essentially registering only one pointer at the beginning of the object. When reusing an object (and removing it from the free list), its bitmap record will go back to the fingerprint of the particular class. This way, the free list pointers will be automatically swizzled with other pointers.

Note that if every object starts with a hidden pointer as happens in DOL, the first four bites of any object are already marked as a pointer in the bitmap. Thus without any special action, the free list is automatically persistent. However, some of the old pointers that may still be in the object image will go through the swizzling uselessly and will make it slower.

Listing 2.12 shows the implementation.

Listing 2.12 Keeping chains of free objects for each class[43]

```
// first 4 bytes of the object represent the 'next' pointer
#define NEXT(P) (*((void**)P))

class A {
    static void *objHead; // first 4 bytes of the prototype
    static void *freeTail;
    // ...
public:
    void* operator new(size_t sz){
        void *p;
            ...
        if(!freeTail) p=allocateFromPage(sz);
        else {
            p=NEXT(freeTail); // from the chain of free objects
            if(p==freeTail)freeTail=NULL;
            else NEXT(freeTail)=NEXT(p);
            NEXT(p)=objHead;
        }
            restoreBitmap(p); // restore bitmap to valid obj.
            return (A*)p;
    }
    void operator delete(void *p) { // does not destroy the object
        setFirstBit(p); //set bitmap to 100..0 for this object
        if(!freeTail) {NEXT(p)=p;} // puts it on the free chain
        else {NEXT(p)=NEXT(freeTail); NEXT(freeTail)=p;}
        freeTail=p;
    }
    int main(){
        A* ap=new A;
        delete(ap);
```

Note that this handles the reuse of single objects but not of arrays.

Note also that memory paging and serialization do not exclude each other. Serialization can traverse all objects regardless of how they were allocated; it is a handy tool which cleans the memory pages of any non-active objects that may be accidentally left there. When deserializing the data we only have to make sure that the new objects are allocated from our pages.

This can be arranged by overloading operator new() for all the application classes and controlled by a global switch, pgAlloc:

```
class Book {
    void* Book::operator new(size_t sz){
        if(pgAlloc) ... // allocate from pages
        else ... //allocate with malloc() or as char[sz]
    }
```

---

[43] The online code does not show the adjustments to the bitmap.

The purpose of pgAlloc is to allow serialization to operate in two modes: standalone or alternating with memory paging. Alternating memory paging with serialization is a good practice, because serialization automatically removes free lists, all garbage, and it defragments the data space.

So far, we have not discussed allocation and free storage of arrays. In C++ there are two types of operators new() and delete(): the static operators which are associated with some class and usually allocate/delete individual objects and the global operators which allocate/delete arrays.

Allocation of arrays brings the following challenges:
1. Can we allocate arrays that are larger than our page?
2. How to reuse arrays? Could we merge or split them?
3. A fast algorithm for finding a free array of the required size is instrumental.

When an array is larger than one page, we can allocate several abutting pages as one large block memory, and allocate the array across the page boundaries. All pages of this set must be marked so that when reading them from disk, they will be again adjacent to each other. Their bitmaps work as usual.

These problems have been well researched, and it depends on you and your application how fancy a management of the free space you chose. Because serialization provides defragmentation and cleanup, we are in favour of a simple free storage.

One possible way to manage free arrays is to use another bitmap,[44] which marks both ends of each free array—see Fig. 2.10.[45] When freeing an array, the bitmap tells us whether the new array butts to a free space on either end, and the record in the adjacent field tells us how large that free space is. Without any search or expensive calculation, we can combine adjacent free spaces.

The assumption for all this is that arrays are allocated from a different part of memory than single objects—always an array abutting on an array, which is a common practice today. Arrays must be at least 16 bytes long, because they have to be doubly linked—when reusing an array we may select an array from the middle of the chain. These arrays must be persistent, which affects the bitmap maintenance while moving arrays to/from the free list.

A more elaborate approach is shown in Fig. 2.11. Single free objects are stored by class, short arrays and strings by size, and large arrays are stored in a height-balanced binary tree, which is O(log n) for lookup, insertion, or removal. For specific differences see Wikipedia. (Knizhnik, POST++, 1999) uses AVL tree; DOL keeps chains of free objects but does not reuse arrays.

A frequently used improvement is an array of entries for short, frequently occurring arrays such as text strings, where entry for index i=(sz/4-1) leads to a chain of short objects of size sz; see Fig. 2.11.

Short arrays including short text strings are allocated and reused in the same way as single objects, without recombining them.

---

[44] This means an additional bitmap which is different from the one we used to mark pointer locations.

[45] Ending beyond the page border.

one box represents 4 bytes, dark is the new free array (16 bytes)

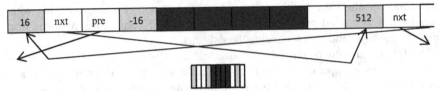

bitmap shows that the new array can combine with a 16-byte space on the left

situation after the two arrays merged

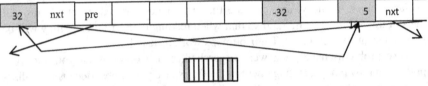

Fig. 2.10 Merging abutting free arrays: we start with two free arrays, one 16 bytes long, the other 512 bytes long, ends marked by *light colour* in the bitmap. *Boxes* shown in *dark colour* represent the free array which we want to add. Bits in the bitmap tell us that we have an abutting array on its left, 16 bytes long. This allows us to merge the two arrays. Pointers nxt and pre form a doubly linked list of free arrays

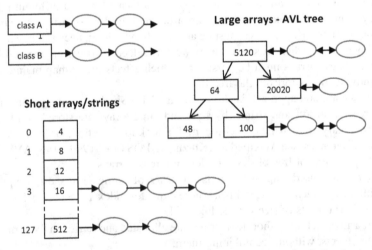

Fig. 2.11 Free storage for arrays including text strings. Short arrays of each size form a singly-linked chain and are allocated from the same part of memory as simple objects. Long arrays are allocated from a different part of memory, and arrays of the same size form a linked list. Their ends are marked by their size and are recorded in the bitmap, and they can recombine with abutting free arrays

2.3 File Mapping

> Many operating systems including Windows and UNIX provide a function which maps a selected section of virtual memory to a disk file. Instead of implementing persistent objects with our own pages, as we did in Chap. 2.2, we can implement it with system pages of the file mapping function—essentially keeping a mirror image between the two entities. However, the data is not transferred as one block, it moves back and forth in system pages. The advantage is that these pages will naturally support transactions. The disadvantage is that you need some knowledge of system programming.

Before we dive into the programming details, let's look at the main concept which is simple. We establish a mapping between a section of virtual memory and a disk file, and then allocate all objects from this section of memory. When the application stops, all the objects are stored on the file. Then when we start the application with the same mapping, the objects magically move back to memory again!

One little detail, though. All this would work if, when reading the data from the disk, we could use the same section of virtual memory. Most of the time, this is not, and We really should swizzle all the pointers by the offset between starting addresses of the old and new memory section.

That again is not trivial. The data does not move between the disk and memory as one block, but as system pages. We could go through the disk data and swizzle the pointers there, but that would not be very efficient. Instead, we have to swizzle the pointers as they are loaded into memory.

It works like this. When the application traverses a pointer, the system checks whether the page with the address stored in the pointer (the address of the target object) is already loaded in memory. If it is not, it triggers a page fault which results in loading the page.

At this point we must swizzle the pointers before the control is returned to the application. For example, we can catch the page fault, copy the page from the disk without leaving this to the system, swizzle the pointers on the page, and return the control back to the application.

That assumes that we can find where the pointers are in the new page, and we have already discussed that at length. Pages may also move in and out of the memory, so it may happen that the page, which re-enters on the page fault already has the pointers swizzled. Swizzling them the second time would make them incorrect. One method to prevent that, is to allow each page to store its own starting address. If this address agrees with the address to which the page is being loaded, swizzling is not required.

ORIGINAL MEMORY & DISK FILE

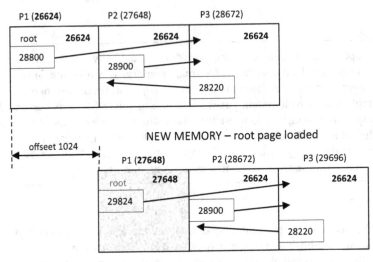

NEW MEMORY – root page loaded

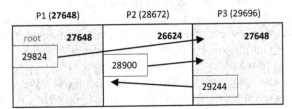

NEW MEMORY – page P3 loaded

NEW MEMORY – page P2 loaded

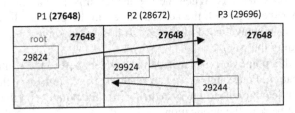

Fig. 2.12 Persistence based on file mapping (the concept). Every page remembers the P1 address (*bold*) at the time of its last pointer swizzling (upper-right corner of the page box)

Figure 2.12 demonstrates the idea. We start with the root page loaded and the 28800 pointer swizzled by the offset of 1024 to 29824. Traversing this pointer triggers page fault because page P3 is not yet loaded. After is it loaded, all its pointers are swizzled by the offset, including the original 28220 which becomes 29244. When traversing this pointer, it triggers page fault for page P2, which is then loaded and its pointers swizzled. The original 28900 is now 29924. That pointer leads to page P3. If it is loaded, there is no page fault and everything runs smoothly and fast. If P3 is not loaded, we get a page fault, we load it, but we do not have to swizzle its pointers because we see that the beginning of the current memory section, 27648, agrees with the number recorded for this page—it is the number recorded at the right upper corner of the page.

The actual implementation is more complicated. File Mapping pages the disk file to file views which are in the virtual memory of individual processes.[46] Several processes may map to the same disk file simultaneously. A view can mirror the entire file or only its section.

This entire feature was clearly designed to facilitate a design of true databases, which may store large amounts of data and be accessed by multiple processes, often simultaneously. The purpose of View is to allow access to only a small part of an otherwise large collection of data, for example in bank or airline reservation transactions.

As explained in Sect. 1.1, this book is about persistent data that are accessed by only a single process at any given time, and for this reason all the following discussion will assume a single process accessing a disk file, and Listing 2.13 shows in code what we explained in Fig. 2.12.

Listing 2.13 is an excerpt from programs List2_13a.cpp and List2_13b.cpp which are online under bk/chap2. Read it without worrying about the numerous parameters that make the use of these functions a bit tricky. It is in the call to MapViewOfFileEx() that you can specify the address where you would prefer the data to start. As we explained, the function may not satisfy the request, but, if it does, there is no need for pointer swizzling.

Listing 2.13 Example of File Mapping under Windows. I order to time and test parts of the algorithm separately, the online version of this program consists of three source files: List2_13a.cpp, List2_13b.cpp, and List2_13c.cpp

---

[46] Each process has its own independent virtual memory.

```
HANDLE fh; // file handle as for normal disk IO
unsigned baseAddr; // requested address for the beginning of the data
void *newBase; // beginning of the data in the virt.memory
char *p;
unsigned vmSZ; // size limit of the data

// Instead of using create() or open() we have to use CreatFile(),
// otherwise CreateFileMapping() does not work.
// Use OPEN_ALWAYS or OPEN_EXISTING when creating or openning file.
fh=CreateFile(fName,GENERIC_READ|GENERIC_WRITE,0,NULL, OPEN_ALWAYS,
              FILE_FLAG_WRITE_THROUGH|FILE_FLAG_RANDOM_ACCESS, NULL);

// create a mapping object for the file, 0=offset on the disk
md=CreateFileMapping((HANDLE)fh,NULL,PAGE_READWRITE,0,vmSZ,NULL);

// Attempt to create a view starting at baseAddr
newBase=MapViewOfFileEx(md,FILE_MAP_ALL_ACCESS,0,0,0,baseAddr);

// If not successful, let the system to chose the new base address
if(newBase==NULL){
    newBase=MapViewOfFileEx(md,FILE_MAP_ALL_ACCESS,0,0,0,0);
}

// Examples of use:
p=(char*)newBase;
*((int*)(p+20032))=1937; // insert 1937 at address (newBase+20032)

float f=(*((float*)(p+11996))); // get float from (newBase+11996)

// flush all remaining pages to the disk
FlushViewOfFile(newBase,totSpace);

// without this, the file remains open
    UnmapViewOfFile(newBase);
```

UNIX (and Linux) has a similar set of functions.[47] Using parameter names as in Listing 2.13, they are

```
// combines CreateFileMapping() and MapViewOfFileEx()
newBase=mmap(baseAddr,vmSZ,protect,flags,fh,offset);

// equivalent of UnmapViewOfFile()
munmap(newBase,vmSZ);

// change size of mapping (Linux specific)
newBase=mremap(newBase,vmSz,newSize,flags);

// equivalent of UnmapViewOfFile()
msync(newBase,vmSZ,flags);
```

Figure 2.13 shows where UNIX maps the file. If you want to play with the Windows functions, beware: possible interaction between processes makes their use trickier and it is, in our opinion, poorly chartered territory. The online rating of

---

[47] For details, see UNIX man pages or http://my.safaribooksonline.com/book/operating-systems-and-server-administration/linux/0596009585/advanced-file-i-o/mapping_files_into_memory

Fig. 2.13 File mapping under UNIX

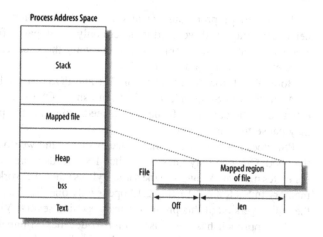

Microsoft documentation ranges from 4/4 to 1/4. Mykhailo Oksenenko recently posted[48] several screens of errors and potential problems in their use, and even the Microsoft documentation for *Reading and Writing from a File View* warns that an attempt to use File Mapping of a sparse file of an NTFS partition may result in an I/O error.

There is also a catch: You can map the disk to the entire virtual memory, but when you open a View, you have to request a certain size. You cannot exceed or increase this size later,[49] so you typically request more memory than you need. However, only the used portion of your data is saved to the disk.

Programs available online (`List2_13a.cpp, List 2_13b.cpp`, and `List2_13c. cpp`) compare the speed of storing 300 MB of data for File Mapping and regular read () and write() with these results in ms[50]:

	Changes on every page	Write	Read[51]	Total
File mapping	194	2682	3008	5884
Read/write	149	2763	2815	5727

It is important to understand that <u>you cannot compare numbers in the first three columns,</u> because the two approaches do different things at different times. When making a change on every page, *file mapping* loads page by page, while *read/write* only changes a memory location. On the other hand, when writing to disk, *file mapping* writes only the remaining pages, while *read/write* writes the entire data space. When starting a program, *file mapping* only has to set up itself without moving any data, while *read/write* reads all the data to memory.

---

[48] http://mikelaud.blogspot.ca/2010/01/shm-hints-windows.html

[49] Under Linux you can, but it may stall the program execution for a while.

[50] Timed on the computer which was used for the benchmark in Chap. 7.

[51] After restarting the computer. If you read immediately after you wrote, the data is still in the system cache, and you get only 80 and 228 ms.

The speed of processing clearly is not the reason to use File Mapping for persistent data, but if we need to access only a few pages from an otherwise large amount of data, File Mapping will move only those pages and will definitely be more efficient than serialization.

Both ObjectStore (c) PSE Pro for C++ and POST++ are based on File Mapping.

As in the old Smalltalk model, when using POST++, the user must supply an estimate of the data size. If the task exceeds this size, the program will crash or it may pause for a long time.[52]

PSE does not require any initial size estimate, and we do not know what is under the hood. One can only guess that when PSE needs more the data space, it perhaps generates multiple Views—in the same style as when we worked with pages of virtual memory in Sect. 2.2.2. Listing 2.13 opens only one File Mapping and one View, but the online version of this program[53] tests opening several Views simultaneously.

This approach has been used for two decades. Singhal (1992) reported on a university project called Texas, to which we did not find any references after 2000. Soukup (1994)[54] showed four pages of code that demonstrated the idea in UNIX. QuickStore was described in White and DeWitt (1995). Free[55] software (Knizhnik, POST++, 1999) also uses this approach and is free to download from their website. For more information on these projects see Sect. 4.2. For more information on ObjectStore look at Lamb et al. (1991), Zikari (2010) and Haradhvala and Weinreb (1991).

2.4 Persistent Pointers

Until now, we assumed that the prime location of data was in memory and the pointers in the disk image stored the original memory addresses, and we had to swizzle pointers after we loaded the data into memory. This section assumes that the prime location of the data is on disk, and the pointers store the disk addresses. This implies a few arithmetic operations when dereferencing a pointer, but no pointer swizzling is required. The secret is a smart pointer class that makes all this transparent.

---

[52] The latter happens specifically under Linux.

[53] bk\chap2\list2_13a.cpp.

[54] pp. 386–392.

[55] POST++ comes in source from which all comments have been removed, and it is rather difficult and time consuming to figure out its inner workings.

2.4.1 The Main Idea

Imagine what would happen if, for every class, we would pre-allocate a large array of its instances, and when we would need an object or an array of that class, we would bypass allocation and simply pick it up from this array—see Listing 2.14.

Normally, pointer stores the starting address of the object to which it is pointing, but if we stored the index into this array, it would be persistent. It would not require swizzling, and we still could access the object very quickly.[56] For the implementation of the smart pointer which does this, see Listing 2.15.

Listing 2.14 Allocating an array of objects for each class

```
class Book {
    static Book *myArr; // preallocated array
    static size_t pool; // next available index
    void* operator new(size_t size) { // for a single object
                        if(!myArr)return (void*)calloc(1,size);
        void* v=(void*)(myArr+pool);
        pool=pool+size/sizeof(Book);
        return v;
    }
    void* operator new[](size_t size) { // for an array of objects
        //...identical with new()
    }
    static void start(size_t sz) {
        myArr=new Book[sz];
        pool=1; // index=0 corresponds to pointer==NULL
    }
};
Book* Book::myArr=NULL;
size_t Book::pool=0;

int main() {
    Book::start(1000);
    Book* bp=new Book();
```

---

[56] The first object in the array could be unused, thus making index 0 equivalent with NULL pointer.

Listing 2.15 Persistent pointer storing the index

```
template<class T> class PersistPtr {
  unsigned index;
public:
  T* operator->() const{
     if(index)return (T::myArr+index); return NULL;
  }
  T* operator*() const{
     if(index)return (T::myArr+index); return NULL;
  }
  PersistPtr& operator=(T *rhs){
     if(rhs)index=((size_t)rhs-(size_t)(T::myArr))/sizeof(T);
     else index=0;
     return *this;
  }
  size_t getIndex(){return index;}
  void setInex(size_t i){index=i;}
};
class Book {
public:
     int id;
     PersistPtr<Book> next; // note no * in the syntax
        ... same as in Listing 2_12
};
Book* Book::myArr=NULL;
size_t Book::pool=0;

int main(){ // examples of different use
     PersistPtr<Book> bp1,bp2; // persistent pointers, no *
     Book *br;                 // regular pointer, use *
     Book::start(100); // start the allocator array for 100 Books
     bp1=new Book; bp1->id=1; // reg. to pers.conversion, use ->
     bp2=new Book; bp2->id=2;
     bp1->next=bp2; // use persistent pointers like reg.pointers
     br= *bp1;      // persistent to regular pointer conversion
     printf("%d %d\n",br->id,bp1->next->id);
```

Using a pre-allocated array of objects has many advantages:

(a) Elimination of unused objects requires reference swizzling but, in this case, such swizzling is simple and fast.

(b) If we want to visit all the objects (as in serialization), instead of traversing the network of pointers, we can traverse these arrays which is much simpler and faster.

(c) Serialization to disk for an array is more economical than for individual objects: it needs only one header.

(d) If we want to move entire pages of data between memory and disk, we don't need a bitmap to locate the pointers. For each class, we can visit the first pointer of all objects, then the second pointer of all objects, and so on.

(e) Page size can automatically adjust to a multiple of the object size, thus reducing problems with large arrays that cross page boundaries.

There are only two issues we have not discussed yet:

(1) Could unstructured, passive[57] objects—with the wide variety sizes such as text strings or arrays of integers—fit this scheme?

(2) When the preallocated array is all used up, can we enlarge it without copying the old array into the new one?[58]

Let's start with implementing each allocation array as a set of pages, which are treated as a "virtual" array. The smart pointer has to perform several arithmetic operations in order to dereference a pointer. That may not have a big impact on the overall performance, but you should be aware of it.

Even if we manage free space for potential reuse, it may be useful to be able to clean up all unused objects and to compress the memory—for example, when ending a session or when we save the data to disk. The following algorithm shows how to do that. After we shrink the arrays for all the classes, we have to swizzle[59] all their pointers, using array conv[] from this algorithm:

Alogrithm: Removal of Unused Objects by Shrinking the Array

Just before saving the data to disk, Book::myArr has free spaces xxxx

```
              0     1     2     3     4     5     6     7     8
myArr[] = obj1  obj2  xxxx  xxxx  obj3  xxxx  obj4  obj5  xxxx
```

We shrink Book::myArr[] and create a temporary conversion array,

size_t Book::conv[]

```
              0     1     2     3     4     5     6     7     8
myArr[] = obj1  obj2  obj3  obj4  obj5  xxxx  xxxx  xxxx  xxxx
conv[] =  0     1    -1    -1     2    -1     3     4    -1
```

We do this for all classes, and then traverse all objects and convert their pointers. When pointer ptr points to a Book object, we convert it like this:

```
PersistPtr<Book> ptr;   // persistent pointer to Book
size_t k=ptr.getIndex();  // the old index
ptr.setIndex(conv[k]);   // index conversion
```

Each object is visited only once, and no search is required

The key to managing the free space is having all free pieces doubly-linked so we can quickly insert and remove both objects and arrays. The key to defragmentation is being able to combine butting free spaces into a single larger space.[60] The following example shows one of many possible implementations.

---

[57] Objects that do not harbour any pointers.

[58] Copying would trigger changes in all objects pointing into this array.

[59] Remember that, in this case, pointers store the integer index into the array, not the object address.

[60] The difference from the normal memory management is that here we deal with arrays of objects that have the same size.

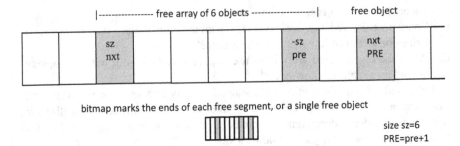

Fig. 2.14 Space representation of free objects and arrays. For a single object, the bitmap is 1, and PRE is an odd number. Left end of the array stores the positive size, right hand stores the negative size. Indexes nxt (=next) and pre (=previous) implement the doubly-linked lists

Example: Let's assume that:

(a) Free object is a segment of memory which we can temporarily use for storing any information such as its size or pointers linking it to other free memory segments.
(b) We can keep a bitmap of our memory space, with one bit per object - see Fig. 2.14.[61]
(c) We allocate all objects so that their space can accommodate at least two integers—at least 8 bytes on 32-bit hardware.
(d) Unstructured memory as text strings will be allocated in chunks of 8 bytes

Figure 2.14 shows the representation of one array and one object. Note that even though nxt and pre form a doubly linked list, they are not pointers but integer indexes—thus they are persistent.

Typically, all single free objects are in one list, and free arrays in another. Another variation is to keep multiple lists, each for certain array size or range of sizes. There can also be a special class for non-structured data, with one object 8 bytes long. Any text, arrays of integers, etc. would be represented as objects or arrays of this class.

Figure 2.15 shows how this data organization detects abutting objects and allows one to combine them into a larger array. It also allows fast splitting of arrays or pulling a single objects from the free array, depending on your allocation strategy.

Until now, we assumed that we pull individual objects from an array of preallocated objects. But what are we going to do if we run out of preallocated objects? Allocating a bigger array and copying the original array in it would not work, because the existing objects would move and pointers to them would become invalid.

Instead, we can use a virtual array which is composed of pages, each a shorter array by itself, but all managed together and indexed as a single array—see

---

[61] Note that bitmaps used in previous chapters kept one bit for every 4-byte location. Here the bitmap is even smaller—how much smaller depends on the size of the object. Object must be large enough to store at least two values: SIZE and PRE, i.e. at least 8 bytes, but is usually much larger.

INITIAL SITUATION: pool=17, free objects=13, free arrays=4

base[ ]	1	2	3	4	5	6	7	8	9	10	11	12	13	14	15	16
size	x	1	x	4			-4	x	x	x	x	1	1	x	x	x
next	x	12	x	0				x	x	x	x	0	2	x	x	x
prev	x		x	0			0	x	x	x	x			x	x	x
bitmap																
....		1		1			1					1	1			

AFTER FREEING ARRAY 8-11, it combines with array 4-7 and single 12 and single 13, resulting in pool=17, free objects=2, free arrays=4

base[ ]	1	2	3	4	5	6	7	8	9	10	11	12	13	14	15	16
size	x	1	x	10									-10	x	x	x
next	x	0	x	0										x	x	x
prev	x	0	x										0	x	x	x
bitmap																
....		1		1									1	1		

AFTER FREEING ARRAY 14-16, it combines with free array 4-13, and thus reduces pool to 4, with free objects=2 and free arrays=0

base[ ]	1	2	3	4	5	6	7	8	9	10	11	12	13	14	15	16
size	x	1	x	-	-	-	-	-	-	-	-	-	-	-	-	-
next	x	0	x	-	-	-	-	-	-	-	-	-	-	-	-	-
prev	x	0	x	-	-	-	-	-	-	-	-	-	-	-	-	-
bitmap																
....		1		-								-				

Fig. 2.15 Allocation and free storage of objects: Array base[ ] for each class . x marks currently active objects. Index 0 is reserved for NULL pointer, and object at that location is never used. "pool" is the index of the first so far unused location; the bitmap is the same bitmap as in Fig. 2.14

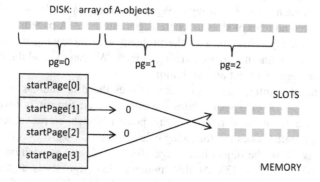

Fig. 2.16 Paging an array of objects from disk to memory. Pages move in and out of a few pre-assigned slots

Fig. 2.16. This is similar to what we discussed in Sect. 2.2.2, except that now we need such a paging system for every application class. That may appear complicated, but the overhead—both in the lines of code and in the required space—is practically the same as when we paged the entire memory.

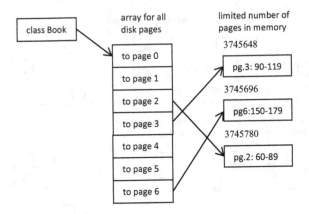

file book.ppf divided into pages with the same number of objects:

pg.0: 0-29	pg.1: 30-59	pg.2: 60-89	pg.3: 90-119	pg4:120-149

Fig. 2.17 Disk as the prime data storage. Pages store the same number of objects (here 30), and are paged to memory as needed

2.4.2 Array on Disk, Paged to Memory on Demand

An example of this approach is the Persistent Pointer Factory (PPF).[62] PPF assumes that the primary storage of the data is an array of objects on a disk file, with a separate file for each class. This array is paged to memory as needed—see Fig. 2.16. There is a limited number of slots to where pages can move. A page is not assigned any slot permanently. This removes the problem with increasing the size of the preallocated array without moving existing objects. We can expand the file gradually by adding pages without any limitation.

Smart generic pointer, `PersistPtr<T>`, stores the disk address of the target object, and its `operator ->` calculates the address each time it is invoked. For example, if we want to dereference the pointer which stores index 103 in Fig. 2.17, the program does the following calculation:

Page size is 30, so the object is on page $103/30 = 3$, and at position 13 within this page ($103 - 30*3 = 13$). At this moment, this page starts at the address 3745648. Figure 2.18 does not say how large one object is; if it were, for example, 24 bytes, then the memory address at which the object resides at this moment is $3745648 + 13*24 = 3745860$

---

[62] A commercial product distributed since 1997; the full source is now available on this book's website.

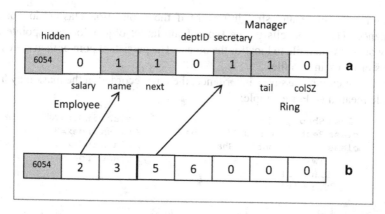

Fig. 2.18 Compared to Fig. 2.2, each class in Objective-C can keep just one mask (**a**). The hidden pointer inserted by the compiler is always in the first field, and pointers of any kind are marked by 1. For faster access, the same information can be converted to format (**b**), with hidden pointer in position 0 followed by the list of indexes for the pointer locations

An interesting question is whether it is better to store the disk address or the object index in the virtual disk array. Listing 2.16 shows the implementation of operator -> for both cases, and storing disk address results in a slightly faster access.[63] However, storing index makes it possible to handle larger data, potentially many times[64] the size of the virtual memory.

Listing 2.16 Disk as the prime storage—what to store in PersistPtr

```
// When storing disk address, the dereferencing is faster
template<class T> class PersistPtr {
    undisgned diskAddr; // disk address in bytes
    T* operator->() const{
        if(index) return pageArray[diskAddr/pageSz]+diskAddr%pageSz;
        return NULL;
    }
};

// When storing disk index, the disk size may exceed virtual memory
// but dereferencing includes additional multiplication
template<class T> class PersistPtr {
    undisgned diskIndex; // object index on disk
    T* operator->() const{
        if(index) return pageArray[diskInd/numOnPage]
                        +(diskInd%numOnPage)*sizeof(T);
        return NULL;
    }
};
```

---

[63] PPF stores disk addresses.

[64] The factor increases with the size of the object size.

This is all simple and straightforward if the application classes do not use inheritance. The mask tells us the type of the target object for each pointer, in other words in which file to look for the object. The persistent pointer then stores the address or index in this file.

If the application class uses inheritance, the type recorded in the mask may have multiple meanings. For example:

```
class Shape {...};                    // class index=7
class Rectangle : public Shape {...}; // class index=8
class Circle : public Shape {...};    // class index=9
class Twin {                          // class index=4
    Shape *s1;
    Shape *s2;
};
```

If all these classes are persistent with the PERSIST_CLASS() statements, then the mask for the Twin class is [7,7]. However, pointers s1 and s2 can lead to a Rectangle or Circle, and these are stored in different files!!! When inheritance is involved, in addition to the disk address, the smart pointer must also store the true target type.

For this reason, PPF uses two types of pointers:

- PersistPtr<T> which stores only the disk address, and can be used only when class T is not using inheritance.[65] It has the same size as regular pointer.
- PersistVPtr<T> stores the target type and the disk address, and can be used under all circumstances. It is the only choice when class T is involved in inheritance. It takes the space of two pointers.

In PPF, user selects the page size and how many pages should be resident in memory for each specific class. Listing 2.17 shows the overall setup and the interface. Macro PERSIST_CLASS(T) overloads operator new() for each class. Allocating one object simply means adding 1 to the pool, and then asking the pager assigned to this class for the memory address. For allocating arrays, we need operator new[], which does the same thing except that it derives the number of the objects from the given size.

Note that pool starts from 1, not from 0. Index 0 is the equivalent of a NULL pointer.

---

[65] Typically when no class is using inheritance.

Listing 2.17 Persistent pointers storing the object index

```
#define PERSIST_CLASS(T) \
friend PersistPtr<T>; \
void* operator new(size_t size){ \
    unsigned u=pool; pool++;
    return pgr->getAddress(u);}\
void* operator new[](size_t size){ \
    unsigned u=pool; pool=pool+size/sizeof(T);
    return pgr->getAddress(u);}\
static unsigned pool; \
static Pager *pgr

#define INIT(T,N) \
T* T::pool=1; \
Pager* T::pgr=NULL

//————————————————————————————
class Library {
PERSIST_CLASS(Library);
    ...
}
INIT(Library,1);

class Book {
PERSIST_CLASS(Book);
    ...
}
INIT(Book,10000);
//————————————————————————————
int main() {
    PersistPtr<Library> lib = new Library;
    PersistPtr<Book>     bk = new Book[250];
```

After a long journey we reached yet another variation of mapping a file to memory. The difference from the mapping discussed in Sect. 2.3 is that all objects there were saved in one file. Now each class has its own data file, but there is no fixed limit on the size of the data.

2.5 Quasi-Single Page (QSP)

When designing a new persistent system that would work with Objective-C, we combined the best ideas from all the existing approaches. The result is simple and efficient. It starts with one page of memory which expands to more pages if more space is required. During the run, discarded objects are reused, and when saving the data to disk, the memory space is all collapsed to a single page, with all unused space eliminated. This is the only completely automatic persistent system—pointer locations are retrieved through reflection, and calls to new() does not require any modifications.

In some chapters we tell you that they are not critical and that you can skip them or skim through them quickly. This chapter is just the opposite. It includes new ideas and algorithms, and we recommend you read it carefully and consider every detail.

Objective-C is the language used by Apple and is thus important for iPhone applications. Under the label of "archiving" it has serialization which requires more manual input than most other languages, and its main flaw—just like in Java and C# serializations—is the recursive internal algorithm which walks through all active objects. If the data includes a long chain of pointers, the system stack overflows easily and the program crashes. The workaround is to maintain a collection of all active objects and to write them individually to disk, which complicates the matters and is a potential source of errors.

The purpose of this chapter is to develop a new approach to automatic persistence which would be simpler to implement yet be as fast, if not faster, than the existing persistent systems. It should run in Objective-C, but the idea should be applicable to C++, C# and possibly other languages.

The method is new, and we believe that it will be highly competitive in performance, flexibility[66] of use, and simplicity of internal design—not only in Objective-C, but also in C++ and other languages.

For the benefit of the majority of readers, this chapter uses code samples mostly in C++. Final implementation in Chap. 6 is written entirely in Objective-C.

This design is a good example of how persistence, data structures, and allocation—when not treated as orthogonal, can be most efficient while working jointly toward the same *objective*.

BUILDING BLOCK 1: Pointer Mask For each class, we can generate the mask showing pointer locations, either by using the approach described in Fig. 2.2 and Listing 2.3, or through reflection as will be explained in Chaps. 5 and 6.

However, this mask will be simpler than that shown in Fig. 2.2. Objective-C is a dynamically typed language and, once we have a pointer, we can determine the type of the target object. We do not need to give ID to each class; we simply mark the pointer locations by 1—see Fig. 2.18. Objective-C uses only one hidden pointer at the beginning of the object. We do not have to record it in the mask but, for convenience, we can keep its value there.

BUILDING BLOCK 2: Making Classes Persistent We will use the simple interface at which we arrived in Sect. 2.1.2, with two statements added to each class[67]:

`PersistInterface;` will insert additional methods[68] needed for the persistence.

`PersistImplementation;` will insert static members and the implementation of the added functions.

---

[66] It supports both storing entire pages and serialization, including the existing Objective-C format.

[67] The names are slightly changed to fit Objective-C terminology.

[68] Mostly static, "messages" in Objective-C lingo.

These two statements will be macros, but clean macros, simply a section of code that repeats for every class. All pointer members will be registered as a `PTR()` statement which, in Sect. 2.2, was in the default constructor:

```
class Library {
PersistInterface;
      Book *books;
      Library *next;
      int telephone;
      char *libName;
public{
      Library(){
          PTR(books,Book); PTR(next,Library); PTR(libName);
          ...anything else you want here
      }
};
PersistImplementation;
```

Some things are simpler in Objective-C. For example, `PersistInterface` and `PersistImplementation` do not need the class parameter.[69] Also, we can use `PTR()` for any kind of pointer, while in C++ we were using `PTR()` for object pointers and `STR()` for strings.

Other things are more complicated in Objective-C. There is no equivalent to the C++ default[70] constructor, which automatically invokes default constructors of its superior (base) classes. In Objective-C, any method can serve as a constructor, but the traversal of the superior classes must be introduced explicitly.[71]

BUILDING BLOCK 3: Replacing Allocation The simplest and most efficient memory management for persistent data is one block (or page) of virtual memory, from which we allocate all the objects. Storing data to disk is reduced to dumping the entire page to the disk, and loading the data back to memory is also very fast. Pointer conversion (swizzling) requires only to add the same offset to all pointers on the page.

We described this method in Sect. 1.4.1 (Old Smalltalk Model), and we pointed out its main weakness—if the data grows beyond the page size, allocation of a larger page and copying of the old page into it would be as complicated operation as storing data to disk. If we move any objects, we have to swizzle all the pointers!

In our new algorithm we will replace one page by a set of pages, but will control these pages and their sizes in such a way that all the data will be on a single page most of the time. We will also collapse multiple pages into a single page any time we'll be saving the data to disk.

Figure 2.19 shows the architecture. Typically, there is only one or a few pages; multiple pages are only a temporary measure for additional data. All pages have the

---

[69] The equivalent from Sect. 2.2 would be `PersistInterface(Library)`.

[70] Constructor without parameters, e.g. `Library(){...}`.

[71] We will show in Chap. 7 how you do that.

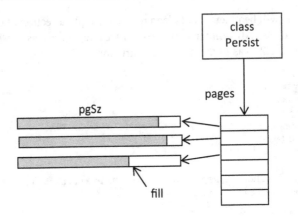

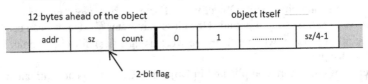

allocation of one object in 4-byte sections:

12 bytes ahead of the object   object itself

| addr | sz | count | 0 | 1 | .... | sz/4-1 | |

2-bit flag

Fig. 2.19 QSP allocation usually involves one or a few pages, which are converted to one page while storing to disk. The lowest two bits of the sz field are used as a type flag: 0 = object or array with no pointers, 1 = object/array of objects with a hidden pointer, 2 = array of pointers. Field addr is a temporary space for internal algorithms

same size pgSz, but different fill. Before saving to disk, pages are sorted by their starting address and converted to a single page.

Before each object or array, the allocation inserts a 12-byte header,[72] which includes the retain count that Objective-C expects to be there. Field addr is a temporary variable that QSP needs in some algorithms. For example, when traversing all active objects, it takes the role of the "next" pointer which builds the queue. Later on, when merging all pages into one, it stores the new address of the object before it actually moves there.

Instances of classes derived from NSObject start with a hidden pointer at the beginning of the actual object. The overhead is 12 bytes per object,[73] which is less than 16 bytes in the standard Objective-C heap.

---

[72] Note that this is still less than the 16-byte header Objective-C uses when allocating from the heap.

[73] Temporarily, while tArr is used, the overhead is 20 bytes.

Field (sz) stores the size of the object, except for its two lowest bits which are used as a special flag. Sizes of objects are always multiples of 4, so the two lowest bits in this field are unused, and we can use them for this flag with values between 0 and 3.

We will allocate all objects—both instances of application classes and large, irregular objects such as blocks of text or pictures from the same data space.

Using one large page instead of smaller multiple pages has a potential flaw. Quoting Mark Bales: *One of our systems worked this way but as designs grew, it required a *very* large block of memory. When we tried to re-load the data back from disk, the read operation failed. This was because there wasn't enough space between various smaller blocks still in use. As a result, I have become convinced that page-based techniques should remain page-based even on re-read.*

Note that this problem can occur for very large data (VLSI design in Mark's case) and for programs that re-read the data within the same run. A simple cure is to provide a smart-read function, which in cases of read failure breaks the data into multiple pages. That by itself is simple but, for multiple pages, pointer swizzling becomes more complicated and time consuming. Instead of applying the same offset to all pointers, we must first find the proper page, and then apply the offset.

Representation of Arrays

The representation of arrays is critical and deserves more explanation. We have three possible styles of arrays. In all three cases, sz stores the overall size of the array in bytes.

(a) Arrays that do not include any pointers are stored and represented in the same way as a block of text, with flg=0.

(b) Arrays of objects that are instances of persistent classes, each object starting with a hidden pointer, are stored with flg=1. A single object derived from NSObject is a special case—an array of objects with only one object.

(c) Arrays of pointers are special, because they do not need any mask. We know that every 4 bytes represent a pointer, and their signature is flg=2.

Listing 2.18 shows the differences in how we use or allocate these different arrays, and what we do with them when we either traverse all objects or swizzle the pointers.

Listing 2.18 Using various types of arrays

```
class Chapter;
class Author;
class Store;
class Book {
    PersistInterface(Book); // registration of the class
    char *name;
    int ISBN;
    Book *next;
    Chapter **chapters; // array of pointers to Chapters
    Author *authors;    // array of Author objects
    Book(){
        PTR(next); PTR(chapters); PTR(authors); PTR(stores);
        ... anything else you want here
    }
};

// Different ways of allocation store the object differently.
// Persist is the persistent utility
bk->name=Persist.palloc(sz); // text or other no-pointer data
bk->next=new Book;  // overloaded new() for a single object
bk->chapters=Persist.allocPtrArr(sz); // pointer array
bk->authors=Book.allocArr{sz}; // method automatically added to B
```

SPECIAL RULE FOR ARRAYS OF OBJECTS:

If you stop using any elements of an array, for example when reducing the number of elements, you must set all the pointers in the released elements to NULL or, safer and easier, simply overwrite these elements with 0s.

The program that controls the persistency has no information about how big a part of the array is actually used. If you don't follow the Special Rule, the program may crash when swizzling or traversing pointers. We recommend that raw arrays of objects such as shown in Listing 2.16 are not used, but instead that they are encapsulated in a special Array class that takes care of overwriting discarded objects with 0.

There are two situations when the algorithms have to traverse pointers of all objects: when we traverse the pointer graph starting from the root in order to find all the active (connected) objects, and then when we are swizzling[74] the pointers of these objects. Assume that we have object obj, and that we want to report all pointers that lead to other objects. The following code which finds all pointers ptr

---

[74] Resetting pointer values after all the objects move to a different place in memory.

in `obj` and calls `fun(ptr)` has interesting logic,[75] which works particularly well in Objective-C[76]:

```
int i,k,mySz; char *obj,**ptr,**msk;
int ptrSz=sizeof(char*);
int flg=getFlg(obj); // get the flag from the allocation record
if(flg==0)return; // there are no pointers in obj
int sz=getAllocatedSize(obj); // get the allocated size of obj
if(flg==1){
    mySz=getClassSize(obj); else mySz=0;
    char *mask=getMask(obj);
}
for(i=k=0; i<sz; i=i+ptrSz, k=k+ptrSz){ // i for obj, k for mask
    ptr=(char**)(obj+i); // *ptr is the value at location i
    if(flg==2){fun(*ptr); continue;} // every location is a pointer
    // k is used only in the next part
    if(k>=mySz)k=0; // repeat the mask for the next section
    if(k==0)continue; // hidden pointer, we exclude them
    msk=(char**)(mask+k);
    if(*msk)fun(*ptr); // if mask is not 0
}
```

BUILDING BLOCK 4: Algorithms A and B The following two algorithms are the heart of this entire approach.

<u>Algorithm A</u> traverses all active objects without recursion. It uses field `addr` as the "next" pointer when building two stacks: One for the objects still to be expanded, the second for those already expanded. A simple check whether `addr==0` prevents the same object expanding again.

Algorithm A can be used for two purposes:

(a) To serialize the data in any of the existing Objective-C formats, simply calling function `writeSingleObject(void* ptr)` which saves the object without expansion.

(b) To set up the data for Algorithm B which eliminates dead space and collapses the data space into a single page. Condition `addr==0` marks an object as a dead space.

For all application classes, the standard allocation is replaced[77] by allocation from our special pages, regardless whether we store the data with QSP or serialization. Being able to alternate between the two styles of saving the data has many advantages.

---

[75] This is more an algorithm description than a functional code.

[76] You will see this in Chap. 7.

[77] The new alloc() method is hidden under `PersistInterface`.

```
                    ALGORITHM A: Serialization
      (mark all active objects with ind=1, possibly write them to disk)
Stage:
ptrSz is the size of pointer, in bytes
The algorithm assumes addr=0 for all objects. Allocator sets
it that way, but if this function is called several times,
this needs a special management.

Algorithm:
    void *stackBeg, *stackEnd; // stack, objects to be expanded
    void *listBeg; // list of active objects
    void *nxtObj; // next object to expand
    void **targPtr; // leads to the next object
    char *p;
    sort pages; // Algorithm B will rely on it
    { place root in the stack, set addr=1}
    stackBeg=stackEnd=root;
    while(stack not empty){
        nxtObj=stackBeg;
        if(option)writeSingleObject(nextObj); // serialization
        int flg=getFlg(nxtObj);
        if(flg>0){ // skip for 0: no pointers, no expansion
            if(flg==1){ // object with hidden pointer
                {get pointer mask, 1 marks regular pointers}
            }
            for(int i=0; i<sz; i=i+ptrSz){ // all ptr locations
                p=(char*)nxtObj+i;
                if(flg==1 && mask[i]!=1)continue;
                targPtr=(char**)p;
                if(*targPtr)==NULL)continue;
                if(addr for *targPtr > 0)continue;
                {add *targPtr to the end of the stack}
            }
        }
        { move nxtObj from stack to list }
        activeSpace=activeSpace+12+sz; // sz for nxtObj
    }
    returns:
        listBeg; // list of active objects
        activeSpace; // space needed for all active objects
    NOTE: Stack and List use addr=1 instead of NULL at the end
```

The Purpose of <u>Algorithm B</u> Is:
- To concatenate all the pages into one.
- To remove discarded or lost objects.

If, after running Algorithm A, we have a single page and the total space is equal to the active space, there is no need to call Algorithm B (Fig. 2.20).

It also does not make any sense to do a big cleanup if there are just a few unused objects. Algorithm B has a flexible, user defined cutoff—for example, it can be

Fig. 2.20 Pass 3 of
Algorithm B

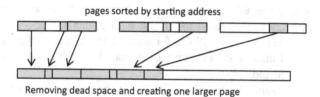

Removing dead space and creating one larger page

bypassed if there is only one page and the dead space is not more than 10 % of the
allocated space (cutoff specified as 0.1 for 10 %).

Algorithm B allocates a new, single page to store all the data without the dead
space. Then it traverses the list of active objects that Algorithm A left behind, and
calculates the future address of each object in this new page. Because the objects are
already sorted, this calculation involves only a gradual accumulation of the memory
shift for the dead space and gaps between pages. In the second pass, the algorithm
traverses the active objects again, and swizzles their pointers to the values stored in
addr of the target object. There are no searches or dictionaries. In the third pass all
the active objects are copied into the new page.

The second and third pass could be combined into a single pass, but we would
not gain much. Leaving them separate allows one to copy the data into an existing
page without allocating a new one, assuming that the old page is large enough to
receive the data.[78]

Algorithm C stores the single page to disk, and it is trivial. It first writes the
header with the overall parameters:

fill = total space required to receive the data,

root = old address of the root,

pageAddress = address on which the old page started and then the table of
registered classes, each entry

class name

size of each instance

pointer mask (includes the value of the hidden pointer)

The hidden pointer is needed for the conversion when loading the data back to
memory, and the mask is for a rough check that the class has not changed.

The page size is not passed; the receiving program can chose any size which is
not smaller than fill.

Finally, there is a binary dump of the entire data space[79] and of the bitmap.

Algorithm D allocates a large-enough page and bitmap, and fills both with the
data from the disk. Without looking at individual objects, it runs through the bitmap
looking for pointer locations, and swizzles them including the root pointer by the
same offset (startOfNewPage − startOfOldPage). When the original pointer does
not fit the old page, it must be a hidden pointer, and it is replaced using the old-to-
new conversion table of hidden pointers. Note that if there are any dead objects,

---

[78] This option is not in the first version of this code.

[79] As a single page.

converting their pointers does no harm, and because there should not be many of them, it may be faster to traverse bitmap than to analyze individual objects.

The conversion allows for some changes of the schema:

(a) If the new data contain additional classes, it does not matter. We can still read the old data.
(b) If some old classes are missing in the new set, but there are no instances of these classes in the old set, that is also fine, but this may require an additional check during the swizzling of pointers.

ALGORITHM B: Cleanup and compression
(eliminates discarded objects and compresses all data into one page).

Stage:
Algorithm A was performed, addr!=0 marks active objects.

Algorithm:
```
    void *nxtObj,*root,*newAddr; int n;
    Using the cutoff condition, decide whether to bypass.
    Sort the array of pages by the increasing page address.
    Allocate a new large page, page0.
    Disassemble the list of active objects.
    // Pass 1: calculate future addresses
    newAddr=page0 + 12;
    Using sz and headerSz, traverse objects page by page {
        if(nxtObj->addr==0)continue; // not active object
        nxtObj.copy(newAddr); // including 12 bytee header
        nxtObj->addr=newAddr;
        newAddr=newAddr+nxtObj->sz+12;
    } // also collect all active objects in char** active[].
    //Pass 2: Swizzle page0 pointers using addr from orig. data
    for(i=0; active[i]; i++){
        nxtObj=active[i];
        newAddr=nxtObj->addr; // swizzle pointers in page0
        {based on the 2-bit flag, decide how to access pointers}
        {get mask from the class, when appropriete}
        traverse pointers of newAddr {
            if(the pointer is neither NULL nor hidden pointer){
                replace pointer value by addr of the target object
            }
        }
    }
    convert the root reference to addr stored on the root object
    // Pass 3: Concatenate active objects (see Fig.2.17)
    newAddr=page0;
    for(i=0; active[i]; i++){
        nxtObj=active[i];
        n=nxtObj->sz + 12;
        memcpy(newAddr,nxtObj-12,n);
        newAddr=newAddr+n;
    }
    delete all old pages;
    set page0 as page[0];
    newAddr is its 'fill'
```

BUILDING BLOCK 5: Special Arrays   So far we have been working with single instances of application classes. What are we going to do with arrays? Arrays of characters or of other basic types such as *int* or *long long*, or even arrays of structures (*struct*) as long as they do not include any pointers are no problem. We allocated each array as an object of the appropriate size, and other objects can refer to it with a pointer. The bitmap corresponding to such an array will be full of 0s, so we do not have to do anything special for these arrays except that we have to make sure they get allocated with the allocator from our Utility class.

Objective-C does not allow arrays of instances, only arrays of pointers. For example:

```
class A {
    int id;
    A *next;
}
int main(){
    A *arr=new A[100]; // array of A instances, not in Objective C
    A **pArr=new (A*)[100]; // array of pointers to A instances
    for(int i=0; i<100; i++){
        pArr[i]=new A;
    {
    printf("arr=%d pArr%d\n",arr[17].id,pArr[35]->id);
```

Instead of calls such as

```
A **pArr=new (A*)[100];
```

the application code will have to call a special function which will not only allocate the appropriate memory from our pages but also fill its assigned area of bitmap with 1s.

BUILDING BLOCK 6: Managing Free Objects   Any saving of data to disk, even if we don't exit our program after that, will remove all unused objects. We can even call Algorithm B without saving to disk, and the unused objects will be removed and all the data will be compacted to a single page. That, however, may cause a pause in the execution of the program, which in some applications may not be acceptable. Also, some applications continuously destroy objects and create new ones, and being able to reuse destroyed objects would help significantly.

It would[80] be easy to arrange chains of free objects organized by size—for sizes corresponding exactly to the application classes, and approximate sizes of all powers of 2—see Fig. 2.21. Any field in the allocated space can be used for the temporary pointer that creates the chain; the beginning of the object seems most appropriate.

In real-life applications, large blocks of memory that are freed and reused are usually in a relatively small range of sizes. Remembering this range leads to the following performance optimization.

---

[80] This feature may not be in the first release of this Objective-C persistence.

Fig. 2.21 Chains of free objects organized by size. The picture assumes instances of all application classes are not more than 24 bytes in size, and all free objects up to that size can be picked up with appropriate size. Larger objects which can only be arrays or long strings, are organized by power of 2

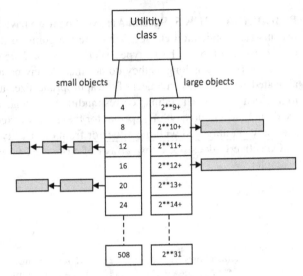

Useful Trick No. 6

When moving larger blocks to free storage or reusing them (see Fig. 2.21) we need to find the right slot for the given size. The binary search seems to be the best choice here, but remembering the range of the stored values makes it super-fast.

Example

slot	value
0	512
1	1024
2	2048
3	4096
4	8192
5	16384
....	
22	214748364
minRange	
maxRange	

We start the run with minRange>maxRange. This is a signal of empty free storage.

When block of size 1048 enters free storage, minRange=1024, maxRange=2044.

When allocating block of size 5000, we do search for a free object, because it is out of range.

When entering the 5000 block to free storage, we search in range 1024-214748364, then adjust maxRange to 8188.

When taking the 1048 block out of the free storage, the range remains 1048-8188; removal from free storage does not change the range.

BUILDING BLOCK 7: Persistent Libraries   In general, persistent data is only as useful as the data structures it supports. This is truer for Objective-C than for other languages, because the NextStep (NS) library is essentially part of the core language. You cannot program in Objective-C without it.

Making a library class persistent is just as easy as making an application class persistent:

STEP 1: Modify *.h by *adding PersistInterface*.

STEP 2: Modify *.m by adding *PersistImplementation* and method *prtList* which registers all the pointers using the PTR() statement.

STEP 3: Search all methods in *.m for any calls that allocate arrays or unstructured memory, and replace them by *allocArr, allocPtrArr*, or *palloc*. (Allocations of single objects with new() require no changes.)

Section 6.2 will describe implementation details specific to Objective-C, NS classes, and to the conversion of the InCode library to Objective-C.

Note that <u>a program may run with persistent application classes, while using NS classes that are not persistent</u> and are allocated from the Objective-C heap. The serialization algorithm (Algorithm A) will save both parts seamlessly. When reading such data from disk, the application classes will automatically allocate from persistent pages of memory, while the NS classes will allocate from the Objective-C heap.

BUILDING BLOCK 8: The Main()   The main() program has to start the persistent utility and all the persistent classes.

```
int main() {
    PersistStart(pageSize);
    myClass1.start();
    myClass2.start();
    ...etc. for all application classes
```

where you normally use pageSize=0 which uses a good default. Selecting this parameter may slightly improve the speed of saving the data to disk especially for very large data sets, but has no impact on the speed of traversing the data. As you save and open the data, the internal algorithms convert all the data to one page anyway, and then the original choice of the page size is irrelevant.

Data Structures, Patterns, and UML

3

Abstract

An essential part of every persistent system are persistent class libraries. Existing class libraries have two flaws: They cannot store bi-directional associations, and they do not treat associations (relations) as first class entities. We need a new paradigm for the proper design of these libraries. We will treat data structures as a database, and implement databases as data structures. The architecture will be controlled by a textual schema, not by the UML class diagram. However, this diagram will be automatically generated from the textual schema. This is just the opposite to what probably expect.

Keywords

Dataless class • Data structures • Class libraries • Associations • Relations • Design patterns • UML • Class diagram • Implementation • Intrusive • Array-based • Pointer-based • Composite • Flywheel • Finite state machine

Why do we include generic data structures in a book on persistent objects? Because, in both cases, the key issue is the safe and transparent handling of pointers.[1] If we design class libraries in the right way, persistency can be more efficient and easier to use. Also, the fact that existing "standard" libraries do not support bi-directional data structures is a disgrace—it complicates programming, makes it more error prone, contradicts UML thinking and often leads to code with inferior performance.

The idea that with the speed and storage capacity of modern computers we do not have to worry about performance is an urban myth. Look at the farms of computers Google is running, or at the problems with the human genome.

Let's establish a few basic facts about building data structures.

---

[1] In this chapter, we use the term *pointer* for both pointers and references.

J. Soukup and P. Macháček, *Serialization and Persistent Objects*,
DOI 10.1007/978-3-642-39323-5_3, © Springer-Verlag Berlin Heidelberg 2014

3.1   Basic Facts About Data Structures

Most of currently used generic containers are based on arrays, while pointer based data structures have been neglected. This section discusses the differences between the two approaches, and it shows what you can do with pointer chains, including sorting, merging, and splitting them.

We can build data structures with array or pointers.[2] Array-based data structures are essentially the 40-year-old Fortran technology which surprisingly still survives in relational databases. Its advantages are:

1. If the data do not change, they takes smaller space—no pointers are needed to create a list.
2. Such data are persistent, indexes are valid even when moving arrays do different addresses.

The disadvantages are severe, especially when the data structures change or grow:

3. If the arrays grow, we have to allocate a larger space than required, which takes away the advantage of the original smaller space.
4. Removing an element from the middle of the array has a major performance penalty.
5. When working with indexes, it is very easy to make an error. Data structures coded in this style are less reliable and harder to debug and maintain.

Object oriented programming combines functions (control) with data, adds inheritance, emphasizing individual objects and their access by pointers. It removes all the disadvantages of arrays but, at the same time, we lose the persistence.[3]

Pointer-based data structures often use lists, either singly or doubly linked. These lists can be either NULL-ended or form a ring. In Chap. 1 (Fig. 1.3) we established that rings are better because they permit inexpensive yet efficient integrity checking, but the for() loop traversing a ring is slightly more complex than the common `for(p=start; p; p=p->next){ ... }`

With a few exceptions, in this book we are always assuming that rings are used.

Many programmers are not aware that linked lists can be sorted with an efficiency comparable to qsort, and that the same algorithm can merge or split lists. We will explain the algorithms with examples. For full running code, look at bk\alib\lib\llist1.cpp (C++), bk\jlib\lib\llist1.jt (for Java), or bk\benchmark\objcLib \lib\llist1.m (Objective-C).

---

[2] Or with a combination of both, but let's keep it simple for now.

[3] Here we have another connection between persistence and data structures.

Algorithm: Sorting a List (Example)

27 3 2 3 5 8 12 7 19 30 6 3 80 79 13 22 40 1 11 2 41 31 32 39

Walking through the list and reversing descending sections[4] gives us the starting set of sorted sublists:

2 3 27, 3 5 8 12, 7 19 30, 3 6, 79 80, 13 22 40, 1 11, 2 41, 31 32 39

When neighbours decrease, it implies a new boundary section. There may be fewer sections now, for example 3 6 becomes automatically one section.

Walk through and merge subsequent pairs of sections

2 3 3 5 8 12 27, 3 6 7 19 30 79 80, 1 11 13 22 40, 2 31 32 39 41

Merging of two sections A and B is a linear process—a parallel walk through them and always selecting the smaller number. For example, for the first two sublists of the starting set

```
A: 2 3 27 result: 2  3 27 result: 2 3  27 result: 2 3 3  27 result: 2 3 3 5
B: 3 5 8 12          3 5 8 12         3 5 8 12        5 8 12

A: 27 result: 2 3 3 5 8  27 result: 2 3 3 5 8 12  27 result: 2 3 3 5 8 12 27
B: 8 12 .                12
```

Repeat this until only one section is left

2 3 3 3 5 6 7 8 12 19 27 30 79 80, 1 2 11 13 22 31 32 39 41 49

1 2 2 3 3 3 5 6 7 8 11 12 13 19 22 27 30 31 32 39 41 49 79 80

Notes: Sort works perfectly for singly-linked list. We can sort doubly-linked list using only the next pointer. When finished, in one pass set the prev pointer—see Fig. 3.1.

Algorithm: Splitting or Merging Singly-Linked Rings The same algorithm can be used to merge or split rings—see Fig. 3.1. When a and b are in the same ring, the algorithm splits the ring into two. When a and b are in different rings, it splices (merges) them together.

```
// a and b are given elements
c=a->next;
d=b->next;
a->next=d;
b->next=c;
```

3.1.1 Working with Lists

It is important to understand the inside workings of lists in various libraries, as shown in Fig. 3.2.

Pointer Array corresponds to the use of STL Vector

```
class D {
    std::vector<L*> ptrArray; // declaration line
};

D* dp=new D;
...
L* lp=dp->ptrArr[17];
int sz=dp->ptrArr.size(); // size of the array
```

---

[4] The breaks between sections are shown as a comma here but not recorded during the calculation.

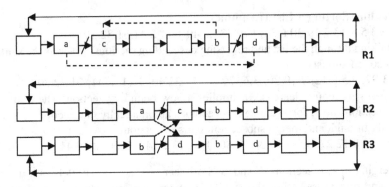

Fig. 3.1 The same reconnection of two pointers splits the ring into two when both objects are on the same ring (R1), or it combines two rings into one (R1 + R2) when each object is on a different ring

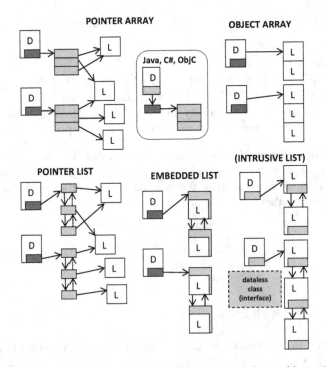

Fig. 3.2 Different implementations of lists. *White boxes* D and L are objects of application classes, *shaded boxes* are objects of library classes. *Lightly shaded boxes* store pointers and other data required for the implementation. *Darker boxes* provide the implementation of the List interface. Intrusive List has its interface implemented in a separate, dataless class. This data structure representation is used only in Code Farms libraries (DOL and InCode)

Here ptrArray is a member of D and contains both data (pointer to the array, its size, etc.) and the implementation of the data structure interface. Nothing is inserted into L. The array (shaded in Fig. 3.2) is transparent to the user.

In other languages, the declaration line would be

```
L[] ptrArray;          // in Java
ArrayList<L> ptrArray; // a better Java implementation
NSMutableArray *ptrArray; // in ObjectiveC
L[] ptrArray;          // in C#
List<L> ptrArray; // a better C# implementation
```

but those languages do not include an instance of the ptrArray object, only a reference. Both the data and the controls become a separately allocated object—see Fig. 3.2.

Object Array corresponds to the use of STL Vector when the array stores entire L objects:

```
class D {
    std::vector<L> ptrArray; // declaration line
};

D* dp=new D;
...
L* lp= &(dp->ptrArray[17]);
int sz=dp->ptrArray.size(); // size of the array
```

This style of array is not allowed in Java or Objective-C. It could exist in C#, but only if L is a structure, not a class.

Pointer List corresponds to STL List using a reference

```
class D {
    std::list<L*> myList; // declaration line
};

D* dp=new D;
...
L* lp=dp->myList.front(); // head of the list
```

Objective-C library does not have a List class.[5] In Java and C# the declaration line would be:

```
LinkedList<L> myList; // in Java
LinkedList<L> myList; // in C#
```

---

[5] GitHub website offers one https://github.com/mschettler/NSLinkedList

Embeded List corresponds to STL List using an instance

```
class D {
    std::list<L> myList; // declaration line
};

D* dp=new D;
...
L* lp= & (dp->myList.front()); // head of the list
```

This is not a recommended type of list because the existence of the application object L is controlled by a transparent object that cannot be accessed by the application.

Intrusive List is often needed in real-life projects, but standard libraries do not provide it. Here is how you invoke it if you use the InCode library:

```
Association LinkedList2<D, L> myList; // declaration line
class D {
    ZZ_D ZZds;
};
class L {
    ZZ_L ZZds;
};

D* dp=new D;
...
L* lp= myList.head()); // head of the list
```

We will be discussing this library later in this chapter. The data structure is controlled by a self-standing dataless class, myList, which also inserts[6] pointers or other variables into participating classes D and L. The declaration line is the same in C++, Java, and in Objective-C.

Why do we claim that this type of list is often needed in real life projects? Look again at Fig. 3.2—Object Array and Embedded List are not suitable for practical use, and both Pointer Array and Pointer List are *collections*. L objects may appear several times under the same D or under several different Ds.

In real life, however, we more often encounter a *set*, where any L can appear only once: Department has Employees, and one Employee normally cannot be member of two Departments. Two customers cannot purchase the same TV screen with the same serial number. A train has ten cars. These cars cannot be, at the same time, in another train. A paragraph in a text document consist of lines. The same line cannot be there twice—it would need a different line number.[7]

Standard libraries have a *set* class, but because they only work with collections they have to do a lot of calculations to make sure that nobody can enter an object more than once. A set is either implemented as a balanced tree which requires O(log N) search for each insertion, or a hash table which needs a constant time but still has an overhead both in the space and time.

---

[6] How to perform this insertion is the prime subject of his chapter.

[7] If the same text appears twice, one of the lines is a copy of the other.

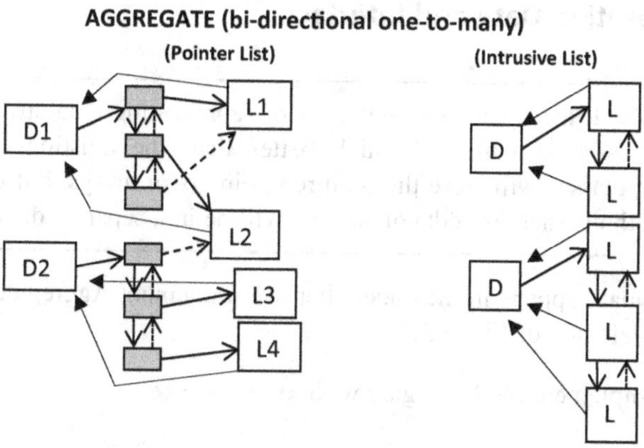

AGGREGATE (bi-directional one-to-many)

(Pointer List)   (Intrusive List)

Fig. 3.3 Aggregate is a bi-directional *association*, even when built with a *collection* which is uni-directional. This mae disadvantage of this implementation is a possibility of an error: D2 thinks that L2 belongs to it, but L2 and D1 think that L2 belongs to D1. In Aggregate, a child can belong to only one parent. Intrusive Aggregate (on the right) is Intrusive List with an additional parent pointer

On the other hand, *Intrusive List* implemented with rings is a natural *set*, where a simple check whether a pointer is 0 tells you whether the object is free to be inserted.

If you find it surprising how the standard *set* is usually implemented, this is only a beginning. All the lists in Fig. 3.2 are *uni-directional associations*: from any D object you can reach its L objects, but these L objects do not know to what D object they have been assigned. In real life application about half the time we need associations that are bi-directional. Teachers have students, and they know who their teachers are. A person has several accounts, and the bank knows, for each account, to whom it belongs. The book may have several authors, and each author knows[8] what books he wrote.

And no standard library supports bi-directional associations! Is that possible, and why?

The reason is that the existing object-oriented languages do not provide a mechanism that would automatically insert the required pointers into more than one class. By definition, class L needs a pointer which would directly or indirectly lead to a D object—see Fig. 3.3.

The left part of Fig. 3.3 shows how using a *collection* (which is not a *set*) we can build *Aggregate* (which is a *set*). When adding an L-object, we check whether its parent pointer is NULL. If it is not, it is already member of this or another *Aggregate*, and must not be added second time.

Imagine that in Fig. 3.3, we are adding L-objects to D1 and D2 from the top down. When adding L1 the second time to D1 (dashed line), the operation is not accepted. Addition of L2 to D2 is also not accepted because L2 is already under D1.

---

[8] Unless he is very very old.

3.1.2 Separating Data and Interface

This section will lead you to a new style of representing data structures and associations, a style which is much better than the existing containers: Participating classes will store the required pointers or arrays, but the overall control—methods such as add() or sort()—will be in a separate dataless class.

Let's see what happens in the code when we implement Aggregate in the style shown on the left side of Fig. 3.3.

Listing 3.1 Implementing Aggregate with `std::list<T>`

```cpp
#include <stdio.h>
#include <list>

template<class P,class C> class Aggregate : public std::list<C*> {
public:
    void add(P *p,C *c) {
        if(c->myPar)return;
        std::list<C*>::push_back(c);
        c->myPar=p;
    }
    ...
};
// ------ library classes above this line, application below ------
class Lecturer;

class Department {
public:
    Aggregate<Department,Lecturer> lecturers; // <<<<<<<
};

class Lecturer{
friend class Aggregate<Department,Lecturer>; // <<<<<<<<
    Department *myPar; // <<<<<<<<<
public:
    Lecturer():myPar(NULL){}
};

int main(){
    Department* dp=new Department;
    Lecturer* lp=new Lecturer;
    dp->lecturers.add(dp,lp);
    return 0;
}
```

Here Aggregate inherits std::list<> and with it both its interface and data—the pointer to the beginning of the list plus possibly the size of the list and other numbers. It also expects that pointer myPar has been inserted into Lecturer. Maintaining such data for possibly many data structures is a recipe for disaster.

Fortunately, if the application inserts `myPar` into a wrong class or uses a wrong name, the Aggregate will not compile, and the compiler tells you where the problem is. That makes this design style relatively safe though a bit tedious.

Besides the Aggregate being a public member of Department, this design has three flaws:

1. The fixed name `myPar` for the member inserted into Lecturer can cause a name collision. For example, if Lecturer can also be a Union member, we have

```
Aggregate<Department,Lecturer> lecturers;
Aggregate<Union,Lecturer> members;

class Lecturer {
    Department *myPar;
    Union       *myPar;
};
```

2. The call to the add() method at the bottom of Listing 3.1 requires `dp` to be mentioned twice, with a potential for introducing an error.
3. Declarations of data structures are spread through the classes, buried in them, and, especially with every class having a separate *.h file, there is no central place where you can see the overall architecture.

We will now address each of these issues separately.

Case 1. We need to use different names for `myPar`, or parametrize it by something typical for each case. For example, we could have

```
class Lecturer {
    Department *Department_Lecturer_myPar;
    Union *Union_Lecturer_myPar;
};
```

but that still may lead to a collision as in this situation

```
Aggregate(Company,Employee) employees;
Aggregate(Company,Employee) retirees;
```

The best parameter to use is the instance name of the data structures, such as

```
Department *lecturers_myPar;
Union *unionMembers_
Company *employees_myPar;
Company *retirees_myPar;
```

That sounds like a good idea, but templates (or generics) do not allow us to parameterize variable and member names. In C based languages we can use macros; in other languages we can use a preprocessor which would provide the substitution:

Listing 3.2 Implementing Aggregate with `std::list<T>` and using a macro for additional parameterization

```
#include <stdio.h>
#include <list>

#define Aggregate(P,C,X)                                \
class X##_Aggregate : public std::list<C*> {  \
public:                                                 \
    void add(P *p,C *c);                                \
}

#define AggregateImplement(P,C,X)      \
void X##_Aggregate::add(P *p,C *c){    \
    if(c->X##_myPar)return;            \
    std::list<C*>::push_back(c);       \
    c->X##_myPar=p;                    \
}

// ------ library include above this line, application below ------
class Lecturer;
class Department;
Aggregate(Department,Lecturer,lecturers);

class Department {
public:
    lecturers_Aggregate lecturers;
};

class Lecturer {
friend class lecturers_Aggregate;
    Department *lecturers_myPar;
};

int main(){
    Department* dp=new Department;
    Lecturer* lp=new Lecturer;
    dp->lecturers.add(dp,lp);
    return 0;
}

AggregateImplement(Department,Lecturer,lecturers);
```

Note how the name `lecturers` becomes the ID of the data structure. This is still not the ideal way of doing it, only the first step.

In Listing 3.2, two characters ## are used to concatenate names. For example:

A##B creates AB.

Cases 2 and 3. The problem with relations spread through the classes is typical for the current way of designing software with STL and other container libraries, but it is still a major problem. Relations (associations, data structures) should have the same visibility in the code as classes. We need associations (relations) to become first class entities, as we have them in the UML class diagrams.

Both this and the problem with `dp` being mentioned twice can be fixed by separating data and interface. The data will reside in the application classes, and the interface will be implemented in a special, dataless class.

Rather than evolving the example based on `std:list<>`, this is easier to explain on the design of the intrusive Aggregate. Let's start with the Aggregate designed in the same style as the popular container classes, i.e. inserting an instance of Aggregate into class Department.[9] In order to make Aggregate generic, we will use a macro, because that is the only way to prevent collision of names.

Listing 3.3 is not easy to read, but it would be useful if you grasp its essence.

Note what happens in the application code. In the beginning you declare what Aggregate you are going to need. This statement creates two classes, `lecturers_AggregateChild` and `lecturers_Aggregate`. These are the types of members you add to classes Department and Lecturer. In both cases you name the member `lecturers`, which is the common name for everything associated with this Aggregate; see the call to add() in the main.

Statement `AggregateImplement(...)` which is at the end of the code contains implementation of all the methods the Aggregate needs. You could also compile it separately.

This implementation is already usable, and it solves two of the problems that we previously mentioned: It avoids the collision of names, and it declares Aggregate as a separate entity,[10] which is just as visible as the application classes.

The disadvantages are the massive use of macros which are always difficult to debug, the need to repeat the relation ID (here lecturers) many times, and the fact that `dp` occurs twice in the call to `add()`. Also we have not touched upon the issue that a library of data structures should derive more complex data structures from simpler ones.

The next improvement[11] of this code is in Listing 3.4. It removes the problem with `dp` and it makes the implementation much more logical. There are three classes now:

1. Aggregate—a dataless class which implements the Aggregate's interface, essentially providing the control of the data structure.
2. AggregateParent—which has no methods (it could even be just a structure) which must be inserted into the parent of the Aggregate, in this example into Department.
3. AggregateChild—which inserts the data into the child of the Aggregate, in this example into Lecturer.

Even though the library file aggregate.h is quite different, the application code remains practically the same (only the bold sections changed), and the problem with the double use of `dp` is solved. Note that this time we named the inserted members differently (_lecturers instead of lecturers). Since lecturers now has a global visibility, using the same name may lead to a collision.[12]

---

[9] This is not the aimplementation style we recommend for intrusive Aggregate, but watch what will happen.

[10] See the line marked with // <<<<.

[11] This is the implementation style we prefer and highly recommend.

[12] We tested that, in this example, using the same name works, but it a general case it may cause problems.

Listing 3.3 Intrusive Aggregate in the style of existing containers

```
FILE: aggregate.h

#define Aggregate(P,C,X)                      \
class X##_AggregateChild {                    \
friend class X##_Aggregate;                   \
    P *par;                                   \
    C *next;                                  \
    C *prev;                                  \
public:                                       \
    X##_AggregateChild(){                     \
        par=NULL; next=prev=NULL; \
    }                                         \
};                                            \
class X##_Aggregate {                         \
    C *first;                                 \
public:                                       \
    void add(P *p,C *c);                      \
    X##_Aggregate(){first=NULL;}  \
}

// list implemented as doubly-linked ring
#define AggregateImplement(P,C,X)                       \
    void X##_Aggregate::add(P *p,C *c){                 \
        C* f=first;                                     \
        first=c;                                        \
        c->_##X.par=p;                                  \
        if(f){                                          \
            c->_##X.prev=f->_##X.prev; c-_##_X.next=f; \
            f->_##X.prev->_##X.next=c; f->_##X.prev=c; \
        }                                          \
        else {first=c->_##X.next=c->_##X.prev=c;}       \
    }
\

APPLICATION:

#include <aggregate.h>
class Department;
class Lecturer;
Aggregate(Department,Lecturer,lecturers); // <<<<<<<<

class Department {
public:
    lecturers_Aggregate lecturers;
};

class Lecturer {
public:
    lecturers_AggregateChild lecturers;
};

int main(){
    Department* dp=new Department;
    Lecturer* lp=new Lecturer;
    dp->lecturers.add(dp,lp);
    return 0;
}

AggregateImplement(Department,Lecturer,lecturers);
```

Listing 3.4 Intrusive Aggregate with the separation of separated data and interface

```
FILE: aggregate.h
#define Aggregate(P,C,X)                         \
class X##_AggregateChild {                       \
friend class X;                                  \
    P *par;                                      \
    C *next;                                     \
    C *prev;                                     \
public:                                          \
    X##_AggregateChild(){                        \
        par=NULL; next=prev=NULL;                \
    }                                            \
};                                               \
class X##_AggregateParent {                      \
friend class X;                                  \
    C *first;                                    \
public:                                          \
    X##_AggregateParent(){first=NULL;}           \
};                                               \
class X {                                        \
public:                                          \
    static void add(P *p,C *c);                  \
}

// list implemented as doubly-linked ring
#define AggregateImplement(P,C,X)                \
    void X::add(P *p,C *c){                      \
        C* f=p->X.first;                         \
        p->X.first=c;                            \
        c->X.par=p;                              \
        if(f){                                   \
            c->X.prev=f->X.prev; c->X.next=f;    \
            f->X.prev->X.next=c; f->X.prev=c;    \
        }                                        \
        else {c->X.next=c->X.prev=c;}            \
    }
```

APPLICATION:

```
class Department;
class Lecturer;
Aggregate(Department,Lecturer,lecturers); // <<<<<<<

class Department {
public:
    lecturers_AggregateParent _lecturers;
};

class Lecturer {
public:
    lecturers_AggregateChild _lecturers;
};

int main(){
    Department* dp=new Department;
    Lecturer* lp=new Lecturer;
    lecturers::add(dp,lp);
    return 0;
}

    AggregateImplement(Department,Lecturer,lecturers);
```

3.1.3 Generalized Templates—Code Generator

Most of the parameterization we need for our data structures can be done with templates, but we also need to parameterize names of certain members—something that templates cannot do but a code generator can. However, if we already use the code generator, we can let it also to expand the templates, and that takes us to new, more general type of templates.

The main problem with Listing 3.4 is the use of macros. They are difficult to understand and debug. Even the simple examples in Listings 3.3 and 3.4 took us a while to debug.

Think what we need to do and what templates and macros provide. We want to parameterize the library classes with types of participating classes just as when you use templates. The only exception is that we also want to manipulate class and member names using one more additional parameter.

Think then what is the compiler doing with templates. Compilers first find for what parameters the templates are instantiated, and expand the templates. For example, if you have an error in

```
Template < class P, class C> class Aggregate {...}
```

and you are using this class for P = Department and C = Lecturer, the compiler tells you that you have an error in class

```
Department_Lecturer_Aggregate
```

After this, the compiler proceeds with the normal compilation.

We can do the same thing, but we can make it simpler and faster by tuning it to what we really need. We can use our expanded templates, and prepare the code for the compiler in the same way as the compiler prepares it with the normal templates. We will use a code generator but will not change the existing code. We will only create files with the expanded templates that can be compiled separately and linked with the application code. This is the method used in the InCode library today.

It uses the special keyword *Association*, which has the same effect as the // comment—the remaining code on this line is removed. However, the code which follows is the instruction for parameterization of templates. We will add this keyword to the lines that invoke the data structure. In Listings 3.3 and 3.4 those are the lines marked with // <<<<<<. Because these lines will be ignored by the compiler, we can change their syntax to look more like templates.

For example, for this original line

```
Aggregate(Department,Lecturer,lecturers);
```

we can use syntax

```
Association Aggregate<Department,Lecturer> lecturers;
```

which better portrays the meaning of this expression, except that `lecturers` is still the id of the interface, and method add() is static

```
lecturers::add(dp,lp)
```

see Listing 3.4.

The next question is how the code generator finds these special lines. You can feed it all the application code, but we recommend placing all these lines into a special small file, which in the InCode library is called ds.def (data structure definitions). The advantage of having them in a single file is not only simple processing. This file becomes a textual form of the UML diagram, the central place that stores the architecture. It further elevates the visibility of relations.

Inside the library, the templates are coded with parameters $\$\$$, $\$0$, $\$1$, $\$2$, ...

where $\$1$, $\$2$, ... are the types of the participating classes, and $\$\$$ is the name of the association and $\$0$ is the same as $\_\$\$$. For example, in line

```
Association Aggregate<Department,Lecturer> lecturers;
```

we have $\$\$$ = lecturers, $\$1$ = Department, $\$2$ = Lecturer. As a shortcut, internally, $\$0$ is used for $\_\$\$$ or, in this example, for _lecturers. This makes the library encoding simple and readable. For example, the macros from Listing 3.4 become what are in Listing 3.5. The application code remains the same, except for the line starting with the *Association* keyword.

Listing 3.5 Intrusive Aggregate with generalized templates

FILE: **aggregate.h**

```
class $$_AggregateChild {
public:
    $1 *par;
    $2 *next;
    $2 *prev;
    $$_AggregateChild(){
        par=NULL; next=prev=NULL;
    }
};

class $$_AggregateParent {
public:
    $2 *first;
    $$_AggregateParent(){first=NULL;}
};

class $$ {
public:
    static void add($1 *p,$2 *c);
};

typedef $$_Aggregate $$;
#define Association /##/
```

FILE: **aggregate.cpp**

```
// list implemented as doubly-linked ring
void $$::add($1 *p,$2 *c){
    $2* f=p->$0.first;
    p->$0.first=c;
    c->$0.par=p;
    if(f){
        c->$0.prev=f->$0.prev; c->$0.next=f;
        f->$0.prev->$0.next=c; f->$0.prev=c;
    }
    else {c->$0.next=c->$0.prev=c;}
}
```

APPLICATION:

```
Association Aggregate<Department,Lecturer> lecturers;

// <<<< marks automatically inserted lines
class Department {
friend lecturers;                            // <<<<
    lecturers_AggregateParent _lecturers; // <<<<
};

class Lecturer{
friend lecturer;                             // <<<<
    lecturers_AggregateChild _lecturers;  // <<<<
};

int main(){
    Department *dp; Lecturer *lp;
    lecturers::add(dp,lp);
```

Generated code is the normal C++ source which can be debugged as usual. The generated code (lecturers.h and lecturers.cpp) has the same number of lines as the library files (Aggregate.h and Aggregate.cpp) in this example. You can either debug lecturers.cpp and transfer each correction to Aggregate.cpp, or you can debug directly Aggregate.cpp.

Note that there is a simple mechanism which allows a quick manual conversion of DOL data structures to InCode.[13]

3.1.4   Transparent Insertion

Now when you are familiar with the Association statements, it is much easier to explain some things. For example, from this

```
Association Aggregate<Faculty,Student> students;
Association Aggregate<Faculty,Teacher> teachers;
Association Aggregate<Teacher,Course> courses;
Association Aggregate<Teacher,Student> advisorOf;
Association Aggregate<Student,Book> booksOnLoan;
Association ManyToMany<Student,Takes,Course> takes;
Association Name<Student> studentName;
```

you immediately see that we have classes Faculty, Student, Teacher, Course, Book and Takes, and you also see the data structures (Associations) that connect them. The only thing we have to add is that even a text string is represented as a special association, called Name.

This block of Association statements is a good example of how complex it would be to insert manually all the required parts. In this case, for example, class Student would look like this:

Listing 3.6 Insertion required for class Student[14]

```
class Student {
friend class students;
friend class advisorOf;
friend class booksOnLoan;
friend class takes;
friend class studentName;
        students_AggregateChild _students;
        advisorOf_AggregateChild _advisorOf;
        booksOnLoad_AggregateParent _booksOnLoan;
        takes_ManyToManySource _takes;
        studentName_Parent _studentName;
        ...     whatever else
    };
```

---

[13] This was the way the InCode library was populated.

[14] This is just a code snippet, with no code on the website.

To handle this on large projects would be a nightmare, but don't worry. These insertions can be performed automatically and transparently. Chapter 5 will show a proposal how, by adding one keyword to existing object oriented languages, this could be done in a simple command. Until this proposal is accepted and implemented, however, we have to find some other way.

Since we were already forced to accept the use of code generator, and the code generator already analyzes the Association statements, we have a great opportunity there. The code generator can easily assemble these statements, and set them up so that Listing 3.6 is reduced to

```
class Student {
    ZZ_Student ZZds;
    ...    whatever else
};
```

This is exactly what the InCode generator does. ZZ prefix was chosen for historical reasons,[15] and *ds* stands for *data structure*.

The library expects that when entering a new association (data structure) you register it in a special registry file. For each association, there is one line which describes its design—see Fig. 3.4.

This record has a little more information than we discussed so far. InCode has two aggregates: Aggregate1 derived from the singly-linked list and Aggregate2 which is derived from the doubly-linked list. Otherwise, Fig. 3.4 is self-explanatory. The directionality and multiplicity record will be needed later for automatic generation of the UML class diagram.

The purpose of $1 and $2 parameters in this line is to connect parameters of the base and derived classes. For example, line

```
Association Aggregate2<Faculty,Student> students;
```

will trigger generation of files for `Aggregate2<Faculty,Student>`, but also for `List2<Faculty,Student>`, and the $.. parameters refer to the Aggregate2 definition. In this case $1 = Faculty, $2 = Student. There are situations where the base class has a different order or fewer parameters than the derived class.

If this appears too laborious, consider that this is done only once when entering the association into the library, and it is well worth it for the simple user interface, the prevention of errors in the application and the ability to generate the UML class diagram about which we will be talking later on.

Besides expanding the classes coded with the $ codes, the code generator also creates files gen.h and gen.cpp. File gen.h provides a mechanism which transparently inserts all the required members. This can have two forms: a macro or involving another level of indirection.

---

[15] All library-related expressions in DOL have prefix ZZ.

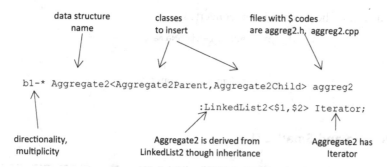

```
            data structure          classes          files with $ codes
               name               to insert        are aggreg2.h, aggreg2.cpp



   b1-* Aggregate2<Aggregate2Parent,Aggregate2Child> aggreg2

                            :LinkedList2<$1,$2> Iterator;


    directionality,          Aggregate2 is derived from      Aggregate2 has
    multiplicity             LinkedList2 though inheritance    Iterator
```

Fig. 3.4 Record of the Aggregate2 class in the InCode registry file

The DOL library uses a macro:

```
// FILE: gen.h
#define ZZ_EXT_Student
fri class students;                                 \
friend class advisorOf;                             \
friend class booksOnLoan;                           \
friend class takes;                                 \
friend class studentName;                           \
students_AggregateChild _students;                  \
advisorOf_AggregateChild _advisorOf;                \
booksOnLoad_AggregateParent _booksOnLoan;           \
takes_ManyToManySource _takes;                      \
studentName_Parent _studentName;

// Application
class Student {
    ZZ_EXT_Student
        ... anything else
};
```

The InCode library uses an intermediary class:

```
// FILE: gen.h
class ZZ_Student {
    friend class students;
    friend class advisorOf;
    friend class booksOnLoan;
    friend class takes;
    friend class studentName;
    students_AggregateChild _students;
    advisorOf_AggregateChild _advisorOf;
    booksOnLoad_AggregateParent _booksOnLoan;
    takes_ManyToManySource _takes;
    studentName_Parent _studentName;
};

// Application
class Student {
public:
    ZZ_Student ZZds;
        ... anything else
};
```

In this case, the $0 code is not converted to

_associationName,

but to

ZZds._associationName

3.1.5 Big and Small, STL

> Examples of how the data structures coded in this style are useful for projects of any size, and a discussion on how to convert STL classes into this representation.

Using this style, you can build data structures of any complexity and involving any number of classes in this style - each as easy to use as Aggregate or List that we just discussed. You can create these data structures using pointers and arrays, or you can use simpler data structures to build the more complicated ones. Details of how you do that are beyond the scope of this book, but you can grasp the main idea by analyzing classes from the InCode library.[16]

Since our objective is to remove all pointer members from the application classes, the library includes

SingleLink = equivalent of a single pointer, or uni-directional 1to1,

DoubleLink = two objects mutually linked via pointer, bi-directional 1to1,

Name = Null ending String attached to the object, an equivalent of char*.

Listing 3.7 shows how these classes are used.

Listing 3.7 Company–Manager–Employee example, InCode style

```
class Employee {
    ZZ_Employee ZZds;
    int phone;
    int salary;
};
class Manager : public Employee {
    ZZ_Manager ZZds;
};
class Company {
    ZZ_Company ZZds;
};

Association Aggregate<Company,Employee> employees;
Association Aggregate<Manager,Employee> subordinates;
Association Name<Employee> employeeName;
Association SingleLink<Manager,Employee> secretary;
```

---

[16] On the website at incode/alib/lib for C++, incode/jlib/lib for Java.

The important question is whether the InCode style library can include STL classes with their original interface, so that programmers who are used to them could still work with them while enjoying the benefits of the additional intrusive data structures.

As an example, let's look at how to represent std::list<> in the InCode style while keeping its original interface.

The standard way to use std::list<> to store Books in a Library is

```
class Library {
    std::list<Book*> myList;
};
```

In order to use the same class with our new interface, we will place myList in the same place, but we will get it there indirectly:

```
class NewListParent {
    std::list<Book*> myList;
};
class Library {
    NewListParent myPar;
};
```

This inserts not only the data that we want to be in Library, but also the STL interface—quite a bit of code which we don't want there but can tolerate it in this special case. Then we code the new dataless class—see Listing 3.8—which consists of short, usually one-line conversions of the old method to the new interface. Note that, compared to the STL interface, the new methods have typically one more parameter—a pointer to the class which holds the STL container. We can use the same method names as in STL, or replace them by new names.

This is more than just the Adaptor Design Pattern, because it combines insertion of data with the conversion of the interface.

Listing 3.8 stl_list coded in the InCode style, the concept of keeping the same interface (general idea, not a generic implementation yet)

```
class NewList { // stl_list, new style
    public:
        static void push_back(Library *lp, Book *bp)
            {lp->myPar.myList.push_back(bp);
        }
        ... // all other methods
};
int main(){
    Library* lp=new Library;
    Book* bp=new Book;
        NewList::push_back(lp,bp); // or add()
```

The generic $-encoding of NewList is simple and clean:

```
using namespace std;
class $$_NewListParent {
    std::list<$2*> oldList;
};
class $$_NewList {
public:
    static void push_back($1 *lp, $2 *bp)
                        {lp->$$.oldList.push_back(bp);}
    ... // all other methods
};
```

This conversion is safe[17] and works fine, but it is tedious because STL containers have quite many of methods.

Example: Airlines, Flights and Airports It's time to show a complete, more realistic example coded in this style. The code is in bk\chap3\list_3-9.cpp, tt9. bat compiles it, rr9.bat runs it.

---

[17] We did not make any changes in the code of stl_list.h.

Listing 3.9 Flights of different Airlines connect Airports, while distinguishing between the arrival and departure flights

```
#include "gen.h" // file generated by incode/codegen.exe
class Flight {
    ZZ_Flight ZZds;
    int flightNo;
};
class Airline {
    ZZ_Airline ZZds;
}; // attached name treated as a data structure
class Arrivals {
    ZZ_Arrivals ZZds;
};
class Departures {
    ZZ_Departures ZZds;
};
class Airport {
    ZZ_Airport ZZds;
    char code[4]; // 3-letter airport code
    Airport(){Departures* d=new Departures; toDept::add(this,d);
              Arrivals*  a=new Arrivals;   toArr::add(this,a);
    }
};

/* ++++++++++ next lines stored in file ds9.def ++++++++++++++++++
Association 3XtoX<Flight,Airline,Departures,Arrivals> flights;
Association DoubleLink<Airport,Arrivals> toArr;
Association DoubleLink<Airport,Departures> toDept;
Association Name<Airline> airlineName;
++++++++++++++++++++++++++++++++++++++++++++++++++++++++++++++ */
int main(){
    Flight *fg; Airline *line; Arrivals *arr; Departures *dpt;
    Airport *dPort,*aPort;
    flights_Iterator it;
    ...
    // print all flights that depart airport 'dPort'
    dpt=toDept::fwd(dPort);
    for(fg=it.from2(dpt); fg; fg=it.next2()){
        line=flights::entity1(fg);
        arr =flights::entity3(fg);
        aPort=toArr::bwd(arr);
        printf("%s %d departs at %2d:%2d for %s\n",
            airlineName::get(line), fg->flightNo,fg->depTime/100,
            fg->depTime%100,aPort->code);
    }
    return 0;
}
Airport::Airport(){
    Departures* d=new Departures;  toDept::add(this,d);
    Arrivals*   a=new Arrivals;    toArr::add(this,a);
}
#include "gen.cpp" // generated by incode/codegen.exe
```

3.1.6 Code Generator and IDE

> Today, programming with a code generator is not considered a bad practice as it was a decade ago, but if you don't know how to set up your IDE properly, it can be a serious deterrent. This chapter describes how to set up a project so that the code generator is called automatically any time you recompile.

It used to be that using a preprocessor or a code generator was considered inappropriate. There were two practical reasons:

1. If preprocessor changed your code, debugging was difficult, especially when line numbers changed.
2. Integrated environments, such as Microsoft's Visual C++, did not integrate well with preprocessors and code generators.

Note also the difference between preprocessing and code generation. Preprocessor changes your original code, while code generator creates additional source files which compile separately and link to your original code.

Code generators are clearly better and they are frequently used today. Many programs quoted in this book use code generators but never a preprocessor.[18]

One of the reasons why code generators are not frowned upon any more is that development environments allow the programmer to register a code generator in such a way that you compile as if there were no code generation. The code generator is invoked automatically and transparently whenever you compile.

If you have never worked with a code generator, here is instruction on how to integrate the code generator for InCode library into VS2010.[19] Don't be discouraged by the fact that ten steps are required. We are trying to explain every detail so that even a complete beginner could do it. Also, remember that once you register the code generator, you compile as if it wasn't there.

1. We assume that the InCode library is stored in c:\InCode , with the code generator in c:\InCode\alib\codegen.exe[20] and the library in c:\InCode\alib\lib
2. Create a project, with or without any source files
3. Create file codeg.bat:

   ```
   mkdir tmp
   c:\InCode\alib\codegen.exe ds.def c:\InCode\alib\lib gen
   ```

   and move it to the directory where you have your new project.
4. In the same directory, create file environ.h, which may even be empty. You don't have to add this file to the project, but the generated files may need it.
5. At the top of main() you need

---

[18] With the exception of the built-in C preprocessor (macros).

[19] The steps are similar in VS2008, and probably in VS2012.

[20] Subdirectory alib is for C++, c:\InCode\jlib is for Java.

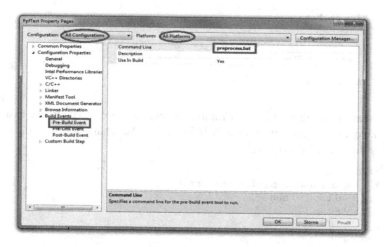

Fig. 3.5 Setting up VS2010 for a project using a code generator

#include "gen.h".

This file still does not exist; the code generator will create it.

6. Display *Properties* of your project by Alt + Enter, or right click in *the Solution Explorer* on your project, and then *Properties*.

7. Using the screen from Fig. 3.5, select *Configuration, All Configurations,* then *Debug* or *Release*.

8. Select *All Platforms*, as in Fig. 3.5.

9. Select Configuration Properties, Build Events, Pre-Built Event.

10. Select Command Line, type the name of the bat file you created, codeg.bat, and click OK.

From now on, you can compile as usual, but before every compilation, codeg.bat will be executed.

As we explained earlier, the full source for most of the examples is available as one large zip file. It unzips into directory bk, which is organized by chapter. More complex examples may be stored in separate subdirectories, with their own readme. txt and files tt.bat to compile and rr.bat to run it in the black CMD window.

As an example, let's take Listing 3.9 which uses the InCode code generator and library. The entire program is in list3_9.cpp, and the block of associations is in file ds9.def:

File tt.bat:
```
mkdir tmp
c:\incode\alib\codegen ds9.def c:\incode\alib\lib gen
cl list3_9.cpp
```

File rr.bat
```
list3_9
```

If you are working with Unix or Linux, you may prepare a makefile or bash file which invokes the code generator only if file ds.def has changed, e.g. if ds.def is younger than get.h. For example[21]

```
#!/bin/bash
#if tmp dir doesn't exist then create it
if [ ! -d tmp ]; then
    mkdir tmp
fi
run_cg=0
#if gen.h exists
if [ -f 'gen.h' ]; then
#if ds.def is newer then gen.h
   if [ ds.def -nt gen.h ]; then
     run_cg=1
   fi
else
   run_cg=1
fi
if [ $run_cg -eq 1 ]; then
  /opt/incode/alib/codegen ds.def /opt/incode/alib/lib gen
fi

gcc myprogram.cpp
```

3.1.7 Arrays (Vectors)

> This section compares arrays of pointers with arrays of objects, and show how to build an Array class in the new style.

Arrays are important in many data structures, for example when building hash tables, and so far we have completely avoided them. As explained in Sect. 2.1.4, in order to make an array persistent, it has to be implemented through a special library class. In the DOL, InCode and PTL libraries this class is called Array and in the STL library it is called Vector. PPF includes class Vector as an example of how to make a STL class persistent. The array class usually represents a dynamic array,

---

[21] Full source bk\chap3\cg.sh.

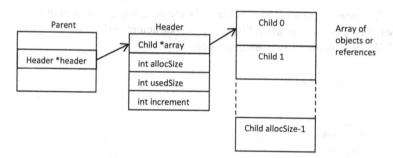

Fig. 3.6 Internal implementation of the Array class. In Java, arrays of objects are not allowed

which automatically increases its size when needed. In Objective-C, it is called MutableArray.

The InCode Array can be invoked in the same way as the pointer-based data structures:

```
Association Array<Parent,Child> name;
```

where Parent is the class to which the array is attached, and the Child is the type of object which forms the array. Child can be an entire object or just a pointer to it, for example:

```
Association Array<Library,Book> books; // array of Books
Association Array<Library,Book*> bookPtrs; // Book pointers
```

This association does not insert anything into the Child class, but it inserts a pointer to a special Header (or a pointer to such Header) into the Parent class— see Fig. 3.4. The Header stores a pointer to the array itself, and the size of the array. When making an array persistent, the Header object is stored to disk in the same way as the instances of the application classes.

The advantage of this arrangement is that, if there is no array attached to the Parent object, only one NULL pointer is wasted—see Fig. 3.6.

Here is an example of using the Array class. Method form() forms the initial array:

```
Array::form(Parent *par, int initialSize, int increment);
```

where increment = 0 specifies an array of fixed size, increment > 0 indicates how many items to add to the array if its size is not sufficient and increment < 0 gives a multiplication factor[22] to increase the size.

```
class Library {
     ZZ_Library ZZds;
     ...
};
class Book {
     ZZ_Book;
     int ID;
     ...
};
Association Array<Library,Book> books;
int main(){
     Library *lib; Book bk, *bp; int i;
     lib=new Library;
     // form array with initial size 10, increase 2x when needed
     books.form(lib,10,-2);
     for(i=0; i<32; i++){
          bk=books.get(lib,i); // equivalent of bk=a[i]
          bk.ID=300-i; // some number
          books.set(lib,i,bk); // equivalent of a[i]=bk
     }
     books.sort(lib);
```

It is much faster to get a pointer to the object inside the array and change the ID directly there, using function ind() which, for a given index, returns the pointer to the object- for example, DOL Array class has such a function. However, this function must be used with extreme care, and only before any other command accesses the array. If the array automatically reallocates, bp becomes invalid:

```
for(i=0; i<32; i++){
     bp=books.ind(lib,i); // equivalent of bk= &(a[i])
     bp->ID=300-i; // immediate use is OK
}
```

Can you figure out what happens with the allocSize and usedSize in this loop? When reaching i = 10 the array reallocates to 20, because the form() method specifies the multiplication factor of 2. Then when i = 20 it reallocates to 40. When the loop is finished, allocSize = 40 and usedSize = 32. When storing the array to disk, only 32 objects are stored.

---

[22] After discarding the negative sign.

3.1.8   Make Them Persistent

> Data structures designed in the new style are easy to make persistent, and by moving all the pointers from application classes to library classes, the application classes also become persistent.

There are three important factors when thinking about persistence:
1. When we stick to the rule that application classes must not have any explicit pointer members, the application data are persistent as long as the library classes[23] are persistent.
2. Each data structure is represented by a dataless class. Since these classes keep no data, it is guaranteed that they do not keep any pointers, and these classes do not need any conversion to become persistent.
3. Remaining library classes are easy to make persistent because we know the pointers they store.

Classes storing the data to be inserted into the application classes are simple, because they typically include a few values and a constructor, no additional methods. As an example, to make Aggregate from Listing 3.5 persistent is to add default constructors to AggregateParent and AggregateChild as shown in Listing 3.10.

Listing 3.10 Making class Aggregate persistent

```
class $$_AggregateParent {
    $2 *first;
public:
    $$_AggregateParent(){PTR(first,$2);}
};
class $$_AggregateChild {
    $1 *par;
    $2 *next;
    $2 *prev;
    $$_AggregateChild(){PTR(par,$1); PTR(next,$2); PTR(prev,$2);}
};
```

When creating a new object with new(), unless other constructors are explicitly called, C++ calls default constructors for all base classes and their members. This guarantees that the PTR statements mark properly the position of all these pointers even in very complex composite objects—see example in Listing 3.11. This is specific in C++, but it does not work in Objective-C.

---

[23] Classes that represent data structures in the style described here.

Listing 3.11 Automatic invocation of default constructors in C++

```
#include <stdio.h>
class A {
    int a;
public:
    A(){printf("A\n");}
};
class B {
    A b;
public:
    B(){printf("B\n");}
};
class C : public B {
    int c;
public:
    C(){printf("C\n");}
};

int main(){
    C *c=new C;
    A *a=new A[5];
    return 0;
}
// It prints ABC and them AAAAA
```

For arrays of pointers we need to use macro ARP() as explained in Listing 2.17.

3.2   Inserting Pointers with Inheritance

Until now, the pointers and other variables that formed the data structures were alway inserted as members of participating classes. Interestingly, we can achieve the same objective with inheritance, at least in C++.

The basic idea of what we did so far was to have dataless class to represent the data structure and to implement its interface. Fpr example

```
template<class P,class C> Aggregate { ... };
```

implemented interface, and classes AggregateParent and AggregateChild stored the data to be inserted into the application classes as their members. We used macros for additional parameterization, but this is still the essence of what we did:

```
template<class P,class C> class AggregateParent{
    C *first;
};
template<class P,class C> class AggregateChild{
    P *parent;
    C *next;
    C *prev;
};
```

However, there is another way to insert data into a class—using inheritance.[24]
The main idea is instead of coding as we did so far:

```
class Library {
    AggregateParent<Library,Book> _books;
    ...
};
class Book {
    AggregateChild<Library,Book> _books;
    ...
};
```

to do this:

```
class Library : public AggregateParent<Library,Book> {
    ...
};
class Book : public AggregateChild<Library,Book> {
    ...
};
```

So far, it is not clear how we will access the data, but let's continue. It is clear
that this approach will lead to a massive use of multiple inheritance, so it will be
possible only in C++, not in Java, C# or Objective-C. For example, consider class
Book which participates in three Aggregates—see Listing 3.12.

Listing 3.12 Class Book participating in three Aggregates

```
Association Aggregate<Library,Book> books;
Association Aggregate<Author,Book> published;
Association Aggregate<Book,Page> pages;

// that implies Book has to inherit from three classes:
class Book : public AggregateChild<Library,Book>,
             public AggregateChild<Author,Book>,
             public AggregateParent<Book,Page> {
    ...
};
```

---

[24] This is how the Code Farms' Pattern Template Library (PTL) works.

Considering that aggregate may be derived from LinkedList, and Link can be derived from Ring2, and Ring2 from Ring1, the use of inheritance is truly massive, we believe beyond what the creators of the language expected.

The advantage of this entire approach is that we don't need any parameterized names. The parameterization is by type. For example, the InCode style aggregate from Listing 3.5

```
class $$_Aggregate {
      void add($1 *p,$2 *c){
           C* f=p->$0.first;
           p->$0.first=c; c->$0.par=p;
           if(f){
                c->$0.next=f; c->$0.prev=NULL;
                f->$0.prev=c;
           }
           else {c->$0.next=c->$0.prev=NULL;}
      }
};
```

now becomes

```
template<class P,class C> class Aggregate {
      typedef AggregateParent<P,C>* pType;
      typedef AggregateChild<P,C>* cType;
      void add(P *p,P *c){
           C* f=(cType)p->first;
           (pType)p->first=c; (cType)c->par=p;
           if(f){
                (cType)c->next=f; (cType)c->prev=NULL;
                (cType)f->prev=c;
           }
           else {(cType)c->next=(cType)c->prev=NULL;}
      }
};
```

Without using the `typedef` statements, the long templates would make this code unreadable, but in this form it is crisp and manageable.

The code would work without casting with cType and pType, but if we don't cast, we open door to a potential error of using a member with the right name but from a wrong class.

There is still one situation though in which this design fails. If there are two associations of the same type, for example aggregates, between the same two classes, then the casting cannot differentiate between the two aggregates:

```
Association Aggregate<Company,Employee> employed;
Association Aggregate<Company,Employee> onVacation;
```

Fortunately, C++ templates allow an `int` parameter which can be used in such situations. The template is declared as

```
template<class P,class C,int i> class Aggregate { ...
```

and is normally used without the last parameter which is 0 by default:

```
Association Aggregate<Library, Book> books;
Association Aggregate<Author, Book> published;
Association Aggregate<Book, Page> pages;
```

but when two Aggregates connect the same classes, we use either

```
Association Aggregate<Company, Employee> employed;
Association Aggregate<Company, Employee, 1> onVacation;
```

or

```
Association Aggregate<Company, Employee, 1> employed;
Association Aggregate<Company, Employee, 2> onVacation;
```

If we assemble manually the multiple inheritance statements such as in Listing 3.12, this library can be used without any code generator which is a definite advantage compared to the approach from Sect. 3.1. However, programming with the library is much easier if, in the fashion similar to the InCode approach, we place all Association declarations into one little file and let the code generator read it and create macros with the inheritance statements.[25] The application code from Listing 3.7 then looks like Listing 3.13:

Listing 3.13 Company–Manager–Employee example, PTL style (compare with Listing 3.7, which is in the InCode style)

```
class Employee : ZZ_Employee {
    int phone;
    int salary;
};
class Manager : ZZ_Manager, public Employee {
};
class Company : ZZ_Company {
};

// ----- either here or in a separate file ds.def -------------
Association Aggregate<Company, Employee> employees;
Association Aggregate<Manager, Employee> subordinates;
Association Name<Employee> employeeName;
Association SingleLink<Manager, Employee> secretary;
// -------------------------------------------------------------

int main() {
    Employee *e=new Employee;
    Manager *m=new Manager;
    secretary::add(m, e);
```

---

[25] The use of code generator in PTL is optional.

As we were writing this chapter, we realized that Code Farms missed a great opportunity to make PTL persistent. All that is needed is to include PTR(), STR() and ARP() statements into the default constructor. For example, adding the two bold lines shown in the following code makes the class Aggregate persistent in the PPF environment:

```
template<class P,class C, int i> class AggregateParent {
    C *first;
public:
    AggregateParent(){ PTR(first,C); }
};
template<class P,class C, int i> class AggregateChild {
    P *parent;
    C *next;
    C *prev;
public:
    AggregateParent(){ PTR(parent,P); PTR(next,C); PTR(prev,C); }
};
```

The only known library using this approach is Pattern Template Library[26] (PTL), which was coded as a proof that a generic library of intrusive data structures can be implemented without a code generator. The library has been available on Code Farms website since 1996, but was the only library never used on a serious, real-life project. It was originally designed as a framework for generic design patterns, and it has the following classes, some of them quite unusual and unique: *Aggregate, Array, Pointer Array, Collection,* pattern *Composite,* pattern *Flyweight* and *Finite State Machine* which can reset its settings while it is running. It would be relatively simple to transfer remaining classes from the InCode and DOL libraries to PTL, because these libraries are coded in the same style.

3.3   Library of Design Patterns

> Structural design patterns are data structures which, besides pointers and arrays, also involve inheritance. This section shows how such patterns can be stored in a class library just like containers or other associations.

Christopher Wolfgang Alexander is an architect noted for over 200 building projects around the world. He was born in Austria, grew up in England and studied at Cambridge and Harvard. For many years, he taught at the UC Berkeley, and he is now retired in Switzerland.

---

[26] www.codefarms.com/ptl

In his search[27] for "quality without a name", he began to record patterns that made buildings pleasant to live in or around. Things such a layout of rooms, doors, windows and stairs, and their specifics depend on the climate and culture and interaction with objects around them. For example, when discussing a street café, we should consider the possible desires of the guests, the working environment of the café owner, but also the people who just walk by.

Alexander's patterns are catalogued in a uniform fashion. They consist of a short name, a rating, a sensitizing picture, the context description, the problem statement, a longer part of text with examples and explanations, a solution statement, a sketch and further references. Patterns recorded in this style are a great communication and teaching tool, and Alexander used them successfully when discussing his projects with the future occupants of his buildings.

Around 1994 a group of software designers began to develop software patterns that would be independent of the programming language and the application domain. The first conference on Pattern Languages of Program Design (PLoP) was in 1994,[28] and the "bible"[29] of this movement by the "Gang of four" was published the same year.

For example, the methodology we are using for bi-directional generic associations in this chapter could be considered a design pattern, and the following example shows the categories that should be recorded. In most situations, individual categories would be much longer; here we assume you understand the subject.

Name: Separation of interface from the attributes that form the data structure (or association).

Motivation: Containers buried in the application classes confuse the architecture, and do not allow the building of generic bi-directional associations as single entities.

Forces: Associations should have the same visibility and importance as application classes. Programming languages limit the implementation. Simple code generation is a practical solution, but is frown upon by purists.

Applicability: Any data structures, structural design patterns.[30]

Participants: The dataless class representing the data structure, and several application classes that store data. Instances of these classes get inserted into appropriate application classes.

---

[27] See his book "The timeless way of building", published by Oxford University Press in 1979.

[28] Proceedings edited by J.O. Coplien and D.C. Schmidt, and published by Addison-Wesley in 1995.

[29] Gamma E, Helm R, Johnson R, Vlissides J (1994) Design patterns: elements of reusable object-oriented software. Addison-Wesley.

[30] The pattern part will be explained later in this chapter.

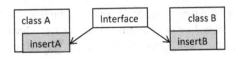

Fig. 3.7 Pattern "Separate interface and data of generic associations", where Interface has the same visibility as application classes A and B manages inserted data, usually pointers or references

Description: ... <detailed description>

Diagram: see Fig. 3.7

Dynamic behaviour: This is a static pattern, but may be applied to dynamic data organizations such as FSM.

Implementation: ... <detailed description>

Variants: Insertion can be either as members or through inheritance.

Consequences: Significant improvement in the clarity and quality of the software. Easier to maintain and evolve. UML class diagram matching implementation.

Limitations: Simple code generator is required.

See also: Separate interface pattern, Reflection in certain OO languages.

Sample code: Listing 3.10.

Known uses: This approach has been supported by Code Farms Inc. since 1989 and was successfully applied to hundreds of projects, some over 100,000 lines of code.

Structural design patterns are a special category of software patterns that can be considered an extension of the classical data structures by adding inheritance to the usual network of pointers and arrays. We have shown already in 1994[31] that these patterns can be implemented in a generic form and stored in a library with other data structures such as Aggregate or HashTable.

For an advanced reader, Listing 3.14 shows the complete implementation of the PTL pattern Composite. Composite is the mechanism that allows one to build a system from bigger and bigger parts. Listing 3.15 demonstrates how to create graphics from lines, text, pictures and smaller sub-designs, we build mechanical designs from plates, bolts, nuts and pre-built parts, and we design silicon chips from transistors, wires, and contacts that connect different layers of wiring. In these and many other applications we design hierarchically, creating larger and more complex designs from smaller and simpler ones—see Listing 3.14.

---

[31] Soukup J (1994) Implementing patterns. PLoP conference, pp. 395–412.

Listing 3.14 Internal implementation of class `Composite` in the PTL library. `Composite` is derived from `Collection`, which is equivalent to `Intrusive List`[32] from Fig. 3.2

```
// file composite.h in directory ptl\lib
// =====================================
template<class P, class C, int i> class CompositeChild :
                          public CollectionChild<P,C,i>{
};
template<class P, class C, int i> class CompositeParent :
                          public CollectionParent<P,C,i>{
};
template<class P, class C, int i> class Composite :
                          public Collection<P,C,i>{
   // all methods of Collection are inherited
};

#define CompositeInherit1(id,par,chi,i)                        \
    public chi, public CompositeParent<par,chi,i>

#define CompositeMember1(id,par,chi,i)                         \
    virtual int isComposite(Composite<par,chi,i> *c){ return 1;}

#define CompositeInherit2(id,par,chi,i)                        \
                          public CompositeChild<par,chi,i>

#define CompositeMember2(id,par,chi,i)                         \
    virtual int isComposite(Composite<par,chi,i> *c){ return 0;}

// file pattern.h produced by code generator ptl\mgr\mgr.exe
// =========================================================
#define pattern_Part \
   CompositeInherit2(comp,Graphics,Part,1) { \
   CompositeMember2(comp,Graphics,Part,1) PTL_COMMENT

#define pattern_Graphics \
   CompositeInherit1(comp,Graphics,Part,1) { \
   CompositeMember1(comp,Graphics,Part,1) PTL_COMMENT

//file mgr.h from ptl\lib that all application source includes
// =========================================================
#define Pattern(A) pattern_##A
#define PTL_COMMENT /##/
```

---

[32] If you want to traverse Composition both up and down, then deriving it from Aggregate would make more sense.

Listing 3.15 Applying Composite to a graphics design

```
class Part : Pattern(Part) {
    int x1,y1,x2,y2; // overall dimensions
};
class Graphics : Pattern(Graphics) {
};
class Line : public Part{ // see footnote33
};
class Text : public Part { // see footnote
    char *txt;
};
class Picture : public Part { // see footnote
  char *fileName;
};
Association Composite<Graphics,Part> parts;
int main(){
    int main(){
    Graphics *g1,*g1; Line *L1,*L2; Text *t; Picture *p1,*p2;

        ...
    parts.add(g1,L1);
    parts.add(g1,t);
    parts.add(g1,p1);
    parts.add(g2,g1);
    parts.add(g1,L2);
    parts.add(g1,p2);
```

Useful Trick No. 7

Macro `Pattern(Graphics)` **on line**

```
    class Graphics : Pattern(Graphics) {
```

adds not only a base class; it also adds a virtual function to class Graphics(!)

```
    #define Pattern(T) \
    public Part{ZZ_##T; virtual int isComposite(...){...}; //
```

where the end comment wipes out the brace at the end of the original line:

```
    class Graphics : public Part{ZZ_##T; virtual int isCompsite(...)
    {...};//{
```

which really is

```
    class Graphics : public Part{
    ZZ_##T; virtual int isCompsite(...){...};
```

---

[33] If class Line participates in some other data structures or patterns, the statement would take this form:
`class Line : public Part, public Pattern(Line) {`

WARNING:

Listing 3.15 can mislead you, because it does not show the key idea of how PTL can access its subparts. This is easier to explain on the Composite[34] class designed from scratch. Note that the types of internal pointers are CT* and PT*, and not C* and P* as one could expect:

```
typedef CompositeChild<P,C> CT;
typedef CompositeParent<P,C> PT;
template<class P,class C,int i> class CompositeChild{
    CT *next;
    PT *parent;
};
template<class P,class C, int i> class CompositeParent{
    CT *first;
};
template<class P,class C, int i> class Composite}
    C *nxt(CT *cp){return (C*)(cp->next); } // <<<<<<<<<<<<<
    ... other methods
};
Association Composite<Graphics,Part> parts;
int main(){
    Part *p; Text *t;
    p=parts.nxt(t);
```

The function finds the right subpart through automatic casting. It is as if writing

$$cp=(CT*)(Part*)t;$$

3.4 Complexity and Errors

> This section explains why the new style of data structures reduces complexity, eliminates errors, and allows rapid software development from a simple prototype that already works like a production-quality product.

The prime purpose of the new approach to building data structures is to increase the productivity of software development and simplify its maintenance, while producing code with the ultimate performance.

These are hard and controversial things to measure. The abilities of programmers vary widely, so letting two people do the same project in different styles may not tell us much. Letting one programmer to do the same project twice

---

[34] This example is for the singly-linked, bi-directional Composite.

does not give meaningful results either, because the programmer learns from the first exercise and is then more efficient the second time.

However, over 2 decades of using this approach on many complex projects, our users reported a two to four times faster development and maintenance for projects without persistence, and three to ten times for projects with persistence. Small groups of developers often outperformed large departments of prestige companies. The larger and more complex the project, the greater was the productivity improvement.

Another personal experience. The author experienced exasperating frustrations when forced to develop without these libraries. Projects that he expected to take a few days, went on for weeks and required extensive debugging.

Everybody offering software tools claims improvements of productivity, and our numbers may appear exaggerated. Why such a large improvement?

The secret is in reducing the code complexity, letting the compiler find errors that we are now debugging in the run time and eliminating hard-to-find run-time errors. It makes it fun to develop software in this new style; it is less stressful.

Let's examine the individual features that, together, have this remarkable effect.

3.4.1 Reducing Complexity

It is now generally accepted that class libraries reduce code complexity and improve productivity. However, about half the data structures needed in real-life applications are bi-directional, and thow are not supported by the existing container libraries. Having generic classes for bi-directional data structures makes a big difference.

The complexity is also reduced, because the Association statements provide a concise description of the entire data organization, especially if they are together, as a block of code or in a special file (ds.def). You can also say that this block of statements defines your *framework*, or that it is a textual form of the UML class diagram.[35] If you get a program written by someone else, and you look at its Association statements, you know instantly what it is all about. Try yourself:

Listing 3.16 Can you see what data is used in this project

```
Association Collection<Library,CD> cds;
Association Hash<Library,Composer> composers;
Association Hash<Library,Performer> performers;
Association Aggregate<CD,Track> tracks;
Association Aggregate<Composer,Work> works;
Association Aggregate<Work,Track> tracksOn;
Association ManyToMany<Track,Link,Performer> playedBy;
```

---

[35] Section 3.5 expands on this subject.

This is a non-trivial organization—a library of CDs that can be efficiently searched by Composer or Performer. Composer composed Works (songs). CD has Tracks and several Performers may participate on one Track. A Work can be recorded several times, with different Performers and on tracks of different CDs.

The block of Associations is also extremely useful when analyzing a section of the code. For example, if you see this line:

```
works_Iterator wit;
```

you know immediately that `wit` will iterate over the Works of a Composer. Or

```
w=trackOn.parent(t);
```

tells you that `w` is a Work that is on Track `t`, even if you are not sure what are the types of `w` and `t`.

The block of Associations is also useful, when you want to see which sections of code are using certain data structures. For example, if looking for the ManyToMany relation between Track and Performer, simply search the code for "playedBy".

Reduced complexity increases the size of the problem you can keep in your mind with all its details, without keeping written records and pictures to guide you when you revisit the program. This is the mode of operation when you are most efficient. Once you reach the point when you don't remember all the parts, the project suddenly takes much more time, and the probability of making a mistake dramatically increases.

When working in a team, a clear communication is essential and, again, the block of Association statements is invaluable: it instantly clears any possible confusion related to the data organization.

3.4.2 Leaving More Work to the Compiler

All the data structures in the new libraries are strictly typed, so mistakes such as placing objects into a wrong data structure are caught by the compiler.[36] For example,

```
Composer *c; Track *t;
performers.add(t,c); //compiler error
```

You can also change, remove or add data structure without analyzing your old code, and the compiler will tell you precisely which lines will need a modification.

---

[36] For InCode, this is true not only in C++, but also in Java and Objective-C.

The Association statements in Listing 3.16 describe the Library of popular music, where each Work is really a song that is always recorded as a CD track. Let's assume that we already have a program running with this data organization, and we want to expand it so it would also support recordings of classical music, where a Work is a composition which usually has several Parts (movements) that are recorded on separate tracks. A CD may have tracks with only some Parts of the Work.

So in Listing 3.16, we replace

```
Association Aggregate<Work,Track> tracksOn;
```

by

```
Association Aggregate<Work,Part> parts;
Association Aggregate<Part,Track> onTracks;
```

Without even looking at the code, you attempt to compile, and the compiler tells you about all places where *tracksOn* was used and which have to be redesigned manually. The new data organizations *parts* and *onTrack* will pass the compilation. They are now empty, and you will likely need them when redesigning the places that compiler picked up.

When replacing an organization it is always safer to use different names, as we did here with *tracksOn* and *onTrack*. However, even if we used the same name, onTrack, the compiler would produce the same errors because of the type differences: <Work,Track> in the original source and <Part,Track> in the new version. For example the original source

```
onTrack::add(w,t);
```

would not compile in the new version because w is not (Part*).

3.4.3 Preventing and Catching Runtime Errors

Pointer (or reference) errors are a potential source of treacherous errors, and we have eliminated all pointer members from the application. These pointers are in libraries that were carefully designed and extensively tested. All pointer chains in our libraries are coded as rings, and the basic rule is that unused pointers are always NULL.

Therefore if an object has a pointer-member which is not NULL, it indicates that the object is connected in some data structure. That provides a protection in two situations:

1. If an object is already in a pointer chain, you cannot move it by mistake to another chain. For example

```
Association Aggregate<A,B> aggr;
A *a1,*a2; B *b;
...
aggr.add(a1,b);
aggr.add(a2,b); // error message, will not execute
```

If you really want to move the object, you have to disconnect it from the old chain and then add it to the new one:

```
aggr.add(a1,b);
aggr.del(b); // dow not need del(a1,b),aggregate knows parent
addr.add(a2,b);
```

2. An object cannot be destroyed until it is completely disconnected

```
aggr.add(a1,b);
delete b; // error message
```

In this case the program may still crash later, but you will know exactly where and which pointer (and organization) was the culprit.

A better solution would be to prevent the destruction and continue in the program run. Unfortunately, once you are in the destructor, you cannot prevent the destruction. Or can you?

We could `throw` an exception, but then making a `try{ }` block around every `delete` call would make an ugly code. However, if we hide all this in a macro, we can use `safeDelete(b);` instead `delete b;` for any class; see Listing 3.17.

But wait a minute! If we are replacing delete by another call, wouldn't this be simpler:

```
class Book {
    Book *next;
public:
    Book(){next=NULL;}
    void safeDelete(){if(next!=NULL)delete this
};
int main() {
    Book *b=new Book;
    b->safeDelete();
```

The difference is that using exception works for all classes, while method `safeDelete()` has to be coded for every class.

Listing 3.17 Bypassing destruction when object is not disconnected

```
#define safeDelete(x)                           \
try {                                           \
    delete x;                                   \
}                                               \
catch (BypassDestruction& bd) {                 \
    printf("bypassed destruction\n"); \

}

class BypassDestruction {
};

class B;

class A {
public:
    B *toB;
    A(){toB=NULL;}
    ~A(){if(toB) throw BypassDestruction();}
};

class B {
public:
    A *toA;
    B(){toA=NULL;}
    ~B(){if(toA) throw BypassDestruction();}
};

int main(){
    A *a=new A;
    B *b=new B;
    b->toA=a;
    a->toB=b;

    safeDelete(a);
    safeDelete(b);
```

3.4.4   Interface: Less May Be More

In order to benefit fully from a data structure stored in a library, its interfaces must
be simple enough to remember without constantly searching the documentation.
For example, InCode and DOL libraries use a much shorter list of commands than
STL, where class *list* has more than a page of methods.[37] Listing 3.18 shows the
methods of the InCode class comparable to stl::list.

---

[37] Plauger PJ, Stepanov AA, Lee M, Musser DR (2000) The C++ standard template Library.
Prentice Hall, pp 290–292.

Listing 3.18 DOL and InCode class similar to stl_list needs fewer methods

```
Child* tail(Parent *p); // get the tail of the list
Child* head(Parent *p); // get the head of the list
void addHead(Parent *p, Child *c); // add c as the head
void addTail(Parent *p, Child *c); // add c as tail
void append(Parent *p,Child *c1, Child *c2); // c2 after c1
void insert(Child *c1, Child *c2); // insert c2 before c1
void remove(Parent *p, Child *c); // remove c from the list
Child* next(Parent *p, Child *c); // returns NULL at the end
Child* prev(Parent *p, Child *c); // returns NULL at beginning
void sort(ZZsortFun cmpFun, Parent *p); // efficient merge sort
void merge(Child *s,Child *t,Parent *p); // merge two sublists

// special commands for ring control, infrequently used
Child* nextRing(Child *c); // wrap around at the end
Child* prevRing(Child *c); // wrap around beginning
void setTail(Parent* p,Child* c,int check); // set c as tail
```

plus there is an iterator which you use like this:

```
Association LinkedList2<A,B> myList;
A *ap; B *bp;
myList_Iterator mit;
...
mit.start(ap);
ITERATE(mit,bp){ // bp traverses B objects
    ...
}
mit.start(ap);
RETRACE(mit,bp){ // reverse traversal
    ...
}
```

The iterators are smart enough to permit removal and destruction of objects while traversing the list without causing a crash or other malfunction.

3.4.5 True Rapid and Agile Development

With data structures designed in this style, you can start with skeleton classes and the Association statements, and your "program" can already compile and run. You plan in code. You evolve and experiment, and with every compilation you can print the new UML class diagram. You can change, remove or add Associations statements, and the compiler guides you as to what changes are needed. All this time you are working with a safe, running code unless, of course, you make an error in your algorithms. There should be no chasing of pointers, no mysterious low-level errors. It takes longer to clear the compiler errors, but then the program runs solid.

3.5 DB Schema and UML Class Diagram

We are treating data structures as a memory-resident database, where the block of Association statements works like a database schema. This block of statements directly maps to/from the UML class diagram, and program called Layout can read this schema and generate the UML diagram.

When working with persistent objects you may treat your data structures as a simple but highly efficient object-oriented database. And if you implemented the data structures as we described it, then the block of Associations statements becomes a schema of this database.

You can also look at the block of Associations from a different angle. Except for the inheritance, it contains the same information as the UML class diagram. You can consider this block as a textual form of the UML class diagram, and that leads to interesting ideas.

Today, tools like Rational Rose allow one to create, in graphics, the UML class diagram. Then a code generator creates a skeleton of classes and relations you entered in graphics. If the libraries of data structures such as we recommend were commonly used, the UML tool would not need a code generator—it could simply generate the block of Association statements!

Another idea is whether it wouldn't be better to have the UML class diagram directly in the code, in a textual form, which would be an integral part of the code. It would be easy and safe to introduce changes, and the diagram and the code would not need any synchronization. It is also much faster to change a few words in the block of the Association statements than to manipulate graphics on the screen. On the other hand, most of us like a diagram when it comes to relations that form a complex network. Note that the idea of entering the information in the textual form is also used by Timothy Lethbridge in the programming environment called UMPLE—see UMPLE (2012).

We prefer to use Association statements to enter and control the relations. At the same time, perhaps with every compilation, we can automatically produce the UML class diagram in a graphical form. This reverses the control flow. Until now, the UML class diagram controlled the data organization. Now the data organization is controlled by the Association statements, and the graphical diagram is demoted to a visual aid.

This arrangement has several advantages: fast and easy initial entry, easy modifications, code and the diagram tightly synchronized, control of the data organization directly in the code—independent of any outside tools.

All[38] Code Farms libraries use a block of Association statements, each library with a slightly different syntax, and they can invoke program called *Layout*, which generates the UML class diagram.

---

[38] DOL, InCode, PTL and the PPF/InCode combination.

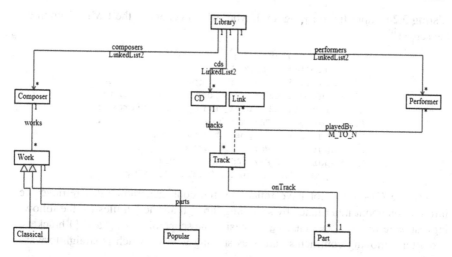

Fig. 3.8 UML class diagram generated automatically from Listing 3.19

For example, Association statements from Listing 3.19 create Fig. 3.8. Listing 3.19 is Listing 3.16 expanded for classical music. Also, in order to make the example more interesting, we added two classes derived from class *Work*, *Popular* and *Classical*.

Listing 3.19 Example for UML class diagram

```
Association Collection<Library,CD> cds;
Association Collection<Library,Composer> composers;
Association Collection<Library,Performer> performers;
Association Aggregate<CD,Track> tracks;
Association Aggregate<Composer,Work> works;
Association Aggregate<Work,Part> parts;
Association Aggregate<Part,Track> onTracks;
Association ManyToMany<Track,Link,Performer> playedBy;
class Classical : public Work
class Popular : public Work
```

How does the Layout program work? In order to draw the diagram, all data structures in the library must be registered in a special *registry* file, which was described earlier in Fig. 3.4. For example, the data structures which we are using in this example are listed with these codes:

```
u1-* LinkedList2  = uni-directional 1 to many
b1-* Aggregate2   = bi-directional 1 to many
R*2* 2XtoX        = bi-directional ManyToMany
```

In addition to the code required for the data structures and persistence, the code generators of the Code Farms libraries[39] combine the Association statements with the registry file, add the information about inheritance and, as a byproduct, generate file layout.inp, which is the input required for the Layout program; see Listing 3.20.

---

[39] InCode, DOL, and PTL.

Listing 3.20 Input file for program Layout which generates the UML diagram on the screen[40]

```
Inherits Popular Work ;
Inherits Classical Work ;
u1-* LinkedList2 Library CD cds ;
u1-* LinkedList2 Library Composer composers ;
u1-* LinkedList2 Library Performer performers ;
B1-* Aggregate2 CD Track tracks ;
B1-* Aggregate2 Composer Work works ;
B1-* Aggregate2 Work Part parts ;
B1-* Aggregate2 Part Track onTrack ;
R*2* M_TO_N Track Link Performer playedBy ;
```

Because C++ does not have reflection, the code generator must retrieve the information about inheritance by searching through all the *.h files for the following test pattern: "class something :" outside the scope of all (), [] and {} brackets, and after removing comments and lines starting with #, which is straightforward and fast.

The Layout program applies algorithms traditionally used in the design of silicon circuits, which is mathematically a similar problem to the one we have here—boxes connected with lines. However, we modified the original objective of the smallest overall area and wires not crossing each other to getting a display which would be pleasing to the human eye. The diagram must reflect the flow of the relations from the root class which is automatically detected. The program first places the boxes in rows, connecting each row before proceeding to the next row. Two labels are added to each line: name of the organization (e.g. *works*) above the line, and the name of the data structure (e.g. *Aggregate2*) below the line.

3.6   Intrusive Data Structures with Aspects

> We have discussed data structures where pointers were inserted as members or with inheritance, but we did not mention Aspects. The key idea behind Aspects is a controlled insertion of code or members, and they can be used for the data structure design we are exploring.

In 2007–2009, two workshops discussed how to implement associations as first class entities:

1. OOPSLA 2007 in Montreal, workshop "Implementing Reusable Associations/ Relationships[41]".

---

[40] Certain permutations of rows in this listing may cause a crash of the Layout program. This is a reported bug scheduled for repair.

[41] Sometimes referred to by the former title "The Popularity Cycle of Graphical Tools, UML, and Libraries of Associations."

2. ECOOP2009 in Genova, workshop "Relationships and Associations in Object-Oriented Languages" (RAOOL'09).

About half of the papers in these workshops were based on Aspects.[42]

Aspects provide another language layer above Java or C++, with their own compiler—AspectJ for Java programs, and AspectC++ for C++ programs.

An aspect is similar to a breakpoint in the debugger. It interrupts the program run at chosen points, allows you to examine or change application data and call a function, and then it returns to the program run. As in the debugger, no code is added to the program. The definition of where to stop and what to do is written on the side in a form resembling a class definition, and that is called *aspect*. Unlike the debugger, the aspect does not stop when interrupting the program. It executes the required actions and returns to the program run.

This type of aspect is called *dynamic aspect*, and its obvious application is a debugging layer with many printouts and checks which may be invoked in a single command but which are transparent to the ordinary user. There are also *static aspects*, which modify the structural part of the program—they can add inheritance or members to application classes.

In general, aspects can simplify programs with objects that combine several independent concerns. For example, an Employee object may store information about the employee, be persistent, and participate in an Aggregate between classes Department and Employee. If the Aggregate is implemented as an aspect, the participation of the Employee is completely transparent. The application code is very similar to what we have been doing, but there isn't even the zz_Employee ds statement which we have used. In case you are not familiar with aspects, we will analyze Listing 3.21 line by line, and explain how it works.

The overall approach is surprisingly similar to the PTL library described in Sect. 3.2 (inserting pointers with inheritance) and, because aspects can insert inheritance, this approach can also be used to implement a library of design patterns as described in Sect. 3.3.

001: Aggregate is designed as an abstract aspect, because it does not have any data, only methods that control the use of this association.

002–003: The data (references implementing the aggregate) is stored in classes AggregateParent and AggregateChild just as we did before. Java does not support multiple inheritance, but it supports multiple inheritance of interfaces. This is critical—otherwise Employee could not participate in more than one association.

004–005: If classes Department and Employee form an aggregate, then Employee must inherit AggregateChild, and Department must inherit AggregateParent, just as in Sect. 3.2.

006–008: Definition of references that form the Aggregate. This is the most tricky part of the Aggregate design. From the syntax of these lines, one would think that they insert head, next and parent into interfaces AggregateChild and AggregateParent, and thus head, next and parent must be

---

[42] Aspect implementation for Java; different implementation for C++ is also available.

static—which is not what we need. However, these lines perform *inter-type member insertion*,[43] which inserts head, next and parent into the classes which inherit from AggregateChild and AggregateParent, in this case into classes Employee and Department. As a result, head, next and parent are <u>not</u> static.

009–016: The code of method addHead () is as you would expect.

020–022: The same definition of Associations as we have been using.

023–024: Application coded in the style we have been recommending.

Listing 3.21 Implementing Aggregate with AspectJ (code obtained from the Victoria University, New Zealand)[44]

```
        // Aggregate itself is an aspect.
001  public abstract aspect Aggregate<Parent,Child> {
002      public static interface AggregateParent {}
003      public static interface AggregateChild {}

004      declare parents : Child implements AggregateChild;
005      declare parents : Parent implements AggregateParent;

006      private Child AggregateParent.head = null;
007      private Child AggregateChild.next = null;
008      private Parent AggregateChild.parent = null;

009      public static void addHead(Parent p, Child c) {
010          if(p.AggregateParent.head!=null){
011              c.AggregateChild.next=p.AggregateParent.head;
012          }
013          else c.AggregateChild.next=NULL;
014          c.AggregateChild.parent=p;
015          p.AggregateParent.head=c;
016      }
017      ...
018  }

     // Application using the Aggregate
019  public class Department {...}// same as if not using Aggregate

     // Declaration of data structures, just like our Associations
020  aspect departments extends Aggregate<Company,Department> {};
021  aspect employees extends Aggregate<Department,Employee> {};
022  aspect boss extends OneToOne<Department,Employee> {};

     // Using the Aggregate
023  Department d; Employee e;
024  employees.addHead(d,e);
```

---

[43] http://www.eclipse.org/aspectj/doc/next/progguide/language-interType.html

[44] Stephen Nelson, David J. Pearce and James Noble.

The drawback of this code is that if the class Employee was a Child in two Aggregates, for example

```
aspect employees extends Aggregate<Department,Employee> {};
aspect inUnion extends Aggregate<Union,Employee> {};
```

then Aggregate::addHead() would not know how to access each part. AggregateChild and AggregateParent really should be generics just like Aggregate:

```
001   public abstract aspect Aggregate<Parent,Child> {
002       public static interface AggregateParent<Parent,Child> {}
003       public static interface AggregateChild<Parent,Child> {}
```

but this version has not been tested.

Nelson, Pearce and Noble developed a library (Nelson et al. 2007; Pearce and Noble 2006) of generic associations with AspectJ, but it did not work in some special cases due to the bugs in 2007 versions of AspectJ, and these authors have not continued in this research since 2009. We also discussed with Olaf Spinczyk (Spinczyk and Lohmann 2007), author of AspectC++, how to implement Aggregate with AspectC++; see Listing 3.22, where AggregateChild, AggregateParent and Aggregate are generic classes, not interfaces. Because AspectC++ does not have inter-type insertion, the declaration of the Aggregate aspect takes four lines, where the line *advice—slice—*... inserts the required pointers into participating classes. However, we can hide these four lines under a macro—see Listing 3.22, and then the invocation of the Aggregate is the same as it was in AspectJ, or all the other libraries we have discussed throughout Chap. 3

Listing 3.22 Aggregate implemented with AspectC++

```cpp
// reusable part
//-------------------
template <typename Aggregation> class AggregateChild {
public:
    typename Aggregation::Child *next;
    typename Aggregation::Parent *parent;
    AggregateChild () : next (0), parent (0) {}
};

template <typename Aggregation> class AggregateParent {
public:
    typename Aggregation::Child *head;
    AggregateParent () : head (0) {}
};

template <typename Aspect, typename _Parent, typename _Child> class
Aggregation {
public:
    typedef _Parent Parent;
    typedef _Child Child;

    static void addHead (Parent *p, Child *c) {
        typedef AggregateParent<Aspect> P;
        typedef AggregateChild<Aspect> C;
        if(p->P::head) c->C::next = p->P::head;
        else c->C::next = 0;
        c->C::parent = p;
        p->P::head = c;
    }
};

#define AGGREGATION(Name, Parent, Child)                             \
    aspect Name : public Aggregation<Name, Parent, Child> {          \
    advice #Child : slice class : public AggregateChild<Name>;       \
    advice #Parent : slice class : public AggregateParent<Name>;     \
}

// application specific part
/ ----------------------------
class Employee;
class Department;
class Union;

AGGREGATION(inDepartment, Department, Employee);
AGGREGATION(inUnion, Union, Employee);

class Employee {};
class Department {};
class Union {};

int main () {
    Department *dp; Union *up; Employee *ep1,*ep2;
    dp=new Department; up=new Union;
    ep1=new Employee; ep2=new Employee;
    ...
    inDepartment::addHead (dp,ep1);
    inDepartment::addHead (dp,ep2);
    inUnion::addHead (up, ep2);
}
```

3.7   Conclusion

Aspects lead to the same simple use of associations as we obtained through other methods, but we are not in favour of adding a complex programming layer just for implementing associations. In our opinion, associations are part of the core programming and we believe they should be supported from within that environment.

Advanced Features, Schema Migration

4

Abstract

Advanced features involve both persistence and data structures. Schema migration deals with changes of classes and their relations when storing data to disk. Extensible property allows one to add class members without changing the class declaration. We also discuss multi-user access to persistent data, ASLR and storing objects in flash memories and smart phones.

Keywords

Schema • Migration • Extensible property • ASLR • Flash memory • Smart phone • iPhone • ZZ_FORMAT • Multi-user • Networks • Aspects • AspectJ • AspectC++

4.1   Schema Migration

> When classes and/or data structures in your application change—and face it, all software eventually reaches this point—you still may want to access the old data stored on disk before the change was introduced. This chapter discusses how to tackle this difficult task.

Over several decades we have met customers from a great variety of applications—coal mining, silicon circuits, telephone switches, networks and stock exchange data—and the most typical customer was a programmer who brought a big, totally messed up program and wanted to clean it up and add persistence to it. Why didn't they use the persistence right from the beginning? Because it had looked so simple! They had thought they'd never need to store the data.

We have not seen real-life software that would not eventually require changes of its classes and data structures. We see software design as a learning process, in which the customer gradually learns what he or she wants, and the programmer

J. Soukup and P. Macháček, *Serialization and Persistent Objects*,
DOI 10.1007/978-3-642-39323-5_4, © Springer-Verlag Berlin Heidelberg 2014

gradually grasps the essence of the problem until, usually after some experimentation, a suitable solution is found.

Whether you are developing a new program or supporting software already used by numerous customers, it is most annoying if you have to change the existing classes and/or data structures and all the storage files suddenly become unusable.

We have already said that the block of Association statements is an equivalent of the database schema. It describes the entire data organization[1] and the data structures from which it is composed. When working with persistent data we face the same problem database designers do: we need to handle, as transparently and automatically as possible, the changes in the schema, and this is called *schema migration*.

Association statements not only describe the data structures; they also give us the participating classes. However, data structures are not the complete schema. Inheritance and individual members of the classes may also change, be added or removed. Let's follow an example of how DOL ASCII serialization does it. The key for the entire process is that the persistence is integrated with the data structure library. The library provides the information about all the pointers it uses—their names, types and locations—the same information other languages provide through reflection.

DOL ASCII serialization does not write out this information for every pointer as does Java serialization. Instead, it writes the description of all the classes at the beginning of the file, and when writing an object, it refers to its class by an index, followed by the values of all members including the pointers. When reading pointers from the file, only pointers with matching name and type move into the target object—see Fig. 4.1. All this happens during the reading process, before swizzling the pointers, and is probably similar to what happens inside Java serialization. As in Java, DOL does this totally transparently and automatically.

Storage and retrieval of members which are integers, floats or characters is controlled by the ZZ_FORMAT statements—see Listing 4.1. This format controls both the read and write functions, so if the classes do not change, the match is always guaranteed.

When some classes change, and some of their members are new or missing, you use the old ZZ_FORMAT to read the old data in the ASCII mode, and then save it in the DOL binary mode which saves entire objects without breaking them into individual members.[2] After that, you can open the data in the binary format and save them with a new ZZ_FORMAT, which reflects the updated situation.

The disk record of old object from Fig. 4.1 may look like this:

```
11 340100 1 6 = class A, addr. 340100, 1 object, 6 pointers
3205688 4084300 0 3695724 3205636 3302004 = all pointers
18.99 6138362327 = cost, phone
```

---

[1] Sometimes the term *framework* is used for this.

[2] In this, DOL binary mode is different from Java or C/# binary modes, which do break objects into their members as in their ASCII/XML modes.

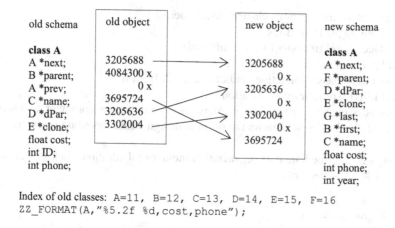

Index of old classes: A=11, B=12, C=13, D=14, E=15, F=16
ZZ_FORMAT(A,"%5.2f %d,cost,phone");

Fig. 4.1 Schema migration in DOL—reading pointers. Pointers marked with x did not find a match

Listing 4.1 shows a problem with three simple classes participating in several data structures, using DOL syntax.

Listing 4.1 Original data organization

```
class Library {
    ZZ_EXT_Library;
};
ZZ_FORMAT(Library,"");
class Book {
    ZZ_EXT_Book;
    int pages;
    float cost;
};
ZZ_FORMAT(Book,"%d %f",pages,cost);
class Author {
    ZZ_EXT_Author;
};
ZZ_FORMAT(Author,"");

// see note(3) about the syntax of these statements
typedef LinkList<Library,Book> books;
typedef LinkList<Library,Author> authors;
typedef singleLink<Book,Author> toAuthor; // equivalent of pointer
typedef Name<Book> bookName;
typedef Name<Author> authName;
```

The website version of Listing 4.1 creates some test data and stores them in the ASCII mode in file1—see bk\chap4\list4_1.cpp and rr1.bat.

---

[3] For the definition of the associations on the next few lines, we use syntax compatible with the previous text; it is slightly different from the DOL syntax on the book website.

We want to make serious changes to this design:
- Remove *pages* from Book.
- Replace[4] *LinkList books* by *Hash allBooks*.
- Add *phone* number to the Author.
- Add a new class Publication, and derive Book from it.
- Add LinkList<Library,Publication>.

This is a bigger change than most of us would trust a computer to handle automatically. Listing 4.2 shows the original design with marked up changes.

Listing 4.2 Intermediate data organization includes all additions, but uses the old ZZ_FORMAT statements

```
class Library {
    ZZ_EXT_Library;
};
ZZ_FORMAT(Library,"");
class Publication {              // introducing new class
    ZZ_EXT_Publication;
public:
    int year;                    // new member
};
ZZ_FORMAT(Publication,"%d,year");
class Book : public Publication { // adding inheritance
    ZZ_EXT_Book;
    int pages;                    // remove it
    float cost;
};
ZZ_FORMAT(Book,"%d %f",pages,cost);
class Author {
    ZZ_EXT_Author;
    int phone;                    // new member
};
ZZ_FORMAT(Author,"");

typedef LinkList<Library,Book> books;                    // remove it
typedef LinkList<Library,Publication> publications;      // remove it
typedef Hash<Library,Book> allBooks;                     // add this
typedef LinkList<Library,Author> authors;
typedef singleLink<Book,Author> toAuthor;
typedef Name<Book> bookName;
typedef Name<Author> authName;
```

With DOL, you convert the old file in three simple steps:
1. Expand your source with all the features you want to add but, temporarily, still retain the features you eventually want to remove. Open the data in the ASCII

---

[4] Replacing something by something else while keeping the same name creates potential problems. When using DOL you must remove the old organization (here *LinkList books*) and add a new association with a new name (*Hash allBooks*).

format, using the old ZZ_FORMAT, then save them in the binary[5] format
(bk\chap4\list4_2.cpp, rr.bat).

2. Open the data in binary and save them in ASCII using the new ZZ_FORMAT
   statements (bk\chap4\list4_3.cpp, rr3.bat).

3. Remove the features you do not want, and open in ASCII using the new
   ZZ_FORMAT statements. Both data and your source have been converted;
   you can save the data in any format you want (bk\chap4\list4-4.cpp, rr4.bat).

IMPORTANT:

In steps 1 and 2 you have in memory <u>both</u> the old and the new data organizations,
but the new one is still unused and empty. This allows you to add a custom
conversion which cannot be done automatically. For example, in this case you
can traverse the old LinkList, and load the same objects to the Hash table. Here is
the snippet from the online file Listing4_2.cpp:

```
Library *lib; Book *bk;
books_iterator bit;

// transfer LinkList to Hash
allBooks.form(lib,100); // form hash table with 100 buckets
bit.start(lib);
ITERATE(bit,bk){
   allBooks.add(lib,bk); // add bk to Hash
   books.del(lib,bk);    // remove it from LinkList
}
```

For the online version of the entire conversion sequence, look at listings
\list4_1_4\readme.txt and the source files in the same directory.

It is much harder to implement schema migration while storing binary images of
objects, as in file mapping or persistent pointers. From all the systems discussed in this
book, ObjectStore (c) PSE Pro for C++ is the only memory mapping system that does
this. All systems that we know that support schema migration are based on serialization.
The penalty PSE is paying for this feature is the use of a code generator.

4.2   Extensible Property

> This is a simple but most useful data structure which allows to expand
> your classes without even recompiling the code or changing the format of
> the disk storage. It is also useful for efficient storage of sparse data.

---

[5] We have to do this because, in DOL, classes cannot have more than one ZZ_FORMAT in one run.

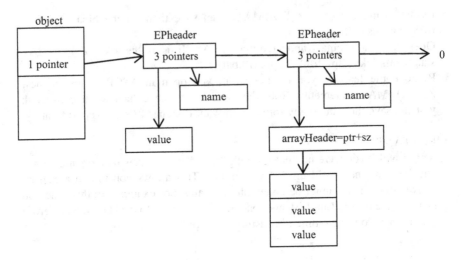

Fig. 4.2 Implementation of the extensible property. Value can be `int`, `float`, `char` or an array of these

It is most interesting that something so useful as Extensible Property (EP) isn't more popular. It deserves to be in any class library.

It is most interesting that something so useful as Extensible Property (EP) isn't more popular. It deserves to be in any class library.

When evolving a project, the data structures usually stabilize fairly fast. However, as programmers keep adding logic, they need to add members which store various values, flags and names. Unless you use serialization for storing the data, any new member makes the old disk files invalid.

EP is a perfect tool to circumvent this problem. For the cost of a single pointer you can add any number of labelled values that act like additional members without making the old disk file invalid. These values are added to an object, not to its class, and for sparsely used values adding this pointer actually saves memory. DOL library provides such EP as a data structure called *Property*—see Fig. 4.2.

If you add such a Property to every class, developing a project is much smoother and better organized. Individual programmers can add values to any class without affecting other team members. The data structures do not change, the software does not have to be recompiled and old disk files are still valid. The only disadvantage is that using a property value is not as efficient as using a true member, but that does not matter much when you are still evolving the code. Once in a while you pause the development and change these values from properties to members, recompile, convert the disk file and continue evolving the software while possibly adding new properties.

For example, in Sect. 4.1, class Book had two members—int `pages`, and float `cost`. If we invoke Property on this class by

```
typedef Property<Book> prop;
```

it creates one NULL pointer on each Book. Then for those books that have an ISBN number, you may add it as property named "ISBN":

```
Book *bk; int inp=321699947;
bk->prop.setProp("int","ISBN",&inp,1);
```

and when you want to retrieve the ISBN number, you call

```
int isbn,size,*ip; char *type;
ip=(int*)bk->prop.getProp("ISBN",&type,&size);
isbn= *ip;
```

Besides the value of ISBN, getProp() also returns `type` and `size`, which tells you whether it is an array and how large it is.

Then later, when someone needs to store number of pages for each chapter with different number of chapters in each book, you can enter it under name *chapPages*

```
Book *bk; inp pages[]={30,55,15,7};
bk->prop.setProp("int","chapPages",pages,4);
```

It is intentional, that DOL Property cannot store pointers. Application should not handle raw pointers; all pointers should be introduced through library data structures.

The fact that named properties are added to objects, not to the class, means that if only a few objects need to store additional information, we do not have to enlarge all objects of their class. In other words, Property is useful not only as a temporary storage for future members, but also as a permanent storage for sparse information.

4.3 Multi-user Access, Data over Networks

> Persistent objects discussed in this book are not required to support these advanced features, but some of the products can support them to a degree. This chapter provides a brief review.

The persistent data as defined at the beginning of this book do not include multi-user access. Their primary purpose is to store internal data to disk in such a way that you can re-activate the data in the next run. However, once you have such persistent data you can do many things with them.

The persistent data as defined at the beginning of this book do not include multi-user access. Their primary purpose is to store internal data to disk in such a way that you can re-activate the data in the next run. However, once you have such persistent data you can do many things with them.

For example, assume that you have a program for star gazing, which has the data about the positions of all stars and planets, and the program displays the view you should have depending on your date, time, latitude and longitude. Anybody on the same computer, or even on the Internet, can get a copy of the file in which you saved the data, and run the same program to display his or her own view of the sky. For this purpose, the file acts as a read-only database. It is not even necessary that everybody would run the same program. For example, the same data file could be used for celestial navigation.

To expand this further, the applications using the same data do not even need identical classes and association. It is enough, if they share the classes and associations which are on the file, and the additional classes and associations satisfy one of the following two conditions:

1. They are temporary and are not to be stored.
2. They are linked to the common classes by a few links that can be temporarily disconnected, allowing one to store the additional classes and associations in a separate file.

We have used this model successfully on CAD systems for the design of silicon chips. The common data held the basic data about components such as transistors, wires, layers, and contact windows that connect these layer, and this data were shared by all the subprojects: graphical display, interactive layout, automatic layout, rule checking and simulation.

The usability of this model is influenced by the type of persistence. When the serialization is used,[6] the program which generates the common file creates it in a short burst, and after that anybody can use it. With persistence based on file mapping or persistent pointers, the program keeps changing the file continuously during its run, and nobody can take a copy of the file until the first run stops.

There is nothing that prevents you from sending the file with persistent data over a network, and we often do that between us—one of us being in Canada and the other in the Czech Republic, and only when sending files over a network do you fully appreciate the importance of the small data footprint. If you are not careful, data from a mass spectrometer can easily overflow the 32-bit address space.

When both the sender and the receiver use the same operating system and compiler, any style of persistence works. When moving data files between different environments, ASCII or XML data are the choice. Generally there is no problem with transferring data from a 32-bit to a 64-bit architecture, but the reverse transfer runs into the problem with numbers, usually pointers, that are too large to read into one 32-bit word.

4.4   Address Space Layout Randomization (ASLR)

> Some persistent systems provide their own memory allocation, and it is important to understand whether this could interfere with ASLR which is performed by all modern operating systems.

---

[6] Memory blasting also falls into this category.

The purpose of ASLR is to improve the security of the computer system against hackers and viruses. When executing a program, we need three sets of virtual memory pages: one set for the executable, one for the stack which stores frames of temporary variables of individual functions and one for the heap which keeps the dynamically allocated data. Each thread gets its stack, but there is only one heap per application.

Typical attacks use one of the following strategies:

1. If the location of the sensitive part of the executable or data is known, they try to alter those locations.
2. They randomly alter many memory locations, hoping that it will hit some sensitive spot.

Strategy 1 aims directly at the destruction of the system. Strategy 2 will most likely crash the run, with a low probability of causing a serious harm.

Without going into detail of how the memory is assigned, the obvious defence against strategy 1 is, with each program load, to use different (random) memory locations both for the executable and the data.

The defence against strategy 2 is not to load executables and data in clusters near a specific location but randomly within the given space. Neither defence is 100 % proof, but they significantly decrease the probability of the random attack hitting a sensitive spot.

ASLR typically generates new space distribution for each load. For example, ARL, the Apple version of ASLR, is performed[7]:

– Per execution: for executable, data, heap, stack, linker.
– Per boot: for libraries.

As long as the data location does not change while the program is running, ASLR should not affect persistence with only one minor performance exception: methods based on memory paging (POST++, ObjectStore (c) PSE Pro) may attempt to load the data to its original location and bypass pointer swizzling, and ASLR will not allow that. However, this is only a matter of occasional performance boost. Our experience with testing POST++ is Windows 7 and Vista which have ASLR but often do not accept the requested location, while Windows XP which does not have ASLR usually accepts it.

There seems to be a similarity between ASLR and persistence. In both cases we have blocks of numbers where some numbers are references to other numbers within the block. In the case of data these references are pointers; in the case of executable the references are either jumps or address locations.

---

[7] Under iOS 4.3 when compiled with PIE; see Zino (2012).

We are not experts on ASLR, but this similarity may be worth exploring. Perhaps using a bitmap[8] for these references could make relocation of the executable so fast that it could potentially be done in a brief interruption while a program is running. On the other hand, perhaps, some of the ASLR techniques may be applicable to the implementation of persistence.

4.5   Flash Memories, Smart Phones

Persistent objects are of special interest for small devices such as smart phones or video cameras that require high speed processing and for which using a database would be an overkill. Compared to hard drives from desktop computers, flash drives used in these devices have different characteristics that are important when working with persistent objects.

Flash memories are storage devices which, due to their construction, have a peculiar behaviour. Information can be stored/restored very fast, but it cannot be overwritten. In order to write into an already filled location the content has first to be erased (zero-filled), but memory can be erased only in large blocks and not in individual bits, bytes or even single objects.

Flash memories are now used to store files and persistent data in mobile phones, handheld computers, digital cameras, portable music players and many other devices.

The speed of USB 2.0 flash drives commonly used today is, according to the specification,[9] up to 35 MB/s. This is the speed of the network; the storage device is much faster. The USB speed limit hides the fact that reading flash memory is faster than writing to it—something that may be important in applications such as smart phones.

Typical flash memory includes a memory management software which allows the user to work with it as if it were another hard drive. The prime purpose of the USB flash drive is to store files, and the software is optimized for this purpose.

Another technical peculiarity of flash drives is that a location may be overwritten only a certain number of times, after which it wears out and becomes unreliable. The software which manages the flash memory must minimize the number of erasures and the level of wear. For more on this see Gal and Toledo (2005), Ku (2011), and Riley (2012).

The failure of a typical flash drive may happen after writing between 10,000 and 1,000,000 times into the same locations, which poses no danger if you only store songs or your MS Word files of your manuscript, but it may become a problem if

---

[8] Such as described in Sect. 2.2.1.

[9] http://en.wikipedia.org/wiki/Universal_Serial_Bus#USB_2.0_.28High_Speed.29

you attempt to use the flash drive as a secondary storage device for a miniature computer system such as a smart phone.

Clearly, all the persistent systems which we discuss in this book can store their data on a flash drive as if it were a hard disk. However, papers (Saxena et al. 2012; Shasha and Toledo 2007) describe persistent systems that keep data structures on a flash drive and move them, on a transactional basis, to memory. Such systems allow a recovery in case of a crash or a sudden shutdown of the device, but their implementation is quite complicated because their main concern is to avoid repeated modifications of the same flash drive location.

> We think that a more practical alternative would be to use one of the persistent systems described in Chap. 2 and save the entire data space periodically, for example any time the user interacts with the system. DOL memory blasting saves 80 MB of highly structured data to a standard hard drive in 630 ms,[10] or 8 MB in 63 ms—fast enough not to affect a typical application.

For example, when considering such alternatives for developing iPhone applications, it would be useful to know their data-space limit and the internal speed of sequential writing to SSD, but this information is not available.

A Web search produced this quote[11]: *It's very difficult to give hard numbers because Apple knows and isn't telling. If your app uses say under 10 MB you are probably OK. If it hits 20 MB it could be a problem. I worked with a memory leak in an app lately and it was killed only when it reached somewhere over 40 MB.*

As a rough guess for the speed of the SSD storage, we can take a big commercial drive, for example Plextor PX-256M5P,[12] with speed of sequential read 520 MB/s and sequential write 442 MB/s.

Considering these numbers, storing the entire data structure used in an iPhone application should be well under 0.1 s. Pointer swizzling is always done when opening the data, thus saving data is relatively fast. Repeated storage of the entire space without potential for a corruption in the incremental saving would provide an ultimate safety, especially when data stored at a few recent time points would provide additional backups.

Let's look at how suitable are the various persistent systems for saving the program data space repeatedly, each time to a different disk location:

- All serialization including DOL binary and DOL ASCII convert internal data to some special format, and write it to disk, object by object. For every object there is additional information, at least the object type and size.

---

[10] These numbers come from the benchmark in Chap. 7, Table 7.4.

[11] http://iphonedevsdk.com/forum/iphone-sdk-development/6606-limit-on-ram-usage.html

[12] http://www.techradar.com/news/computing-components/storage/best-ssd-10-of-the-top-ssds-on-test-994095

- DOL mb writes the data space with the bitmap (overhead of 1/32 of the data) as a block of bytes, straight to disk.
- SQLite moves constantly between the external storage and memory; it is not suitable for this type of storage.
- QSP reduces the data space to one page and writes it to the external storage, which is very fast. If the page size exceeds the data-space limit, the speed of saving should be comparable to DOL mb - still fast enough for this purpose.
- The systems based on memory paging (PPF, POST++, QSP, PSE) would have to run in a mode, in which all the data space would be in memory. QSP always fulfills this condition. In PPF, we have control over the page size and over the number of pages in memory, so this is not a problem. We believe that PSE has controls that can do this, but we are not sure about POST++ which uses the page size 512 - a fixed value derived from the size of the system pages.

Languages, Their Features and Limitations

5

Abstract

The implementation of persistence and class libraries depends on features provided by the programming language. Even though C, C++, C#, Objective-C and Java are quite similar in many aspects, they are significantly different in what they allow us to do about persistence and class libraries.

Keywords

Laguages • Persistence • Limitation • C • C++ • C# • Objective-C • Java

The first four chapters explored various approaches to implementing persistent objects and bi-directional associations, including tricks that make the persistence more efficient and make it easy to use. This chapter looks at individual languages and their features that may help to develop such systems.

Figure 5.1 sums up the features required for the basic styles of persistent objects:

A: When saving object-by-object, we can use normal allocation, but when saving entire blocks of memory, we have to replace the allocator.

B: Regardless of how we save the objects, we need to know the locations of all pointers.

C: When saving object-by-object, we need to know the type (the class) of the target object. Without this information, the algorithm could not collect all objects by following the pointers.

D: Members other than pointers are needed only when saving in the ASCII mode.

J. Soukup and P. Macháček, *Serialization and Persistent Objects*,
DOI 10.1007/978-3-642-39323-5_5, © Springer-Verlag Berlin Heidelberg 2014

175

special allocator	pointer location	target class	other members	virtual funct.	insert members	type of persistence
		C	D	E		ASCII serialization
	B				F	binary images serialization
A						block of memory

Fig. 5.1 Features required for the basic three types of persistency

E: When collecting all objects by traversing the pointer links, we need virtual functions that detect the true type of each object. When saving blocks of memory, inheritance is transparent (irrelevant).

F: The library of intrusive associations requires coordinated insertions into participating classes, regardless of how the data is stored to disk.

5.1   Plain Old C Language

> This section describes the internal design of Data Object Library (DOL). This library is a proof that we can implement a full fledged persistence in plain C, but we have to be smart about it and use a code generator with a lot of macros.

The first version of DOL was released in 1989, and it worked only in C. It included a library of intrusive associations such as described in Chap. 3 Today, DOL supports persistent C++ objects, but most of its internal design is still the original C code. Code Farms does not support the C version any more; if you wanted to use it, you would have to back several years to some earlier version. The new InCode library uses the same data structures with only improved parameterization and avoiding macros. The main difference from C++ is that we work with structures, not classes, and the generic functions which control the data structures are macros parametrized by the association ID, not class methods.

Figure 5.2 shows the information (chequered boxes) that cannot be obtained automatically, and must somehow be entered by the user. In C we do not have to worry about inheritance and virtual functions, there is no problem with writing our own allocator and we can insert members with macros. If we plan to implement persistence based on a block of memory, all we need are the pointer locations. Binary serialization also needs the type of target objects, and for ASCII serialization we need information about all the members, not just for the pointers. DOL provides all three types of persistence, and you can switch between them within one program run.

allocate	pointer locations	target class	other members	virtual funct.	insert members	type of pesistence
		C	D	N/A		ASCII serialization
	B				F	binary images serialization
A						block of memory

Fig. 5.2 In C, we do not need virtual functions, but pointer locations and target class are more difficult to obtain. Checkered information must be provided by the user; it cannot be obtained automatically. However, areas B and C are needed only when you are constructing the library. When you program with DOL, only D must be supplied by the user. Information from checkered boxes cannot be obtained automatically

OVERALL CONCEPT

DOL comes with an extensive library of generic intrusive data structures, and its persistence assumes the strategy which we still recommend and which was described in Chap. 3, namely that application classes have no pointer members; if there are any pointers that are a part of a data structure, they are transparently inserted by the library.

The generic library classes are implemented with macros, and, besides the types of participating classes, they are also parameterized by the data structure ID. For example, if you declare[1]

```
ZZ_ORG_SINGLE_AGGREGATE(books,Library,Book);
```

and then use it like this

```
struct Library *lib;
struct Book *bk;
...
ZZ_ADD(books,lib,bk);\
Note that the parameters are not only Library and Book, but also books.
```

the parameters are not only `Faculty` and `Student`, but also `students`.

The code generator called *zzprep* creates short segments of code that pull it all together. This preprocessor creates additional code. It does not modify the application code, so you use a debugger as usual.

When you program with DOL, you do not have to identify pointers because there are none in the application classes, at least not explicitly. Pointers are controlled by the library, and they were identified and described when the class was added to the library.

---

[1] This corresponds to the syntax we have been using in this book: Association SingleAggregate <Library,Book> books; Note that DOL includes the directory "test" with many programs that test all the features of this library. Tests that use ZZ_ORG_¼ are the C tests; C++ tests use ZZ_HYPER_¼ instead. For example, test0a.c is a C test.

Most users may never create new library classes. Because that is done only once, such registration of data structure and its pointers does not have to be particularly efficient or elegant. DOL The library keeps a *master*[2] file, where all the data structures (associations) and their pointers must be manually registered.

Listing 5.1 shows a section of this file, and what we have to do to register new data structure SINGLE_AGGREGATE, which works with pointers from 4 to 6: they are ZZp (from child to parent), ZZt (tail of the children ring) and ZZs (from child to its next sibling). In the C version of DOL, associations or data structures are called "organizations".

The last section[3] of the Listing 5.1 records methods of each association and the file where their source is stored.

Listing 5.1 Adding SINGLE_AGGREGATE to the master file where associations DOUBLE_LINK and DOUBLE_RING are already recorded

```
ZZorganization {
        0 DOUBLE_LINK                    0  1
        1 DOUBLE_RING                    2  3
        2 SINGLE_AGGREGATE               4  6
}

/* ind usedOn pointTo type ptrName, type=a means a pointer */
ZZpointer {
        0  0  2  a  ZZf     /* forward link */
        1  0  1  a  ZZr     /* reverse link */
        2  1  2  a  ZZf     /* forward ring */
        3  1  1  a  ZZb     /* reverse ring */
        4  2  1  a  ZZp     /* parent aggregate */
        5  1  2  a  ZZt     /* tail aggregate */
        6  2  2  a  ZZs     /* sibling aggregate */
}

/* function organization fileName */
ZZfunction {
        add       0  adddlink
        del       0  deldlink
        fwd       0  fwddlink
        rev       0  revdlink
        addTail   1  addtdrin
        next      1  nextdrin
        prev      1  prevdrin
        ...
        addTail   2  addtsagg
        next      2  nextsagg
        parent    2  parsagg
        ...
}
```

---

[2] In DOL, it is file macro/zzmaster.

[3] This section shows the concept, not the exact format.

For example, when the code generator reads these definition of these associations

```
ZZ_ORG_SINGLE_AGGREGATE(books,Library,Book);
ZZ_ORG_SINGLE_AGGREGATE(published,Author,Book);
```

it retrieves the names of all the structures and it gives them an index: 0 = Library, 1 = Book and 2 = Author. It also combines this information with the *master* file, makes a list of pointers that have to be inserted into these structures and creates file zzincl.h with ZZ_EXT_.. macros that insert the required pointers:

```
#define ZZ_EXT_Library \
        Book *_books_ZZt
#define ZZ_EXT_Book               \
        Library *_books_ZZp;   \
        Book *_books_ZZs;         \
        Author *_published_ZZp;\
        Book *_published_ZZs
#define ZZ_EXT_Author \
        Book *_published_ZZt
```

Note that this arrangement always positions all the pointers at the beginning of the object. When swizzling them or writing them to disk, we do not need a bitmap to identify their locations—we only need to know how many pointers we have at the beginning of the object.

The following code is an example of using DOL in a C application:

```
#include "zzincl.h" /* generated by the code generator */
struct Library {
        ZZ_EXT_Library;
        ... other members as usual
};
struct Author {
        ZZ_EXT_Author;
        ... other members as usual
};
struct Book {
        ZZ_EXT_Book;
        ... other members as usual
};

ZZ_ORG_SINGLE_AGGREGATE(books,Library,Book);
ZZ_ORG_SINGLE_AGGREGATE(published,Author,Book);

int main(){
        Library *lib; Author *auth; Book *bk1,*bk2;
        ZZ_PLAIN_ALLOC(Library,1,lib);
        ZZ_PLAIN_ALLOC(Book,1,bk1);
        ZZ_PLAIN_ALLOC(Book,1,bk2);
        ZZ_PLAIN_ALLOC(Author,1,auth);

        ZZ_ADD(books,lib,bk1);
        ZZ_ADD(books,lib,bk2);
        ZZ_ADD(published,auth,bk1);
        ...
}
#include "zzfunc.c" /* generated by the code generator */
```

where ZZ_PLAIN_ALLOC (T, 1, p) is the C equivalent of p=new T() in C++,
    ZZ_PLAIN_ALLOC(T, n, p) is the C equivalent of p=new T[n] in C++,
    ZZ_ADD(org, p1, p2) is the C equivalent of org.add (p1, p2) in C++.

The code generator prepared the definitions of macros ZZ_PLAIN_ALLOC and ZZ_ADD so that they are readily available through the include file, zzincl.h. The internal implementation is rather complex, but the following code samples show the general idea how it all works. In order to understand the concatenations (##), look above for the example of ZZ_EXT_.. statements:

```
/* macro from the library */
#define ZZ_PLAIN_ALLOC(TYPE,N,PTR) \
PTR=(TYPE*)calloc(sizeof(TYPE),N);

/* line generated specifically for this project */
#define ZZ_ADD_books ZZ_ADD_SINGLE_AGGREGATE

/* prepared by the code generator, ## concatenates */
#define ZZ_ADD(ID,PAR,CHI) \
ZZ_ADD##ID(ID,PAR,CHI,_##ID##_ZZp,_##ID##_ZZt, _##ID$$_ZZs)

/* macro from the library, parent and child */
#define ZZ_ADD_SINGLE_TRIANGLE(id,par,chi, \
                               parent,tail,sibling) \
    if((chi)->parent!=NULL || (chi)->sibling!=NULL){\
        .:. error exit or do nothing
    }\
    else {\
        if((par)->tail==NULL){\
            (par)->tail=(chi);\
            (chi)->parent=(par);\
            (chi)->sibling=(chi);\
        }\
        else  {\
            (chi)->sibling=((par)->tail)->sibling;\
            ((par)->tail)->sibling=(chi);\
            (chi)->parent=(par);\
        }\
    }\
}
```

We do not need to know any details about *other members* (see box E in Fig. 5.2) if we want to run an ASCII serialization. We only need to know how to write and read back these members from the disk.

For that DOL has an elegant solution. For each class the user has to supply a ZZ_FORMAT statement. For example:

```
class Book {
    ZZ_EXT_Book
    int ISBN;
    float cost;
};
ZZ_FORMAT(Book,"%d %6.2f,ISBN,cost");
```

This statement contains enough information for the code generator to create the write and read functions that will always match, yet it has the flexibility to handle any interpretation of numbers and text.

5.2   C++ Language

C++ is excellent for implementing persistent data except for one thing: It does
not support reflection. Since Chaps. 2 and 3 were built on C++ examples, we do
not have to discuss the capabilities of the language itself, but we can look at the
different approached used in the available C++ products.

Over the past 2 decades, most of the work on persistency was done in C++, and
the history details of all these projects are interesting. Under the name of Organized
C (orgc), DOL has been commercially distributed since 1989. Pointer swizzling at
the page fault was first proposed by Wilson (1990). Singhal et al. (1992) reported on
a university project called Texas, to which we could not find any references after
2000. Soukup (1994)[4] introduced memory blasting. Free[5] software (Knizhnik,
POST++, 1999) is available for download. The Boost persistence was designed
during 2002–2004 without its author being aware of the Code Farms libraries
(DOL, PPF, InCode). Figure 5.4 shows the time progress of these projects.[6]

File mapping has been used in the **ObjectStore** line of products since the
inception of the company as described in Lamb et al. (1991). Recently, Zikari
(2010) confirmed the company still uses the same methodology. When using
ObjectStore (c) PSE Pro for C++, the user must replace all calls to new() throughout
the application.[7] The user does not have to identify pointer members, and neither
published papers nor the documentation explain how PSE does it. Our guess is that
the PSE code generator performs a partial syntax analysis of the application
classes—essentially what you get through reflection in languages like Objective-
C or Java. To verify this hypothesis is difficult because the PSE code generator
produces a binary file, not a source you could examine visually.

Figure 5.3 shows the information (chequered boxes) that cannot be obtained
automatically in C++ and must somehow be entered by the user.

Data Object Library (DOL) supports three styles of persistence (*binary serialization, ASCII serialization* and *memory blasting*). The serialization is automatic
and supports schema migration. DOL combines persistence with an extensive
library of data structures (associations) which include bi-directional associations
not supported by STL—see Fig. 5.5. It provides a more extensive protection against
pointer errors than Java, and all classes have iterators which allow to delete objects
while iterating the containers. The total space for its executables (code generator
and compiled library) is under 400 kB.

---

[4] pp. 386–392.

[5] POST++ comes in source from which all comments have been removed, and it is rather difficult
and time consuming to figure out its inner workings.

[6] Code Farms were incorporated in 1988 and ObjectStore in 1989.

[7] Compare this to PPF which re-defines operator new() and makes this transparent.

allocate	pointer locations	target class	other members	virtual funct.	insert members	type of pesistence
		C	D			ASCII serialization
	B			E	F	binary images serialization
A						block of memory

Fig. 5.3 In C++, virtual functions that we may need when inheritance is involved can be inserted with a macro. Otherwise the situation is similar to C, where the main problems are boxes B, C and D. Information from checkered boxes cannot be obtained automatically

year	DOL	ObjSt.	Texas	PPF	POST	Boost
1989	S					
1990	S	M				
1991	S	M	M			
1993	SB	M	M			
1997	SB	M	M	P		
1998	SB	M	M	P	M	
2000	SB	M		P	M	
2004	SB	M		P	M	X

Fig. 5.4 History of persistent systems, commercial projects in bold. Legend: S = automatic serialization, both binary and ASCII, M = memory mapping, B = memory blasting, P = persistent pointers, X = binary, ASCII and XML serialization. Information from checkered boxes cannot be obtained automatically

DOL assumes that application classes do not store any raw pointers and participate only in data structures (associations) from DOL. DOL includes some unusual classes, for example class **Pager** which stores nonstructural information such as text, pictures or tables of numbers in a separate file, and pages it to memory as needed. Class **Property** is useful in two situations. (1) When you may need, sometimes in the future, to add members to applications classes without adjusting the schema. (2) When some members are only sparsely used. For more details, see Sect. 4.2.

Persistent Pointer Factory (PPF) uses a completely different style of persistence, see Sect. 2.4.2. It is based on persistent pointers which page disk to memory on demand. Because these pointers store the disk address and not the memory address, they are persistent and do not require swizzling when moving the data to or from the disk. This library being written is proof that C++ persistence can be implemented in pure C++ without any code generation or using system specific

ring (singly and double linked; sort, merge, and split functions)
collection (singly and double linked; sort, merge, and split functions)
aggregate (singly and double linked; **OneToMany** association)
trees (singly and double linked)
name (variagle length string)
single and double **link** (pointer link, or **OneToOne** association)
LIFO and **FIFO** queues
reference (similar to Java reference)
array (array of object or array of pointers, also **binary heap**)
hash table (use default or your own hashing)
graphs (directed, not directed, singly or doubly linked)
ManyToMany (including two iterators)
type (essentially a form of reflection)
pager (persistent storage of large non-structural information, texts)
property (run-time expansion of objects by any number of named members)

Fig. 5.5 Persistent data structures supported by DOL

functions such as file mapping. It has been offered on the web for over a decade, but in spite of being elegant and compact,[8] it did not become popular, probably because it originally did not include any data structures, and programmers looking for persistence chose DOL with its extensive library.

While writing this book, we paired PPF with InCode library,[9] which is a modern library of bi-directional associations, but does not have persistence. The result is the **PPFIC library**. For the performance comparison with other libraries, see Chap. 7 (Benchmarks).

The main difference between PPF and POST or PSE is that PPF works with soft pointers which require a short arithmetic calculation on each pointers access, while PSE and POST use hard pointers which are swizzled when the page is loaded to memory.

Boost is an open source library of data structures which also includes serialization. The serialization requires too much user input to qualify, in our terms, to be considered an automatic persistence, yet it was recently proposed as a C++ standard. Because of that, and because of its massive use worldwide, we treat it as one of the serializations that are part of the language, such as Java serialization or C# serialization. For more on Boost, see Sect. 1.5.5.

---

[8] Based on C++ templates, total source 2700 lines including comments, executable 164 kB.
[9] See Sect. 3.1.3.

Just for your curiosity, let's look at how much the syntax of working with DOL improved when moving from C (Sect. 5.1) to C++ here:

```
#include "zzincl.h" /* generated by the code generator */
class Library {
    ZZ_EXT_Library;
    ... other members as usual
};
class Author {
    ZZ_EXT_Author;
    ... other members as usual
};
class Book {
    ZZ_EXT_Book;
    ... other members as usual
};

ZZ_HYPER_SINGLE_AGGREGATE(books,Library,Book);
ZZ_HYPER_SINGLE_AGGREGATE(published,Author,Book);

int main(){
    Library *lib; Author *auth; Book *bk1,*bk2;
    lib=new Library;
    bk1=new Book;
    bk2=new Book;
    auth=new Author;

    books.add(lib,bk1);
    books.add(lib,bk2);
    published.add(auth,bk1);
    ...
}
#include "zzfunc.c" /* generated by the code generator */
```

In file zzincl.h, code generator prepared ZZ_EXT_... statements the same way as it did in C, but it added the friend statements which allow the relevant interface classes to reach inside class Book. It also replaces operator new() depending on whether the persistence uses memory blasting or serialization. MB_ALLOC(Block) is a macro which not only allocates the object from special pages, but it also updates the corresponding bitmap with the location of pointers embedded in each Book.

```
#define ZZ_EXT_Book \
friend class ZZHbooks;\
friend class ZZHpublished;\
    Book * _published_ZZs;\
    Book * _book_ZZs;\
    Author * _published_ZZp;\
    Library * _books_ZZp;\
public:\
    void * operator new(size_t size){\
        if(memoryBlasting) return MB_ALLOC(Book);\
        else return calloc(size,1); /* serialization */\
    }\
    ...
```

Internally, the interface class is renamed, using the association name. For example
`ZZ_HYPER_SINGLE_AGGREGATE(books,Library,Book)` becomes `ZZHbooks`
`ZZ_HYPER_SINGLE_AGGREGATE(published,Author,Book)` becomes `ZZHpublished`

Internally, individual methods can either call the original C macro (STYLE 1), or be fully coded in C++ (STYLE 2):

```
// STYLE 1: new interface hiding the macro design
#define ZZ_HYPER_SINGLE_AGGREGATE(id,pType,cType) \
class ZZH##id { \
public: \
     void add(pType *p,cType *c){ ZZ_ADD(id,p,c); } \
     ... all the other methods \
} id;
```

```
// STYLE 2: true C++ code
#define ZZ_HYPER_SINGLE_AGGREGATE(id,pType,cType) \
class ZZH##id { \
typedef tail _##id##_ZZt; \
typedef sibling _##id##_ZZs; \
typedef parent _##id##_ZZp;\
public: \
     void add(pType *par,cType *chi){\
          if(chi->parent!=NULL || ch)->sibling!=NULL){\
               ... error exit or do nothing
          }\
          else {\
               if(par->tail==NULL){\
                    par->tail=chi;\
                    chi->parent=pa);\
                    chi->sibling=chi;\
               }\
               else {\
                    chi->sibling=(pa)->tail)->sibling;\
                    (par->tail)->sibling=ch);\
                    chi->parent=par;\
               }\
          }\
     }\
     ... other the other methods \
} id;
```

Note that the syntax in which application uses this interface can be set up in two ways. When it is as we just described, the application calls are

```
books.add(lib,bk);
published.add(auth,bk);
```

which is the style used in DOL.

If we set up the interface class like this

```
#define ZZ_HYPER_SINGLE_AGGREGATE(id,pType,cType) \
class id { \
     ... \
};
```

the application calls would be

```
books::add(lib,bk);
published::add(auth,bk);
```

5.3   Java Language

From the viewpoint of data structures and persistence, Java is significantly simpler than C++, and very much like C#:

- It does not have pointers, only references.
- A member can be a reference, but not an object (instance of some class).
- Multiple inheritance is not allowed.
- It has *reflection* which solves the problem with finding reference members.
- There is no equivalent of C macros.

Internally, references store object addresses, but their values are not available to the application programmer, and operator new() cannot be overloaded. From Fig. 5.6 we can conclude that implementing serialization should be easy, but persistence based on the block of memory would be difficult or impossible to design.

It's not surprising that Java has built-in serialization which saves the data in a special byte-encoded format; see Sect. 1.5.2 What is surprising is that the ObjectStore company now has PSE Pro for Java.

Blog (Weinreb 2007) describes how the original PSE Pro for Java was implemented, but the past tense is being used—perhaps meaning that the existing implementation is different: *The PSE Pro for Java had its own storage engine which is used just for object-level faulting with a specialized lightweight, small footprint, storage engine. However, it did not support concurrent access between separate Java processes.* The idea of injecting JVM instructions into Java class files is also mentioned.[10]

Besides Java built-in serialization—see Sect. 1.5.2, there are several systems that store Java objects in a database which is not the type of persistence we cover in this book. An example of such a system is Hibernate.

UMPLE (2012) is a model-programming technology which resembles the InCode library in that it represents associations as first class objects, includes a library of data structures (associations) and alternates between controlling them with a textual schema which is in the code or controlling them with the UML class diagram—see Sect. 3.5. It runs with Java, PHP and Ruby, but it does not support persistence.

---

[10] JVM—Java Virtual Machine; this is an equivalent of inserting machine code instructions into an object file.

allocate	pointer locations	target class	other members	virtual funct.	insert members	type of pesistence
			D			ASCII serialization
	B	**C**		**E**	**F**	binary images serialization
A						block of memory

Fig. 5.6 C# and Java are similar. Their reflections allow one to identify references, their target types and other members, but you cannot overload operator new() or get the address stored inside the reference. Inserting members is difficult, there are no macros and instances cannot be inserted as members. Information from checkered boxes cannot be obtained automatically

5.4   C# Language

From the viewpoint of data structures and persistence, C# is significantly simpler than C++, and very much like Java—see Fig. 5.6:

- It does not have pointers, only references.
- A member can be a reference but not an object (instance of some class).[11]
- Multiple inheritance is not allowed.
- It has *reflection* which solves the problem with finding reference members.
- There is no equivalent of C macros.

Internally, references store object addresses, but their values are not available to the application programmer, and operator new() cannot be overloaded. From Fig. 5.6 we can conclude that implementing serialization should be easy except for the insertion of pointers required for intrusive data structures. However, persistence based on the block of memory would be difficult if not impossible to design.

C# has a **built-in serialization** which supports both binary and XML formats. The advantage of the XML format is that it can read the stored data even if the

---

[11] This is easiest to explain on a C++ example:

```
class A {...};
class B {
    A *ap; // corresponds to reference in Java
    A aa; // is not allowed in Java
};
```
Note that ap leads to an object allocated separately, but aa is allocated as a part of any B object.

structure of the serialized objects are changed, for example if we add or remove members from some classes. The disadvantage of the XML format is a larger size of the data file. For more details see Sect. 1.5.3.

The **C# library of associations (Osterby** 2000) is not persistent, but it is interesting because it inserts the references that form the association without using a code generator or Aspects. It uses runtime type instantiation, which is not available in Java. This was a university research project which is not active any more. The C# version of Java Hibernate is called NHibernate. Commercial product DevXPress also provides persistency which is using a database.

5.5 Objective-C Language

Of all the languages discussed in this book, Objective-C is the most suitable for building persistence.[12] It has all the advantages of C and C++ including access to addresses of objects and pointers, but it also has reflection which can identify pointers and their locations without any user input.

There are no chequered boxes in Fig. 5.7 because all the steps are easy. You cannot replace operator new() but you can code your own method *alloc*. The reflection gives you all the members, and tells you what the types are. You do not need information about the pointer target type, because each object, in this case the target object, can tell you its type. All methods in Objective-C are virtual, so there is no special problem with virtual methods. You cannot insert an object instance as a member, but a member can be a struct—which is all we need when we built intrusive data structures.

We know only one implementation of persistent objects for Objective-C, the built-in serialization called *Archiving,* which generates XML, ASCII or binary output as we explained in Sect. 1.5.4. To support archiving, a class has to implement the NSCoding protocol which has methods to encode (to archive) and decode (to unarchive) instances of that class which, as we said at the beginning of this book, is something we want to eliminate. Also quoting[13] the Apple documentation:

> Cocoa archives can hold Objective-C objects, scalars, arrays, structures and strings. They do not hold types whose implementation varies across platforms, such as union, void*, function pointers, and long chains of pointers.

If it cannot handle long chains of pointers it cannot handle intrusive data structures.

---

[12] It is also a young language only about 10 years old which has little in common with Objective-C from the 1990s.

[13] http://developer.apple.com/library/mac/#documentation/cocoa/conceptual/Archiving/Articles/archives.html

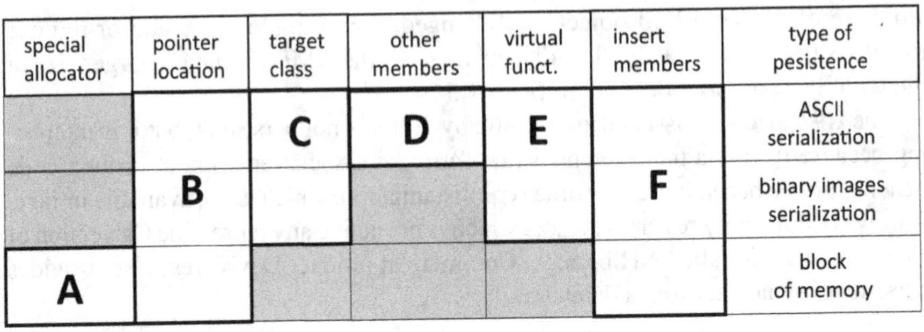

special allocator	pointer location	target class	other members	virtual funct.	insert members	type of persistence
		C	D	E		ASCII serialization
	B				F	binary images serialization
A						block of memory

Fig. 5.7 Of all the languages discussed in this book, Objective-C is the most suitable for building persistence—in addition to all the useful features of C++, it also supports reflection. Its weak point is the NextStep (NS) library. Note that all the information can be obtained automatically (there are no checkered boxes)

The following chapter (Chap. 6) will take us through the implementation of fully automatic persistence for Objective-C, with code examples in Objective-C only. Objective-C syntax is quite different from the C++ or Java, and not all readers will be familiar with it. The remaining part of this chapter will introduce Objective-C syntax, just enough that you should be able to read the code samples in Chap. 6. It will also show some algorithms that are conceptually different from C++.

You can compile Objective-C programs with gcc under Windows or Linux, or with iOS on any Apple hardware, e.g. Mac. Look at Listing 5.2 for the comparison of the C++ and Objective-C syntax.

Normally all application classes are derived, directly or indirectly, from class NSObject. For example, in Listing 5.2, class Publication might have been derived from it:

```
@interface Publication : NSObject
```

Reserved keyword *id*, usually written as (id) means "pointer to any Objective-C object", not just "pointer to any object derived from NSObject". The advantage of deriving object from NSObject is that NSObject implements support methods required by runtime. In Listing 5.2, method *init* returns (id).

Listing 5.2 Comparing syntax of C++ and Objective-C

C++ file: Book.h
```
class Author;

class Book : public Publication {
  int pages;
public:
  char *title;
  Book *next;
  static int ID; // class ID
  Book();
  int getPages();
  void setBook(int pg,char *tit);
  static int getID();
};
```

C++ file: Book.cpp
```
int Book::ID=13;
Book::Book(){pages=0;title=NULL;}
int Book::getPages(){
  return pages;
}
void Book::setBook(
            int pg,char *tit){
  pages=pg;
  title=tit;
}
int Book::getID(){return ID; }
```

C++ file: main.cpp
```
int main(){
  Book *bk1,*bk; int sz;
  char *t="C++ Manual";
  bk1=new Book(;
  bk1->setBook(120,t);
  sz=Book:getID();
  // ...more books form a chain
  for(bk=bk1; bk!=NULL;
              bk=bk->next){
    printf("%s\n",bk->title);
  }
  return 0;
}
```

Objective-C file: Book.h
```
@class Author;

@interface Book : Publication
{
@private
  int pages;
@public
  char *title;
  Book *next;
}
- (id) init;
- (int) getPages;
- (void) setBook: (int) pg
              title: (char*) tit;
+ (int) getID; //size of object
@end
```

Objective_C file: Book.m
```
@implementation Book
static int ID=13; // class ID
-(id) init {
  self=[super init];
  pages=0; title=NULL;
  return self;
}
-(int) getPages {
  return pages;
}
-(void) setBook: (int) pg
            title: (char*) tit {
  pages=pg;
  title=tit;
}
+ (int) getID {return ID;}
@end
```

Objective-C file: main.m
```
int main(){
  Book *bk1,*bk; int sz;
  char *t="C++Manual";
  bk1=[[Book alloc] init];
  [bk1 setBook: 120 title: t];
  sz=[Book getID];
  // ...more books form a chain
  for(bk=bk1; bk!=nil;
              bk=bk->next){
    printf("%s\n",bk->title);
  }
  return 0;
}
```

The main difference from C++ is that classes are not abstract, untouchable entities: they are objects. You can examine them during the program run or pass them as function or method parameters. Keyword Class (without *) means "pointer to a class". This concept opens magical possibilities about which you could not dream in C++, for example:

```
Book *bk=[[Book alloc] init];
(id) v=bk;
Class cls=[v class];
const char* className = class_getName(cls);
NSLog(@"yourObject is a: %s", className);
```

An instance of a class cannot be used as a member of another class. This is similar to Java; however, unlike Java, Objective-C allows members which are instances of a structure. Compare the rules with this C++ code:

```
class A {...};
typedef struct myStruct {
    void *mask;
    int maskSize;
} myStruct;

class B {
    A a;              // not allowed in Objective-C
    myStruct ms;      // works in Objective-C
    A *ap;            // works in Objective-C
};
```

For any Objective-C object, its hidden pointer (first 4 or 8 bytes) points to the class object. Keyword *self*, when used in an object method, has the same meaning as *this* in C++. For example, see the return of method *init* in Fig. 5.1. However, inside a class method[14] it represents the class.

Unlike in C++, Objective-C programmers often use C-style, free floating functions. The following example demonstrates this style of design where *self* represents the class. This is a situation where we want to add the same simple method

createMask to every application class and let all these methods call one C-style function which actually does the job. The example is shown for application class Book:

---

[14] Method that would be static in C++ and in Objective-C starts with '+'.

Listing 5.3 C-style function implementing multiple methods, with self representing a class, not an object

```
(id) createMaskGeneral(Class cls);

@interface Book : NSObject
   // ...
   + (void) createMask; // one line added to every application class[15]
   + (void) checkMask;
@end

// C-style function which actually creates the mask
void *createMaskGeneral(Class cls){
   (id) obj=[[cls alloc] init];
   // ... more code
   return obj;
}

@implementation Book
   static Book *mask=nil;
   + (void) createMask {
      mask=createMaskGeneral(self); // <<<<<<<<
   }
   + (void) checkMask {
      if(mask==nil) printf("error: Mask remains unset\n");
      else {
         Class cls=[mask class];
         printf("mask is an instance of class=%s\n",
                              class_getName([cls class]));
      }
   }
@end

int main(){
   [Book createMask];
   [Book checkMask];
   return 0;
}
```

The penalty for the dynamic typing and all the magic we can do with the classes is that programs coded in Objective-C are more error prone and more difficult to debug. We will discuss that at the end of this chapter.

An important part of Objective-C is the NextStep (NS) library, which provides NSObject that all the application classes should inherit, basic arrays and collections, and also the Objective-C version of the String class NSString, which can store either C-style text or Unicode:

```
char *s="abcd"; // C-style string
NSString *ns= @"abcd"; // Objective-C type string
char *c=[ns cString]; // conversion from NSString to C-string
printf("%s %s\n", s, [ns cString]);
```

---

[15] This method can be added at runtime through a utility which uses reflection.

Objective-C also has reference counting which is similar to Java. Each object keeps the count of pointers that lead to it. If the count drops to 0, it means nobody refers to it, and it can be discarded or reused. Compared to Java where this counting is completely transparent and is an integral part of a complex memory management scheme, Objective-C permits custom allocation and a manual control of this count. If you wonder where objects keep this count, it is part of the memory used by the allocator, outside of the object, just before the address where the object starts—see Fig. 6.2.

For more on the garbage collection in Java which was introduced to simplify programming, and now "*its tuning is a long exercise which requires lot of profiling and patience to get it right*"; see Javin (2011).

The Automatic Reference Counting (ARC) was introduced to Objective-C in 2001. It does static code analysis, and automatically inserts retains and releases for objects created by the code.

> Note that Objective-C ARC does not provide a cycle collector; users must explicitly manage the lifetime of their objects, breaking cycles manually or with weak or unsafe references.

ARC may be explicitly enabled with the compiler flag `-fobjc-arc`, or disabled with the compiler flag `-fno-objc-arc`.

The key issue when designing persistence for Objective-C is how to use introspection (reflection) to detect pointers, and then convert this information into the pointer mask. Listing 5.4 shows the trick.

The mask is one of the pieces of information about the class that we keep in structure *persist_params*. *CreateMask* creates one instance of the class and calls *assignIvarValue* with 1. This 1 is the value we want to use to mark the pointers in the mask. Call to *class_copyIvarList* returns an array with one entry for each variable[16] of the class. With it, we get *encoded Type*, and its first character tells us whether it is or isn't a pointer. If it is a pointer we set its value to 1, if not then under default we set it to 0.

This loop does not affect the value of the hidden pointer which is already there. It is not considered to be a variable.

---

[16] *variable* is Objective-C lingo for C++ *member*

Listing 5.4 Automatic generation of the pointer mask through reflection

```
// Copyright (c) 2013 Raj Lokanath. All rights reserved.
// Modified by Jiri Soukup, 2013

@implementation Util
+ (void) createMask: (Class) klass params: (persist_params*) data {
    data->mask = [[klass alloc] init];
    [self assignIvarValue:1 inObject:data->mask];
}

+ (void) assignIvarValue: (int) value inObject: (id)object {
    unsigned int ivarCount = 0; int ivarIndex;
    Class cls = [object class];
    Ivar *allIvars = class_copyIvarList(cls,&ivarCount);
    for (ivarIndex = 0; ivarIndex < ivarCount; ivarIndex++) {
        Ivar ivar = allIvars[ivarIndex];
        const char *encodedType = ivar_getTypeEncoding(ivar);
        // NSLog(@"%s type %s",ivar_getName(ivar),encodedType);
        switch (encodedType[0]) {
            case '@':// reference of object
            case '*':// pointer to native type
            case '^'://pointer to type
                object_setIvar(object, ivar, (void*)value);
                break;

            default:
                object_setIvar(object, ivar, 0);
                break;
        }
    }
    free(allIvars);
}
@end
```

Note that the code in Listing 5.4 does not detect pointers which are inside struct instances. In the following sample, pointers *name* and *item* will not show in the mask for class Produce. This is something that is feasible to do; it just needs more code.

On the other hand, since ARC does not allow object references (pointers) inside struct, it is questionable whether the persistence should support it.

```
typedef struct bunch {
    int cost;
    char *name;
    (id) item;
} Bunch;

@interface Produce
{
    float weight;
    Bunch myBunch;
}
@end
```

The other thing missing in Listing 5.4 is that it records only pointers at the level of the given class—and no pointers of its superior classes. If we need all the pointers, we have to go through the entire inheritance hierarchy—see the recursive implementation in Listings 5.5 and 5.6.

Listing 5.5 shows the C++ implementation, in which each application has method *createMask* which creates the mask but only at the level of this class. The code is taking advantage of the default constructor automatically invoking all superior default constructors. The Util class holds flag allocControl which is essentially a nicer form of a global variable. If this flag is 0, default constructors perform normal allocation. When it is 1, *createMask* is invoked.

Listing 5.6 shows the Objective-C implementation,[17] in which not only the mask generation but also the recursion is extracted to a common C-style function (you could use the word "generic") *createMaskGeneric()*. The main concept is the use of the superior class[18] from which this class inherits.

Note the different order in which the inheritance levels are traversed. The order makes no difference when constructing a mask.

Listing 5.5 output	Listing 5.6 output
Before creating the mask	Create mask for C
Create mask for A	Create mask for B
Create mask for B	Create mask for A
Create mask for C	
Create mask for D	

---

[17] In Objective-C, method init is used as a constructor, but init does not automatically traverse the inheritance hierarchy. Even if we wanted to use the C++ approach, we cannot use it. It would not work.

[18] Keyword or class method *super*.

Listing 5.5 Recursive mask generation, C++ style

```
class Util {
public:
     static int allocControl;
};
int Util::allocControl=0; // 0=normal allocation, 1=mask generation

class A {
     static void createMask(){ printf("create mask for A\n"); }
public:
     A(){if(Util::allocControl) createMask(); /* …other code… */}
};

class B : public A {
     static void createMask(){ printf("create mask for B\n"); }
public:
     B(){if(Util::allocControl) createMask(); /* …other code… */}
};

class C {
     static void createMask(){ printf("create mask for C\n"); }
public:
     C(){if(Util::allocControl) createMask(); /* …other code… */}
};

class D : public B, public C {
     static void createMask(){ printf("create mask for D\n"); }
public:
     D(){if(Util::allocControl) createMask(); /* …other code… */}
};

int main() {
     D *d=new D;
     printf("before creating the mask\n");
     Util::allocControl=1;
     d=new D;
     return 0;
}
```

Listing 5.6 Recursive mask generation, Objective-C style

```
void createMaskGeneric(Class cls){
    printf("create mask for %s\n", class_getName(cls)); // see 19
    Class superClass = class_getSuperclass(cls);
    if([superClass isEqual: [NSObject class]]) return;
    createMaskGeneric(superClass);
}

@interface A : NSObject
    + (void) createMask;
@end
@implementation A
    + (void) createMask{ createMaskGeneric(self); }
@end

@interface B : A
    + (void) createMask;
@end
@implementation B
    + (void) createMask{ createMaskGeneric(self); }20
@end

@interface C : B
    + (void) createMask;
@end
@implementation C
    + (void) createMask{ createMaskGeneric(self); }
@end

int main() {
    [C createMask];
    return 0;
}
```

5.6   Errors and Debugging

In a more sophisticated language, the errors will also be more sophisticated, and some of them will show up at the run time instead of the compile time. That means more difficult debugging, and safety issues with software which simply must not fail (space shuttle, computer driven surgery, control of nuclear reactor).

A typical example is what happened to us when we began to test QSP persistence on the benchmark example from Chap. 7. The program crashed in the middle of the run with memory fault on a line which looked quite normal and was coded by all the rules. Only after several days (!) we realized that we did not include <objc/runtime.h> at the

---

[19] If this line is placed at the end of the function, the order in which the sub-masks are created would be the same as in the C++ version.

[20] Instead of doing this, Objective-C allows one to inject this method at runtime through reflection, without any need to modify the application class.

top of one source file.[21] Compiler in C++ or Java would catch the problem, and we could corrected it within seconds, but Objective-C did not complain about it because there, with its relaxed rules, there was some (remote) possibility of using the particular function even without objc/runtime.h.

Another thing to watch for is that Objective-C classes cannot have an equivalent of C++ static class member—a value associated with the class, not with any object. Variable *data->mask* which we use all through this Chap. 5, is a member of static struct *persist_params* with the scope of the given *.m file. Program using such variables must strictly maintain a separate *.m file for each class.

The Apple variety of Objective-C[22] supports <u>associated object</u>, which is another alternative to this type of object, but it must be created dynamically, unlike the static member in C++.

---

[21] When a method is not declared or imported, Objective-C assumes a return type id, and that was likely the cause of the crash in this case.

[22] The Windows/gcc variety of Objective-C does not support it yet.

Automatic Persistence for Objective-C

6

Jiri Soukup, Raj Lokanath, and Martin Soukup

Abstract

This chapter describes the implementation details of the QSP persistence. It starts with a single page from which all the objects are allocated. When more space is needed, additional pages are automatically allocated. When storing data to disk, all data are collapsed into a single page, and the unused objects are eliminated. During each program run a temporary management of free objects is used.

Keywords

QSP • Quasi Single Page • Objective-C • Persistence • NS Foundation class • Reflection • Memory management • Paging • Allocation • Reference count • Retain count

J. Soukup (✉)
Code Farms Inc., Richmond, ON, Canada
e-mail: jiri@codefarms.com

R. Lokanath
Tata Consultancy Services, Santa Clara, CA, USA

M. Soukup
Irdeto Canada corp., Ottawa, Canada
e-mail: the.martin.soukup@gmail.com

J. Soukup and P. Macháček, *Serialization and Persistent Objects*,
DOI 10.1007/978-3-642-39323-5_6, © Springer-Verlag Berlin Heidelberg 2014

The QSP persistence was implemented in two phases:

1. Using Objective-C syntax but C++ design style, where all classes must be derived from the same PersistObject class with all pointers registered through the PTR() statements.
2. Taking the advantage of the Objective-C features and reflection, the two restrictions are removed, arriving to a remarkably automatic and efficient persistent system.

We will start with a practical instruction how to use QSP persistence. The next part will provide technical notes on implementation details, focusing on the more tricky parts of the Objective-C implementation. The last part will discuss how to make existing class libraries persistent, with emphasis on the NextStep (NS) Foundation classes.

All code samples in this chapter are in Objective-C. If you are not used to this language, the basic information about it is in Sect. 5.4. If you are interested only in the main idea or the algorithms, read Sect. 2.5 again.

Note that the two phases differ only in the initial setup and how the information about references is recovered, and thus there is no difference in their runtime performance. The persistent algorithms are identical.

For the record, the benchmark tests on Apple/Mac reported in Chap. 7 used the Phase 1 version of QSP.

6.1   Practical Guide to QSP Persistence

The **implementation** of both phases is light and simple. You don't have to install anything – you only download two files *Persist.h* and *Persist.m* then compile and link with them. They are small, 100 and 800 lines of code[1] (5 kB and 45 kB). QSP was tested on the Chap. 7 benchmark with more than a million objects and six intrusive associations, but it is still only a prototype that has not been used on real-life projects and should be used with caution.

The source of the Phase 1 implementation of the benchmark from Chap. 7, including files *Persist.h* and *Persist.m,* is in bk/chap6/bench. It uses the InCode library where only the classes required for the benchmark are converted to Objective-C; see bk/chap6/objcLib.

This library includes a code generator (*codegen*), which works both for C++ and for Objective-C. For Objective-C, use

    codegen -objc ...

The templates of individual data structures are in bk/chap6/objcLib/oclib.

---

[1] These counts exclude blank lines and comments.

Files *.h and *.m are templates for the converted classes, files*.h and *.cpp are still the original, uncoverted C++ data structures.

6.1.1 QSP Phase 1

In Phase 1, QSP persistence was implemented in Objective-C but using what we could call the "C++ coding style", which assumes that references embedded in all classes are registered with PTR() statements. This is the technique described in Sect. 2.1.3.2.

All application classes must be derived from class PersistObject, which is derived from NSObject.[2] That class has no members, so it does not increase the size of the application classes.

```
@interface Book : PersistObject
{
    int salary;
    Book * next;
    char *name;
}
   Persist Interface;
@end

@implementation Book
   Persist Implementation:
   Book_ptrList
   -(id) ptrList(){ PTR(next); PTR(name); return self;}
@end
```

When using InCode library, its code generator prepares the prtList line for you, so instead of

```
   -(id) ptrList(){ PTR(next); PTR(name); return self;}
```

you code

```
            ptrList_Book
```

Note that the format of the additions required to make a class persistent is simpler in Objective-C than it is in C++. *Persist Interface* and *Persist Implementation* are not parameterized by the name of the class; the PTR() statement is used for all pointer types—for pointers to objects, pointers to strings and pointers to arrays (now shown in this example). The persistence is transparent and easy to use. All you have to do is to call

```
[Persist save: myFile root: myRoot]; // to save data in myFile
root = [Persist open: myFile];   // to load data back to memory
```

---

[2] This requirement is specific for Objective-C; it would not be required in the C++ implementation.

In this manner you can register even pointers embedded in a struct, for example,

```
strict info {
    char *name; // see3
    int phone;
};
@interface Student
    Student *next;
    struct Info info;
@end
@implementation Student
- (id) ptrList {
    PTR(next);
    PTR(info.name);
    return self;
}
@end
```

Allocation. Single objects of classes coded in this style are allocated as usual, for example,

```
Book *bk = [[Book alloc] init];
```

Blocks of data without embedded pointers, text, numbers or arrays of number must be allocated with [Persist palloc]

```
size_t sizeInBytes = 50;
char *name = [Persist palloc: sizeInBytes];
```

Array of pointers must be allocated with [Persist allocPtrArr]

```
size_t NumOfPointers = 50;
char *name = [Persist allocPtrArr: numOfPointers];
```

You can even allocate an array of objects from the heap,[4] using allocArray for the appropriate class

```
size_t numOfObjects = 50;
char *name = [Persist allocArray: numOfObjects];
```

6.1.2 QSP Phase 2

In Phase 2, application classes do not have to be derived from the same class, and the registration of pointers is not required. However, in the current implementation of Phase 2, a line with an empty *prtList* is required:

---

[3] This should be avoided because ARC does not work with struct that hides a pointer.

[4] This is an addition to the standard Objective-C, which has no mechanism for this. The established way of doing this is to use class NSArray.

```
@interface Book : NSObject
{
    int salary;
    Book * next;
    char *name;
}
Persist Interface;
@end

@implementation Book
    Persist Implementation:
    -(id) ptrList { return self; }
@end
```

This is a truly automatic and persistent system, which requires to add only one, always the same line to the *.h file, and another, again always the same line to the *.m file. The use is the same as for Phase 1:

```
[Persist save: myFile root: myRoot]; // to save data in myFile
root = [Persist open: myFile];   // to load data back to memory
```

Allocation. Allocation is identical to Phase 1, using methods alloc, palloc, allocPtrArr, and allocArray.

The advantage of keeping *ptrList* even if we normally don't need it is that we can manually supplement pointers which the automatic detection would miss, for example pointers embedded through a struct.[5] For example,

```
struct BookInfo {
    int pageCount;
    Font *font;
};

PersistInterface;
    BookInfo bkInfo;
    Author *author;
    Book *nextBook;
@end

@implementation Book
    PersistImplementation;
    -(id) prtList{ PTR(bkInfo.font); return self; }
@end
```

---

[5] The line with *prtList* may be eventually removed, assuming the automatic pointer detection proves reliable and covering all possible situations.

6.2   Technical Notes on Objective-C Implementation

The implementation of QSP allocation and persistence follows the algorithms from Sect. 2.5. It is essentially a C-code disguised as class methods of the *Persist* class. There isn't anything Objective-C specific, and class *Persist* has only 29 methods, less than a typical class in the NS library. The code is short (under 800 lines, with comments and references to Sect. 2.5).

6.2.1   Notes to Phase 1

6.2.1.1   Creating Pointer Mask from PTR Statements

The implementation follows exactly the algorithms described in Sect. 2.5. We used that Section as the master plan for coding, and the QSP always refers to its individual steps and lines. It would make boring reading to describe this code, which is essentially a C++ code in an Objective-C disguise, and class Persist encapsulating all the persistence logic.

The only exception is the conversion of the PTR() statements into the masks. For each class we have to walk through all its superior classes and merge the corresponding masks—see Fig. 6.1.

In C++, we could do this:

```
#define PTR(P) \
        if(Persist::aFlg == 0) ((size_t)P=0; else (size_t)P=1;

class Employee {
        float salary;
        char *name;
        Employee *next;
public:
        Employee() {PTR(name); PTR(next);}
};
class Manager : public Employee {
        static int mySize;
        int deptID;
        Employee *secretary;
public:
        Manager() {PTR(secretary);}
};
int main() {
        aFlg=1;
        Manager *mask=new Manager;    // mask of for the Manager class
        aFlg=0;
        Manager *aManager=new Manager; // Manager object
```

The default constructor automatically traverses all the ascendants; thus when creating a new Manager with aFlg = 1 (generating a mask, not a normal object), this happens not only for the Manager but also for the Employee from which the Manager is derived.

```
// Employees working for a Manager form a Ring
@interface Employee
    int salary;
    char *name;
    Employee *next; // next on Ring
@end
@interface Manager : Employee
    int deptID;
    Employee *secretary;
    Employee *tail; // tail of the Ring
    int colSZ; // collection size
@end
```

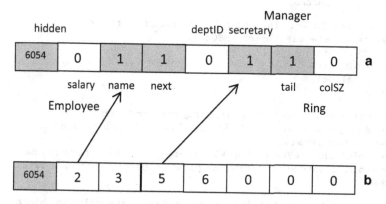

Fig. 6.1 (a) Mask for the Manager class. (b) The list derived from it. Note the hidden pointer in the beginning of the object, and the regular pointers marked by 1. Hidden pointers are always multiples of 4. This figure is a copy of Fig. 2.18 from Sect. 2.5

Objective-C does not support default constructors that would behave like that, but it has a mechanism that allows us to reach the super class, e.g. from class Manager we can get to class Employee—see Fig. 6.1. When using this recursively, we can traverse all the inheritance levels and get the complete mask.

Listing 6.1 shows the recursive function that does it.[6] This listing is long, but you may look only at the critical part—the highlighted method *create Mask*. The rest of the code is needed in case you want to see how it all works together.

This code is also another example of Useful Trick No. 2 from Sect. 2.1.1. Macros *PersistInterface* and *PersistImplementation* inject only a few lines. The *mask* and the main info about the class (struct *persist_params*) are set outside by the methods of *Persist* class.

This listing is far too long for this book, but its core, which is worth reading, is the highlighted method to create Mask.

After all this, we wondered whether there would be a performance penalty for additional function calls that make the macro shorter. We ran the benchmark[7] from

---

[6] For another interesting example, see bk\chap6\testinit.m.

[7] One million books, without abstracts, five runs for each coding style.

Chap. 7 with persistence implemented in long and short macros. With the shorter macro (Useful Trick No. 2), the creation of all objects took about 10 % more time.

Listing 6.1 Generating mask from PTR() statements

```
FILE: Persist.h

// important class info ready for fast access
typedef struct persist_params {
     void* mask;
     u_int mySz;
} persist_params;

// all persistent classes must be derived from this class
@interface PersistObject : NSObject
-(id) ptrList;
+(void) start;
+(id) alloc;
@end

// Utility that controls everything related to persistence.
// What you see here is only its small part, it is a big class.
@interface Persist
+ (void) outsideStart: (id) klass params: (persist_params*) data;
+ (void) create Mask: (id) klass params: (persist_params*) data;
@end

// no need for aFlg, PTR() is never used in constructing an object
#define PTR(P) (P)=(void*)1

// +++++++++++++++++++++++++++++++++++++++++++++++++++++++++++++++
// Useful trick No.2: only two short sections inserted by macros
// +++++++++++++++++++++++++++++++++++++++++++++++++++++++++++++++
#define Persist Interface \
- (id) ptrList; \
+ (void) start; \
+ (id) alloc ;

#define Persist Implementation \
static struct persist_params params= { nil, 0 }; \
+ (void) start{ [Persist outsideStart: self params: &params];}
// +++++++++++++++++++++++++++++++++++++++++++++++++++++++++++++++

FILE: Persist.m

@implementation Persist
+ (void) outsideStart: (id) klass params: (persist_params*) data {
     if(data->mask != NULL) return;
     data->mySz=class_getInstanceSize(klass);
     [Persist create Mask: klass params: data];
     const char *cName=class_getName([klass class]);
     [Persist reportClass: cName sz: data->mySz mask: data->mask];
```

```
+ (void) createMask: (id) klass params: (persist_params*) data {
    void *sMask; Class superClass,*p; int i,sz,sSz; char *m,*s;
    // if the mask exists, this method was already called
    if (data->mask != NULL) return;
    data->mySz=sz=class_getInstanceSize(klass);
    // allocate mask as a true object
    p = (Class*)calloc(sz,1);
    *p = klass;
    data->mask= (void*)p;
    // prtList is a constructor, sets pointers but not for ascendents
    [(id)data->mask ptrList];
    superClass = class_getSuperclass([klass class]);
    if (superClass != nil &&
                        ![superClass isEqual:[PersistObject class]])
    {
        // recursive call to the next base class
        [superClass start];
        /* merge the two masks */
        sMask=[superClass getMask];
        sSz=class_getInstanceSize(superClass);
        s=(char*)sMask;
        m=(char*)data->mask;
        for(i=sizeof(char*); i<sSz; i++) {m[i]=m[i] | s[i];}
    }
}
...
@end
```

```
// FILE B.h - application class
// ++++++++++++++++++++++++++++++++
@interface B : PersistObject
{
    NSString *p1;
    NSString *p2;
    B *ptr;
    int val1;
    int val2;
}
PersistInterface;
@end
```

```
// FILE B.m - application class
// ++++++++++++++++++++++++++++++++
@implementation B
Persist Implementation;
- (id) ptrList { PTR(p1); PTR(p2); PTR(ptr);}
@end
```

Note that in the C++ implementation of the same algorithm (Sect. 2.1.3.2, Listing 2.5), the user had to supply more information about the pointers. We did not use PTR for all pointers. We had PTR for pointers to single objects, STR for strings, ARR for arrays of objects and ARP for arrays of pointers. In these statements we also had to supply the type of pointer, for example PTR(Employee, secretary), not just PTR(secretary).

allocation of one object in 4-byte sections:

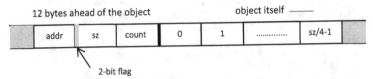

Fig. 6.2 QSP allocation: the lowest two bits (the size of objects is always a multiple of 4) of the sz field are used as a type flag: 0 = object with no pointers, 1 = object/array of objects with a hidden pointer, 2 = array of pointers. Field addr is a temporary space for internal algorithms, and count is reserved for the Objective-C reference counting. Pointers in the unused section of any array must be set to nil. This figure is a section of Fig. 2.19

In Objective-C we do not have to supply the type. By dereferencing the pointer we get to the target object which, as every object in Objective-C, can tell us its own type. Also, as we allocate objects[8] we store the information whether it is an object, string or array in a two-bit flag in the space preceding the object—see Fig. 6.2.

6.2.1.2   Allocating Objects from Pages of Memory

Serialization and persistence based on memory paging are generally considered as two completely different approaches to storing objects, yet combining them brings mutual benefits:

- Memory pages are faster to store and restore, but serialization allows data transfer between different operating systems or environments. They complement each other in different situations.
- It is easier to implement schema migration for serialization than it is for memory pages.
- If you allocate from pages of memory and then save with serialization, the algorithm of collecting active objects is much simpler: you can walk through the memory[9] and collect objects that way rather than using recursive functions, searches and other complex algorithms. The result is a faster serialization.
- Saving objects by serialization automatically removes all dead space and re-formats the pages, thus helping the memory management which otherwise is a problem.

QSP is primarily a page-based system, but we added to it a function which walks through the memory, collects all active objects, and allows one to save them using the standard formats of Objective-C Archiving, including XML.

Listing 6.2 shows the basic idea of how to reserve a larger page and then allocate individual objects from it. A running version of this code is in bk.chap6/testallo.c.

Note that a system like this takes over the memory management, bypassing the retain counting and managing free objects fully automatically. Nevertheless, we reserve the field required for Objective-C for retaining counting—if we used the field for something else, some unexpected interaction could overwrite that field and damage our records.

---

[8] This is our allocation scheme, not a part of standard Objective-C.

[9] As QSP does.

The highlighted section allocates an instance of class A. The class (here A) is never explicitly mentioned in this method; if you copy this code into another class it will work without any modifications. The key trick in it is the line

```
*p = self;
```

which copies self into the beginning of the object or, in other words, it is setting the hidden pointer and thus turning the section of the memory into a valid object.

Listing 6.2 Basic idea of allocating objects from a private page of memory. Real systems use multiple pages

```
@interface Persist : NSObject
+ (char *) palloc: (int) sz;
+ (void) start: (int) pgSz;
@end

@implementation Persist
static char *page = (char*)nil;
static int pgSz = 0;
static char *pool = (char*)nil; // next free address
+ (char *) palloc: (int) sz {
    printf("start: pgSz=%d page=%u pool=%u\n",pgSz,page,pool);
    pool=pool+sz;
    return (pool-sz);
}
// start allocation, set up pageSz
+ (void) start: (int) pageSz {
    pool=page=calloc(1,pageSz);
    pgSz=pageSz;
}
@end

// Example of the application class
@interface A : NSObject {
    int val;
}
+ (id) alloc; // replacing system allocation
- (id) init; // constructor
@end

@implementation A
- (id) init { val=0;}
+ (id) alloc {
    int sz=class_getInstanceSize(self);
    Class *p = (Class *)[Util palloc: sz];
    *p = self; // replace the beginning of the object <<<<<<<
    return (id)p;
}
@end

int main()
{
    [Persist start: 1024];   // start with page size =1024
    A *ap = [[A alloc] init]; // allocate a new object
    return 0;
}
```

6.2.1.3 Main Part of the QSP Algorithm

The key to quick and safe debugging is a function which prints memory pages and the images of individual objects in a human-readable format. Figure 6.3 shows such a printout for the benchmark problem from Chap. 7, with relations from Fig. 7.1 and reduced to a small number of objects (five books and one author). The classes are *Library, Author, Book* and a "link" class *BooksToAuthors* which is needed for the *ManyToMany* relation between *Book* and *Author*.

The printout shows everything you may possibly want to know about allocation, object types, pointers and how the objects connect.

Each object mask starts with the hidden pointer, which is a unique class signature. The printout then shows the memory space as in Fig. 2.19, page by page, and within each page object by object.

The image of each object is

```
+ (0)aux (0)[flg]sz (0)count [addr] = (0)hidPtr (1)regPtr (0)number
```
where
aux is the auxiliary address,
flg = 0 no pointers, 1 = embedded ptrs, 2 = pointer array
sz is the size of the allocated area without header (2 bits used for *flg*)
count is the retain count (not used),
addr is the starting address of the object
hidPtr is the hidden pointer
regPtr is a regular pointer
number is numerical value or text, no pointers

If you analyze the first object, [1]12 tells you that it has embedded pointers, and its size is 12 bytes. It starts at address 6565700 and it is an instance of Library.

The first pointer leads to address 6566148 which, judging by the hidden pointer 4249696, is a Book. The second pointer leads to address 6565724 which, judging by the hidden pointer 4250528, is an Author.

This Author (the second object) is 20 bytes, and its fourth field 6565756 points to the third object, with [0] which means no pointers, 12 bytes long. It is probably one of the strings, most likely author's name.

If you compare the difference between *fill* and *page* with *pageSz* you will see that most pages are almost full, except for the last page,

Note that when you add *PersistInterface* to some class, say X, it automatically adds two allocation methods:
[X alloc] allocates a single object of this class,
[X allocArr] allocates an array of objects of this class.

Arrays of pointers and unstructured blocks of memory including text must also be allocated through class Persist:
[Persist palloc] allocates a block of memory without embedded pointers,
[Persist allocPtrArr] allocates an array of pointers.

Internally, all these methods just call *palloc* but then set the 2-bit flag differently.

```
DEBUGGING PRINT: Alg.b finished
=========================================
format:  (mask bit) [flag] value_or_size
flg=0 unstructured, =1 obj with ptrs, =2 array of ptrs

root=6565700
class records:
i=0 class=BooksToAuthors sz=28 mask=4251360 1 1 1 1 1 1
i=1 class=Author sz=20 mask=4250528 1 1 1 1
i=2 class=Book sz=28 mask=4249696 1 1 1 1 0
i=3 class=Library sz=12 mask=4248896 1 1

pgSz=128 pgArrSz=50 objCount=18

Page[0] page=6565688 fill=6565808 pageSz=128
 +(0)7357532 (0)[1]12 (0)0   [6565700]=(0)4248896 (1)6566148 (1)6565724
 +(0)7357556 (0)[1]20 (0)0   [6565724]=(0)4250528 (1)6565724 (1)6565724
(1)6565756 (1)6566380
 +(0)7357588 (0)[0]12 (0)0   [6565756]=(0)1629503824 (0)1869116533
(0)3219570
 +(0)7357612 (0)[1]28 (0)0   [6565780]=(0)4249696 (1)6566284 (1)6565900
(1)6565836 (1)0 (1)6565860 (0)26502

Page[1] page=6565824 fill=6565952 pageSz=128
 +(0)7357652 (0)[0]12 (0)0   [6565836]=(0)1646282575 (0)543911791 (0)49
 +(0)7357676 (0)[1]28 (0)0   [6565860]=(0)4251360 (1)6565860 (1)6565860
(1)6565780 (1)6565972 (1)6566380 (1)6565724
 +(0)7357716 (0)[1]28 (0)0   [6565900]=(0)4249696 (1)6565780 (1)6566148
(1)6565940 (1)0 (1)6565972 (0)30090
 +(0)7357756 (0)[0]12 (0)0   [6565940]=(0)1646284615 (0)543911791 (0)50

Page[2] page=6565960 fill=6566064 pageSz=128
 +(0)7357780 (0)[1]28 (0)0   [6565972]=(0)4251360 (1)6565972 (1)6565972
(1)6565900 (1)6566108 (1)6565860 (1)6565724
 +(0)7357820 (0)[1]28 (0)0   [6566012]=(0)4249696 (1)6566148 (1)6566284
(1)6566052 (1)0 (1)6566108 (0)15706
 +(0)7357860 (0)[0]12 (0)0   [6566052]=(0)1646287448 (0)543911791 (0)51

Page[3] page=6566096 fill=6566200 pageSz=128
 +(0)7357884 (0)[1]28 (0)0   [6566108]=(0)4251360 (1)6566108 (1)6566108
(1)6566012 (1)6566244 (1)6565972 (1)6565724
 +(0)7357924 (0)[1]28 (0)0   [6566148]=(0)4249696 (1)6565900 (1)6566012
(1)6566188 (1)0 (1)6566244 (0)3722
 +(0)7357964 (0)[0]12 (0)0   [6566188]=(0)1646282568 (0)543911791 (0)52

Page[4] page=6566232 fill=6566336 pageSz=128
 +(0)7357988 (0)[1]28 (0)0   [6566244]=(0)4251360 (1)6566244 (1)6566244
(1)6566148 (1)6566380 (1)6566108 (1)6565724
 +(0)7358028 (0)[1]28 (0)0   [6566284]=(0)4249696 (1)6566012 (1)6565780
(1)6566324 (1)0 (1)6566380 (0)18741
 +(0)7358068 (0)[0]12 (0)0   [6566324]=(0)1646286155 (0)543911791 (0)53

Page[5] page=6566368 fill=6566408 pageSz=128
 +(0)7358092 (0)[1]28 (0)0   [6566380]=(0)4251360 (1)6566380 (1)6566380
(1)6566284 (1)6565860 (1)6566244 (1)6565724
```

Fig. 6.3 Debugging print shows the pages and the images of individual objects

6.2.2 Notes to Phase 2

6.2.2.1 Creating Pointer Mask with Reflection

Would it be possible to detect pointers without using PTR() statements? If we could do that, the interface would be much simpler. We would have to use some features of Objective-C which are not available in C++, because we know that in C++ we had to use these statements.

Listing 6.3 shows how Objective-C reflection allows us to create array *alliVars* with information about individual variables (members) of the class. The loop traverses these variables and uses the first character of *encodedType* to decide whether it is a pointer and what kind of pointer it is. Object *object* here is the mask, and we set its pointers to 1. The remaining variables (members) are set to 0.

Listing 6.3 Object mask by an automated detection of pointers[10]

```
@implementation Persist
+ (void) createOneMask: (Class) klass params: (persist_params*) data
{
        data->mask = [[klass alloc] init];
        [self assignIvarValue: 1 inObject:data->mask];
}

+ (void) assignIvarValue: (int) value inObject: (id) object {
        unsigned int ivarCount = 0; int ivarIndex;
        Class cls = [object class];
        Ivar *alliVars = class_copyIvarList(cls, &ivarCount);
        for (ivarIndex = 0; ivarIndex < ivarCount; ivarIndex++) {
            Ivar ivar = alliVars[ivarIndex];
            const char *encodedType = ivar_getTypeEncoding(ivar);
            switch (encodedType[0]) {
                case '@' : // reference to object
                case '*' : // pointer to native type
                case '^' : //pointer to type
                    object_setIvar(object, ivar, (void*)value);
                    break;

                default:
                    object_setIvar(object, ivar, 0); // <<<<<<
                    break;
            }
        }
        free(alliVars);
}
@end
```

This code works, but it has two limitations:

1. It gets pointers only at the inheritance level of the given class.
2. It does not get pointers that are embedded in a struct.

Problem (1) is easy to correct. In method *create Mask*, we replace the following call to *ptrLinks* which generates the mask with PTR statements

---

[10] For a running example see directory bk\chap6\autoPtrs

```
                         [(id)data->mask ptrLinks];
```

by call to a new method

```
        [self assignIvarValue:1 inObject:(id)data->mask];
```

see the first highlighted section in Listing 6.4.

Listing 6.4 Generating the pointer mask automatically

```
@implementation Persist
+ (void) createMask: (id) klass params: (persist_params*) data {
    void *sMask; Class superClass,*p; int i,sz,sSz; char *m,*s;
    // if the mask exists, this method was already called
    if(data->mask != NULL) return;
    data->mySz=sz=class_getInstanceSize(klass);
    // allocate mask as a true object
    p = (Class*)calloc(sz,1);
    *p = klass;
    data->mask= (void*)p;

    // [(id)data->mask ptrList];
    [self assignIvarValue:1 inObject:(id)data->mask];

    superClass = class_getSuperclass([klass class]);
    if(superClass != nil &&
                       ! [superClass isEqual:[PersistObject class]])
    {
        // recursive call to the next base class
        [superClass start];
        /* merge the two masks */
        sMask=[superClass getMask];
        sSz=class_getInstanceSize(superClass);
        s=(char*)sMask;
        m=(char*)data->mask;
        for(i=sizeof(char*); i<sSz; i++) {m[i]=m[i] | s[i];}
    }
}
```

We know the solution to **Problem (2)**, but we may not have the code before the book goes to print. The workaround, and actually a good solution, is not to comment out the call to ptrList in Listing 6.4, but to leave both the highlighted lines active and comment out line marked // <<<<<< in Listing 6.3. That way, not only can the mask be created by either method, but prtList may add[11] pointers that automatic detection would miss, such as pointers embedded in a struct.

Useful Trick No. 8.
Creation of the pointer mask has no effect on the overall performance, and doing it twice—first automatically and then with PTR() statements—opens possibilities for handling unusual cases such as pointer members embedded in a struct.

---

[11] With this arrangement, ptrList may provide only some pointers, or no pointers if no struct is used.

6.2.2.2 Removing Dependency on PersistObject

The requirement of deriving every class from a new base class is a major obstacle when converting existing library classes. However, the only reason why we introduced PersistObject in Phase 1 was that, when we compiled without it, we got a screen full of warnings related to NSObject not having method *start*. However the second highlighted place in Listing 6.5 prevents calling this method on NSObject. If we can live with these warnings, then we can go back to NSObject as shown in Listing 6.5, and the benchmark works flawlessly.

Listing 6.5 Critical section of Listing 6.1 where PersistObject was replaced by NSObject

```
@implementation Persist
+ (void) createMask: (id) klass params: (persist_params*) data {
    void *sMask; Class superClass,*p; int i,sz,sSz; char *m,*s;
    // if the mask exists, this method was already called
    if(data->mask != NULL) return;
    data->mySz=sz=class_getInstanceSize(klass);
    // allocate mask as a true object
    p = (Class*)calloc(sz,1);
    *p = klass;
    data->mask= (void*)p;

    // [(id)data->mask ptrList];
    [self assignIvarValue:1 inObject:(id)data->mask];

    superClass = class_getSuperclass([klass class]);

    if(superClass != nil
            //&& ! [superClass isEqual:[PersistObject class]])
            && ! [superClass isEqual:[NSObjectt class]])
    {
        // recursive call to the next base class
        [superClass start];
        /* merge the two masks */
        sMask=[superClass getMask];
        sSz=class_getInstanceSize(superClass);
        s=(char*)sMask;
        m=(char*)data->mask;
        for(i=sizeof(char*); i<sSz; i++) {m[i]=m[i] | s[i];}
    }
}

...
@end
// FILE B.h - application class
// ++++++++++++++++++++++++++++++++
// @interface B : PersistObject
@interface B : NSObject
{
    NSString *p1;
    NSString *p2;
    B *ptr;
    int val1;
    int val2;
}
```

Fig. 6.4 Shot of the iPhone screen shows the interface

6.3 Testing QSP on iPhone

We first tested the QSP version of the benchmark program on Mac, with the results and technical details reported in Chap. 7, Table 7.6. Then, because iPhone Apps cannot write directly to disk, we converted all the file I/O code to read/write from the documents folder, and added a user interface that allows to input the test parameters – see the screenshot of iPhone 5 in Fig. 6.4. This interface allowed us to set number of Books and the run number.

You can download the source of this App from www.codefarms.com/book.

6.4 Converting Existing Libraries

6.4.1 Libraries Available in Source

Assuming that library classes are derived from NSObject and their full source is available, such classes are just as easy to make persistent as application classes[12] using the following steps. For each newClass we do this:

STEP 1: Modify newClass.h by adding *PersistInterface*.
STEP 2: Modify newClass.m by adding *PersistImplementation*.

---

[12] See Sect. 6.1.

STEP 3: Add prtList which is normally empty; only in special[13] situations not covered by the automatic handling must you provide PTR() statements.

STEP 4: Search methods in newClass.m for any calls that allocate arrays or unstructured memory, and replace them with *allocArr, allocPtrArr* or *palloc*.[14] (Allocations of single objects with new() require no changes.)

This was the way we converted the InCode classes required for the benchmark. The conversion was simple and straightforward because we had access to its source.

6.4.2 Difficulties with NS Classes

The NS classes are an essential part of Objective-C, and unless we can convert them, our QSP persistence will not be very popular. The problem is that the full source of NS classes is not public. That means not only no access to important classes such as NSString.m, but also that NSString.h which you include with Foundation.h may not be the same NSString.h which is used when compiling the system library. This is something Objective-C specific. For example, a String class in C++ stores a pointer to the actual string, and you can see that pointer if you look at String.h. If you look at NSString.h, there are no variables (or members in C++ lingo).

Before we dig into the complexities of the NSString class, let's explore its behaviour by experimenting. Perhaps that could help us to guess what is under the hood.

After allocating two NSString objects with some strings, we got the memory layout shown in Fig. 6.5. NSString objects are true objects complete with their hidden pointers, but the allocator left no space for the retain counter! The same happened to strings themselves, which are allocated on a 2-byte boundary!

This raises many questions. Is NS library allocating and reusing NSString objects and strings in a different way than other objects? Where does NSString store the information whether the string is Unicode or ordinary ASCII? Can it store strings that are not ending with \0? What is the minimum length of a string?

Some of the answers are on the Stackoverflow website.[15] NSString is one of the cluster classes,[16] and its conversion will not be trivial.

The Apple source of the NSString class is not public, but the GNU version of the class is an open source, and we retrieved NSString.h and NSString.m from there. The source is under bk/chap6.

---

[13] At the moment we believe that pointers embedded in a struct are the only situation not covered.

[14] It does not matter where the call is, it only matters what it allocates.

[15] http://stackoverflow.com/questions/7376261/are-nsstrings-stored-on-the-heap-or-on-the-stack-and-what-is-a-good-way-to-initi

[16] http://developer.apple.com/library/ios/#documentation/general/conceptual/CocoaEncyclopedia/ClassClusters/ClassClusters.html

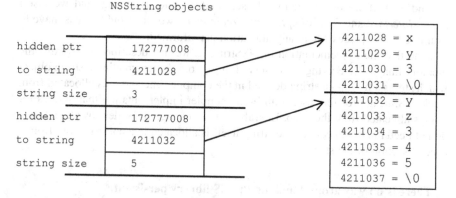

Fig. 6.5 Example of the layout for two NSString objects. Note contiguous strips of memory, one for NSStrings and one for the strings "xyz" and "yz345". Strings always start on <u>even</u> address

Only when you look at this code do you understand the complexity and size of these classes. NSString.h has 885 lines of code and comments, with over 300 methods and no variables (no members)!

NSString is an intelligent class which can handle any text including non-European alphabets, but compare it with the Name class in InCode library where Name.h has 33 lines of code, with 7 methods and 1 pointer member as you would expect. It is not as intelligent as NSString, but it allows one to work comfortably with C-like strings, and its methods are easy to remember and use. It is also easy to make it persistent.

As a cluster class, NSString may hide additional classes – and it probably does hide them – that are invisible to the application programmer but share the NSString interface. It works like this:

```
@interface NSString : NSObject
    ...
+ (id) stringWithCharacters: (const unichar*)characters
                   length: (NSUInteger)length;
+ (id) stringWithCString: (const char*)byteString
                 length: (NSUInteger)length;
+ (id) stringWithCString: (const char*)byteString;
+ (id) stringWithFormat: (NSString*)format,...;
+ (id) stringWithContentsOfFile: (NSString*)path;
@end
@interface GSMutableString : NSString
{   ???   } // unknown pointers of integers
@end
```

where each of these methods creates an object of some hidden class, possibly of a different class for each method. In this case all the methods create an object of GSMutableString. So in order to make NSString persistent, we have to make GSMutableString and possibly other classes persistent. And these classes are likely to be at least as large and complex as NSString.

And even if we detect all the classes hidden under NSString, and we insert *PersistInterface* and *PersistImplementation* in them, we still would at least have to examine all the places where any allocation is performed.

Note that the implementation of NSString as we just described it explains the memory image of NSStrings as observed in Fig. 6.5. When creating a string object which stores a literal—a string defined in the compile time and thus allocated from stack, NSString probably uses a different, simpler implementation than it does for strings allocated from the heap. Literals will not change or be destroyed, and they do not need the retain count. The string itself is allocated in a compact way from a special section of the stack.

> **There is no way around making the NS library persistent.**
> It is possible to do it, and the method is simple and clear. However, it will be a tedious job considering the size of these classes, and it should be attempted only by someone thoroughly familiar with the internal design of the library. And that probably is the reason why the full source of this class is not available to public.

6.4.3   Pointer Detection

We do not suggest that a conversion of a library should be performed automatically, but Listing 6.6 is an interesting example of how powerful Objective-C is. It allows us to detect pointers in an object of any class, without adding anything to the class itself, not even the *PersistInterface* and *PersistImplementation* statements.

Look again at how the pointer mask is assembled in Listing 6.4. In the first part of this listing we create the mask for class *klass* and we fill its pointers for this class with the call to *assignIvarValue*. After that we find the super class of klass, superClass, and call

```
[superClass start];
sMask = [superClass getMask];
```

These two calls form the recursion which assembles the mask, but they are also the reason why all classes so far needed the *PersistInterface* and

PersistImplementation statements. We have to code this part in a way which avoids additional methods.

Listing 6.6 A better recursion of creating the mask. First call (msk = NULL) allocates the mask, and returns the finished mask. Subsequent calls just keep recording the pointers[17]

```
+ (void*) createMask: (Class) klass mask: (void*) msk {
    Class superClass, *mask; int sz;
    if (msk == NULL) {
        sz=class_getInstanceSize(klass);
        // allocate mask as a true object
        mask = (Class*)calloc(sz,1);
    }
    else mask=(Class*)msk;

    *mask = klass; // make it the object of this class
    [self assignIvarValue:1 inObject:(id)mask];
    superClass = class_getSuperclass([klass class]);
    if (superClass != nil) {
        // recursive call to the next base class
        [Util createMask:superClass mask:(void*)mask];
    }

    *mask = klass; // reset hidden pointer back to what it was
    return (void*)mask;
}
```

If we have class LibClass to which we don't have the source, and we want to get its pointer mask, we can now do it using the approach from Listing 6.6 (for a full running code see bk/chap6/possible). We derive class PerClass from LibClass

```
@implementation PerClass : LibClass
    PersistInterface;
@end

@implementation PerClass
    PersistImplementation;
@end
```

and then use it like this which makes a persistent LibClass object:

```
int main() {
    LibClass *lib = [PerClass alloc];
    [lib foo];
```

The mask for PerClass is the same as for LibClass, except for the hidden pointer.

---

[17] For a running example, see directory bk/chap6/possible

Unfortunately, this would not help us to detect pointers used in the implementation of the NSString objects. As we explained, there are no pointers in NSString as such. We can do this though:

```
@implementation PRString : NSString
    PersistInterface;
@end

@implementation PRString
    PersistImplementation;
@end
```

and we get an empty mask with just the hidden pointer as we would get for an NSObject. A similar thing happens if we apply the same approach to the NSArray class.

Benchmark

7

Abstract

All authors of persistent systems claim that their systems are super fast. This chapter compares the performance of ten major persistent systems on a benchmark which involves up to one million books and a many-to-many relation between books and their authors. The books can be with or without abstracts. The results are most interesting and intriguing.

Keywords

Performance • Testing • Persistence • Benchmark • Persistent system • Persistent data structures • DOL • Memory blasting • PPF • Boost • PSE Pro • SQLite • Java serialization • C# serialization • QSP • Post++

7.1 History of this Benchmark

We, the authors, met for the first time at the Department of Biochemistry, South Bohemia University, Nové Hrady, Czech Republic, when discussing the architecture of software[1] for processing the output of liquid mass spectrometers.[2] In this project, 2 GB of data must by restructured, stored and analyzed by complex algorithms on standard PC hardware within 3 minutes. The calculation involves removal of random noise and conversion of the raw data into a spectrum of peaks. The work is supported by E.U. and is still in progress at the time of writing.[3]

Each of us comes from an opposite corner of the programming profession. Petr is a young application programmer who is always on lookout for new, better ways of

---

WARNING: Comparing times shown in this chapter without considering features of each system as discussed in the previous chapters may lead to a wrong conclusion about what is the "best" persistent system—if there is such a thing.

[1] Urban et al. (2009, 2012).

[2] http://en.wikipedia.org/wiki/Liquid_chromatography-mass_spectrometry

[3] E.U. grant CENAQUA CZ1.05/2.1.00/01.0024.

J. Soukup and P. Macháček, *Serialization and Persistent Objects*,
DOI 10.1007/978-3-642-39323-5_7, © Springer-Verlag Berlin Heidelberg 2014

223

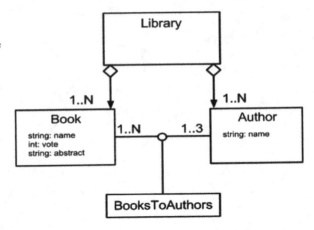

Fig. 7.1 ER diagram of the benchmark. Except for small aesthetic differences, also the UML class diagram

programming and Jiri spent the past 24 years designing tools for a new, more efficient software design, with emphasis on automatic persistence and advanced class libraries.

Later on, when we began to work on this book, we discussed how to compare the performance of the various persistent systems, and we decided that Jiri should not be involved in their evaluation; it would be difficult for him to remain unbiased. All the code, testing, and most of the text in this chapter, was produced by Petr.

Our first benchmark was based on the mass spectrometer project, which used numerous bi-directional associations (one-to-many and many-to-many) that are not supported by any standard library. Except for DOL and PPF, running this benchmark with the existing persistent system required extensive custom modifications— essentially replacing all the bi-directional associations by several containers or pointers. We planned to test about ten typical persistent system, and doing everything ten times was not only beyond our capacity—the testing would depend very much on how we would modify each system.

We eventually decided to strip the benchmark to the bare bones as described in Sect. 7.2 and Fig. 7.1, using class names that would be more familiar to the average reader. We believe that the ManyToMany association should be in the benchmark in order to reflect the complexity of real-life projects, and that blocks of unstructured text (here book abstracts) often occur in practical problems.

We also added a step in which one quarter of the objects is removed. We believe that removal of objects is critical in many applications, and should be part of any benchmark.

The steps which we observed are the same as in our original benchmark. We test the time to build the data organization, traverse and sort them, search, remove data, store them to disk, and then—in a separate run, retrieve them from the disk. We also observe the size of the disk file and check the integrity of the data.

When displaying the results graphically, we ran into the problem of numbers falling into a wide range where linear graphs show clearly which programs are the worst rather than which are the best. In such cases, we use logarithmic scale. When analyzing the results, always watch for what type of scale is used! It may appear that one system is twice as fast as another, but when you interpret the scale correctly you see it is ten times faster.

7.2 Persistent Systems Tested

In alphabetic order:

- Boost C++ library with STL containers or Boost data structures
- C# serialization, as implemented in .NET
- DOL (Data Object Library) library of persistent data structures (Code Farms)
- Java serialization, as implemented in java.io
- Java serialization combined with InCode data structures
- ObjectStore © PSE Pro for C++ combined with InCode data structures
- POST++ (Persistent Object Storage for C++) with STL containers
- PPF (Persistent Pointer Factory) with InCode data structures (Code Farms)
- QSP (Quasi Single Page) persistence for Objective-C[4] combined with InCode
- SQLite database for both persistence and data relations (no data structures used)

In graphs and tables, we abbreviate the names of some technologies, for example P++ stands for POST++, J for Java, B for BOOST or PSE for "PSE Pro"

Since persistent objects are an alternative to using a database, we included SQLite in our testing. It is a relational database which requires one either to match the benchmark data structures to the database format or to forget about object-oriented programming and remain in the realm of relational thinking—essentially to replace all the data structures by the database.[5]

The InCode library includes bi-directional associations, and we used it in environments where the persistent system does not support such associations. Using the same library helps to reduce dependency of the results on the implementation of the data structures.

We find the tables and graphs presented below most interesting. However, when comparing individual technologies, it would be a grave mistake to look just at the speed of the processing or the size of the output files. The performance is important, but sometimes the flexibility to support evolving software or the ability to transfer data between different operating systems may outweigh the performance. For the features of individual products see Tables 7.1 and 7.2.

The value of measuring performance is twofold:

1. It tells us how the different approaches to persistence, rather than the individual products compare to each other: serialization vs. working with memory pages, XML serialization vs. binary serialization or primary data storage in memory vs. on disk.
2. If you choose any particular product because of the features it offers, the performance results tell you what penalty you are going to pay for those features.

Notes
- We also wondered whether there should be a column for integrity checking, but then we decided not to include it. Integrity checking is usually performed by the

---

[4] The prototype described in Sects. 2.5 and 6.5.
[5] This is what we did when testing with SQLite.

Table 7.1 Persistent systems and the features they offer—look for more explanation in the text

	Change or add to class/alloc (a)	Persistence needs code generator (b)	Reuse of free objects (c)	Schema evolution/portable data (d)	Pointers soft/hard (e)	Loads only data actually needed (f)	Trans-actions (g)
DOL (3 modes)	+class	Y	free list OS	Y/Y	hard		
PPF +InCode	+class		free list		soft	Y	
Java +InCode	+class		OS		hard		
POST++	+class		memory manager	limited/N	hard	Y	Y
Java serialization	+class		OS	Y/Y	hard		
C# serialization	+class		OS	Y/Y	hard		
PSE Pro	+alloc	Y	memory manager	Y/N	hard	Y	ACID
Boost	+class		OS	Y/Y	hard		
SQLite	DB		OS	Y/Y	soft	Y	ACID
Objective-C QSP	+class		memory manager		hard		

Table 7.2 Persistent systems and class libraries

	Data structure libraries
DOL (3 modes)	Integrated with an extensive library of intrusive and bi-directional associations
	Other libraries: would have to be re-coded
PPF	Has no special library, works with InCode (only some classes so far)
	Other libraries: replace pointers by the PPF smart pointer
Java serialization	Designed to work with Java Collections
	Other libraries: may be used without conversion
POST++	Integrated with JudyLibrary, STL with serious limitations
	Other libraries: pointers must be registered by a special statement
C# serialization	Designed to work with Java Collections
	Other libraries: may be used without conversion
PSE Pro	Has its own collection classes and a version of STL
	Other libraries: all allocation calls must be converted
Boost	Integrated with the extensive Boost libraries and STL
	Other libraries: user must code serialization methods
SQLite	Does not have data structures, only a limited choice of relations
	Other libraries: cannot be used
Objective-C QSP	Has no special library, works with InCode (only some classes so far)
	Other libraries: register pointers as in POST

data structure library, not by the persistence. Libraries that come with DOL and InCode do provide integrity checking.
- We did not test Objective-C with Archiving because it would take too much work to prepare the benchmark in that style.

Columns in Table 7.1

Column (a) When making a program persistent, most systems require the application to add something to its classes (to make classes persistent). That does not apply to SQLite which is a database. PSE Pro does not require any additions to the classes; instead, all allocation calls within the application code must be modified.

Column (b) Usually when code generator is used it implies a simpler user interface. InCode library always uses a code generator, but that is for data structures, not for the persistence.

Column (c) Serializations usually leave the management of free objects to the operating system. All the systems based on memory paging manage free objects, but we suspect that sophistication and performance differs significantly from one system to another. The benchmark only checks whether the removal of some objects will reduce the disk file which is an indication that some memory management is in place.

Column (d) This column combines two related features: support for schema evolution[6] and the ability to transfer data between different environments, e.g. between Windows and Unix. In DOL, it is the ASCII mode that supports schema evolution. In Java serialization and C# serialization the XML format supports it.

Column (e) Hard pointers are traversed at the same speed as if you don't use persistent objects. Soft pointers perform some arithmetic on each dereference. Note, however, that the benchmark results for PPF later in this chapter are surprisingly good in spite of using soft pointers.

Column (f) When processing certain types of data, for example in reservation systems, we need the ability to work with only a small subset of the data. In other situations such as VLSI CAD systems, all the data is needed in memory.

Column (g) As defined in Chap. 1, the scope of this book does not include multi-user systems. However, in some application, support of transactions is a bonus. ACID stands for *Atomicity, Consistency, Isolation, Durability.*

7.3   Description of the Benchmark

The benchmark includes classes Library, Book, Author and BooksToAuthors; see Fig. 7.1.

---

[6] Sometimes also called *schema migration.*

Class *Book* has three non-structural members[7]:
- **name** is randomly generated title of the book in format "XX book N", where XX are two random ASCII characters and N is a random number.
- **vote** is the number of votes by the readers, random integer.
- **abstract** is a text of random length, max. 512 characters.

Class *Author* has one non-structural member:
- **name** is randomly generated similar name of the author, in format "XX author N".

Class *BooksToAuthors* represents the link in the ManyToMany relation, and it has only structural members.

There are 5-times fewer Authors than Books. A Book can have up to three Authors, an Author can have any number of Books. The Books in the Library are sorted by vote. In real application, Books would likely be stored in a dictionary indexed by the Book's name. Considering the tests we performed, this was not necessary.

As we expected, participants questioned the usefulness of the benchmark and whether it reflects the characteristics of real life projects. The fact that the performance of several products were significantly improved (more than an order of magnitude) as the result of this competition—see Sect. 7.9, we believe, is the ultimate proof of its value.

7.4   Monitored Data

We monitored time needed for individual tasks performed in the benchmark. For each number of books, we repeated the run five-times and recorded minimum, maximum and average values. As can be seen from the graphs, the difference between the runs was insignificant (Sects. 7.4, 7.5, 7.7 and Figs. 7.3 and 7.9).

We tested three sizes of problem:

N = 50,000, 250,000 and 1,000,000 books

all three with/without book abstracts.

We did not perform any monitoring or processing involving abstracts. We only wanted to see their influence on the size of the disk file, and possibly on the times of individual tasks due to increased system paging.

Each tests consisted of two runs:
- The first run executed tasks 1–4.
- The second run executed tasks 5–10.

We tested separately the performance for the data with/without abstracts.

Checksums were used to make sure that the data was stored and retrieved without corruption and in full size.

Hardware used for the testing:
- CPU—AMD Phenom II, X4 965 3.4 GHz (4 cores), 64 bit;
- RAM—KINGSTON DDR3 2000 MHz CL9, 6 GB (3 × 2 GB);

---

[7] Numbers or text, anything but references (or pointers).

Table 7.3 Monitored tasks

No.	Task	Description
1	Create	Time to create the library of N books
2	Sort	Time to sort books by vote[a]
3	Save	Time to save the data to disk
4	FileSize 1	Size of the disk file
5	Open	Time to read the data from disk, swizzle pointers
6	TopVoted	Time needed to find five books with the top votes
7	Traverse	Time to search all books for a substring in their name
8	Delete	Time to remove every fourth book
9	Save 2	Time to save the reduced data
10	FileSize 2	Size of the disk file after the data reduction[b]

[a]Collections in the InCode library are mostly based on intrusive linked lists. Sorting a linked list is a massive and random pointer exercise
[b]Some persistent systems do not reduce the data space

- HDD—MAXTOR DiamondMax 23, SATA II NCQ 7200 rpm 32 MB, 1000 GB;
- OS—Windows 7 Home Premium, 64 bit.

The programs were compiled for ×86 architecture (32 bit). The C++ and C# programs were compiled with VS2010, the Java programs with JDK 1.7.0_02. Objective-C programs were compiled with GNUstep under Windows 7. Additional details will be discussed later.

During testing the benchmark was always the only program running, with all the RAM and CPU at its disposal. Each output file had a unique name combining the technology with the number of books and the repetition index; for example library_ppf_50000_1.dat.

7.5 Specifics of Individual Technologies

The performance of a persistent system depends on the implementation of the data structures. We had two choices:

1. To enforce identical data structures for all the persistent systems we tested. [That could produce misleading results for the systems where special data structures are a part of the solution.]
2. To measure each persistent system with the data structures it normally uses. [This is a more realistic overall evaluation.]

We favour approach 2, and for those persistent systems that do not have any specific library of data structures we used the InCode library which, in our opinion, provides the best performance for this type of the problem.

The main issue was the implementation of the ManyToMany association. DOL and InCode libraries already have a generic ManyToMany class. In environments to which InCode has not yet been ported, we implemented ManyToMany as two containers, and tested various combinations as shown in Listing 7.1. Only the best implementation for each technology is shown in the final results.

Note the difference between implementations A and B. Under A there are no references between classes Book and Author in either direction. Under B, such references are used. As we began to test, we quickly found that the B-style is unusable with Java and with C# exporting to XML. We were getting stack overflow caused by the recursive implementation of Java serialization. This was discussed in Sects. 1.5.2, 1.5.3 and 1.5.4 including examples demonstrating the problem.

Listing 7.1 Tested implementations of ManyToMany. Names of containers are generic. For example HashMap<> used here is Dictionary<> in C#, HashMap in Java and std::map<> in C++

```
(A1)    class Library {
                HashMap<Book, Vector<Author>> booksToAuthors;
                    HashMap<Author, Vector<Book>> authorsToBooks;
        }
(A2)    class Library {
                HashMap<Book, LinkedList<Author>> booksToAuthors;
                    HashMap<Author, LinkedList<Book>> authorsToBooks;
        }
(A3)    class Library {
                HashMap<Book, HashSet<Author>> booksToAuthors;
                    HashMap<Author, HashSet<Book>> authorsToBooks;
        }
(B1)    class Book {
                Vector<Author> authors;
        }
        class Author {
            Vector<Book> books;
        }
(B2)    class Book {
                LinkedList<Author> authors;
        }
        class Author   {
        LinkedList<Book> books;
        }
(B3)    class Book {
                HashSet<Author> authors;
        }
        class Author {
                HashSet<Book> books;
        }
```

7.6   Benchmark Rules

1. When coding the benchmark, we asked each author or person responsible for the product (participant) to review our design.
2. Participants could submit their own implementations in source so that we could check it and run it on our testing hardware.
3. When several implementations using the same product[8] were available, the best results would be used in the final tables and graphs.
4. When a participant improved his/her system beyond the official version, the improved results would be accepted only if the participant revealed technical details of the improvement.
5. Participants would be continuously informed about the results of others, and about the improvements others decided to share.
6. The competition ran for several months, and there was no time limit. In order to prevent incorrect or inefficient use of the tested systems we encouraged their authors or their support groups to cooperate with us on coding the benchmark.

7.7   Testing Details

7.7.1   Java Serialization

In Java, the best performing implementation used pattern A3. The tables also show the results for the combination of Java serialization with the Java version of InCode library.

The serialization used objects ObjectInputStream and ObjectOutputStream from package java.io.

Many containers in the InCode library are intrusive and create long chains of references. As discussed in Sect. 1.4.2, Java serialization cannot handle this type of data and crashes with stack overflow. As a workaround we expanded InCode containers with a method that explicitly writes to disk all its objects, which is essentially the method whereby Java handles its own containers.

When running on Java virtual machine (JRE) we used parameter Xmx1000m, which allows Java to use 1 GB of RAM.

7.7.2   C# Serialization

The implementation of ManyToMany used pattern A3.

Tests show that C# binary serialization is very slow, especially the de-serialization where the time increases rapidly with the number of books. We have already mentioned in Sect. 1.4.3 that its prime use is in .NET Remoting. It is

---

[8] For example, using different class libraries or different data structures.

unsuitable for the type of data we have in the benchmark. The results are not included in the book but they are on the website.

Besides the binary serialization, we also tested the XML serialization which, to our surprise, proved to be much faster. We used two styles of formatting the disk data:

- Binary format, invoked by object BinaryFormatter in namespace System. Runtime.Serialization.Formatters.
- XML format, invoked by object DataContractSerializer in namespace System.Runtime.Serialization.

Serialization based on DataContractSerializer is not fully automatic. The user must add attribute DataContract() to every class, and attribute DataMember() to every member to be serialized. In order to minimize the disk space we exported all members with one-character names. For example, class Library was exported as XML element L.[9]

7.7.3 DOL (C++)

DOL has its own library of persistent data structures which includes ManyToMany. For the relation between Library and Book we used DoubleCollect, which is a doubly-linked intrusive linked list which protects data integrity.

The benchmark tested all three persistent modes supported by DOL:

- Binary serialization, each object storing its binary image—fast and space efficient.
- ASCII serialization member by member, in a portable format which also supports class changes. The disk file is larger than for the binary serialization.
- Memory blasting[10] which allocates objects from memory pages, which are then stored without looking at individual objects, and is super fast.

7.7.4 PPF (C++)

Originally PPF did not have its own library, but now there is a version of InCode which works with PPF. Note that the prime data storage in PPF is not memory but disk; the data is paged to memory on demand. Pointers are swizzled any time they are dereferenced. This naturally leads to a longer traversal time, but very short time for open and save. Each class has its own file, so there are as many output files as there are classes in the application.

---

[9] This is done by using attribute DataContract(Name="L").

[10] See Sect. 2.2.2; for more details (Soukup 1994, p. 379); how to use it http://www.codefarms.com/docs/dol/index.htm, Sect. 13.2, *Memory management.*

7.7.5 POST++ (C++)

POST++ library allocates data from one large block of memory, and it does not come with data structures required for this benchmark. It can store STL containers but under a rather restricting condition: when opening the disk file, the block must be stored at the same base address where it was before saving to disk. In other words, values of all pointers must remain the same. No swizzling required.

We did not find this approach very practical. For data using 100 MB of memory or more, the mapping to the same address often did not work, and we had to restart the program several times.

The author[11] of POST++ recommends use of an address which is not occupied by other DLLs. It sounds simple, but starting from Windows Vista, operating systems randomize locations of DLLs. This also would not work when transferring data between two different computers that use different DLLs.

ManyToMany was implemented using pattern B3.

7.7.6 SQLite (C++)

Code of this benchmark is quite different from all the other technologies. Instead of data structures such as List or Array, it uses the relational database, with the schema from Fig. 7.2. SQLite supports many features including transactions.[12]

SQLite was set to work as fast as possible by using:
PRAGMA journal_mode = MEMORY[13]
PRAGMA synchronous = OFF[14]

7.7.7 PSE Pro for C++ from ObjectStore (c)

Our benchmark would not be complete without this well established commercial product from the company which on their website claims "performance beyond reach", "world's highest performance" and "fast, instant access". PSE Pro is a single-process, small footprint object database management solution based on memory paging. PSE stands for Personal Storage Edition, and it is a light complement of the main ObjectStore product, which is a full-fledged OODBS, ObjectStore © Enterprise.

---

[11] Konstantin Knizhnik, Russia.

[12] http://www.sqlite.org/features.html

[13] http://www.sqlite.org/pragma.html#pragma_journal_mode

[14] http://www.sqlite.org/pragma.html#pragma_synchronous

Fig. 7.2 Benchmark schema
when using SQLite

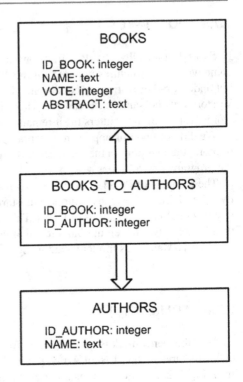

As with the other products, we aimed for the best results PSE Pro can produce, and we coded the benchmark jointly with the PSE Pro support group, which guaranteed that PSE Pro was used properly. The PSE Pro license does not allow users to publish results of any benchmarks, but we received a special permit from the company to include PSE Pro in this chapter. Do not confuse PSE Pro with the main product of ObjectStore company, the ObjectStore Enterprise (TM).

7.7.8   BOOST (C++)

We tested both the *binary* serialization and the *text* serialization. The *text* serialization is somewhat similar to DOL ASCII mode, but requires more manual input. The *binary* serialization isn't similar to binary DOL though. BOOST *binary* stores member by member using binary format, while DOL *binary* stores binary images of entire objects without breaking them into members.

As one could expect, binary BOOST was faster than text BOOST. Under "BOOST", graphs and tables in this book show the results of binary serialization. The book website shows results for both serialization styles.

We used BOOST persistence version 1.52.2, and ManyToMany was implemented using pattern A3.

7.7.9   QSP (Objective-C)

Objective-C and its NS library provide a built-in serialization called *Archiving*, which requires so much manual input that it does not fit our definition of automatic persistence—see Sect. 1.4.4.

In Sect. 2.5 we explained new, not previously published persistence based on memory pages, called Quasi-Single-Page persistence, and in Chap. 6 we explained how this new approach can be used for truly automatic persistence in Objective-C.

The QSP benchmark used a prototype[15] of this persistence combined with InCode data structures.

7.8   Results

From the book website www.codefarms.com/book, you can download complete results of the benchmark, with more details than it was possible to show in this chapter. You can view these results either with MS Excel 322 (files with type xls) or with OpenOffice, LibreOffice 325 (files with type ods). You can also download the benchmark implementation with various products and languages, including batch files which compile and run them.

Most of the results that follow are for one million books without abstracts. We do not show results for C# binary serialization because it was so slow that the results were completely out of the range for the other technologies.

Some tables show total times for several tasks, for example for 2(sort) + 6 (topVoted) + 7(traverse). The total is more meaningful when individual technologies use different data structures.

Observation: PPF, and POST++ page disk to memory on demand. PPF is using soft pointers, POST++ uses hard pointers. One would expect that, in traversal, PPF would be slower. Why is it significantly faster in Table 7.4? The only explanation we can think of is that the softness of the PPF smart pointer is only a few arithmetic operations, which may be less overhead than the paging and transaction management performed in P++.

---

[15] The source is available on the website, but be aware that, except for this benchmark, it has not been used on any serious project yet.

Table 7.4 Overall results for one million books without abstract

Technology/ test	Create (s)	Open (s)	Sort+ TopVoted+ traverse (s)	Save (s)	Delete (s)	FileSize 1 (MB)	FileSize 2 (MB)	Total mean time (s)
DOL (bin)	1.34	18.7	2.17	4.72	0.32	112.71	84.99	31.11
DOL (mb)	2.31	1.20	2.17	0.48	0.20	78.51	78.51	6.85
DOL (ASCII)	1.32	25.09	2.19	11.40	0.33	196.85	152.94	49.29
PPF[a]	3.07	1.30	2.73	0.53	0.54	88.07	88.07	8.67
P++(set)	3.26	3.67	0.65	3.37	0.58	320.26	320.26	14.89
J (set)	14.49	50.12	1.34	33.67	3.79	81.47	63.63	127.63
J (InCode)	11.24	29.51	3.48	22.01	0.32	43.84	34.41	82.05
C# XML (set)	11.92	30.73	5.80	15.19	0.58	644.15	496.23	76.13
SQLite	6.88	0.03	45.69	<0.01	159.48	131.72	131.72	212.08
PSE Pro	2.99	1.51	1.52	1.46	1.39	106.48	106.48	10.65
Boost (bin)[b]	5.63	6.45	0.39	8.86	0.79	84.46	65.48	28.35
ObjC (QSP)	2.66	2.08	1.99	6.98	1.10	133.72	103.39	21.16

Follow footnotes for the stories of products that were significantly improved during the benchmark competition—this table already shows the improved results

[a]The overall time for PPF was reduced 12.5 times by taking advantage of the cache on the modern hard drives. The information was shared with other participants. For full story and technical details, see Sect. 7.9.1

[b]The overall time for Boost was reduced 7.5 times by correcting a performance bug in Boost serialization. For full story and technical details, see Sect. 7.9.2

We also tested the benchmark on Mac[16] and on iPhone[17]. The results are for general interest only; we cannot compare with Tables 7.3 and 7.4 because of the differences in the hardware:

MacBookPro10.2 with Intel Core i5, 2.5 GHz.

APPLE SSD SM128E with 121.33 GB

Observation: In Tables 7.3 and 7.4, as expected, traversal time for technologies based on memory paging is longer. The result is that for intensive algorithms the overall time will become more favourable for technologies that, between open and save, keep the data in the same memory location.

Konstantin Knizhnik ran the benchmark with POST++ under Linux, using a computer with an SSD which is faster than normal HDD. His result for "Top voted

---

[16] For the full source see directory bk/chap7/benchApple.

[17] For more information, see Sect. 6.3.

Table 7.5 Overall results for one million books with abstracts

Technology/ test no	Create (s)	Open (s)	Sort+ TopVoted+ traverse (s)	Save (s)	Delete (s)	FileSize 1 (MB)	FileSize 2 (MB)	Total mean time (s)
DOL (bin)	2.17	29.83	2.21	6.38	0.39	380.44	285.78	46.00
DOL (mb)	2.71	3.74	2.49	2.72	0.23	343.01	343.01	14.38
DOL (ASCII)	2.14	38.50	2.21	16.29	0.39	489.48	368.22	72.73
PPF	5.88	4.12	2.86	1.90	0.63	359.29	359.29	16.22
P++(set)	4.40	7.59	6.10	6.90	1.08	679.18	679.18	32.98
J (set)	17.62	59.17	1.47	42.95	6.09	212.04	161.53	157.66
J (InCode)	17.74	35.66	3.62	29.89	0.25	301.59	227.76	105.57
C# XML (set)	13.39	32.57	5.99	15.48	0.60	762.83	585.25	80.30
SQLite	23.64	0.02	50.08	<0.01	182.85	452.42	452.42	256.59
PSE Pro	4.96	4.22	1.52	6.87	2.18	371.40	371.40	28.72
Boost (bin)	6.52	8.15	0.41	9.35	0.82	337.41	255.20	31.97
ObjC (QSP)	3.08	4.71	2.14	10.91	1.14	396.97	300.83	30.75

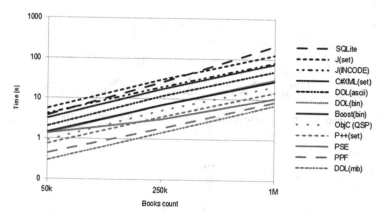

Fig. 7.3 Average total times, <u>without</u> abstracts. When there is no dark top, there was no file reduction

books" and 1 M books with abstracts was 5.6 sec compared to 27 sec in Table 7.5. This can be a rough indication of how much the performance can be improved by using different hardware and operating system (Figs. 7.3, 7.4, 7.5, 7.6, 7.7, 7.8 and 7.9; Tables 7.6 and 7.7).

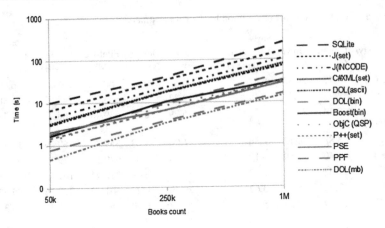

Fig. 7.4 Average total times, with abstracts

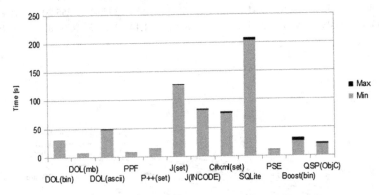

Fig. 7.5 Minimum and maximum total times, one million books, without abstracts

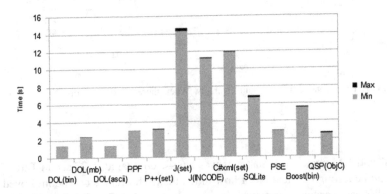

Fig. 7.6 Minimum and maximum times to create data, one million books without abstracts

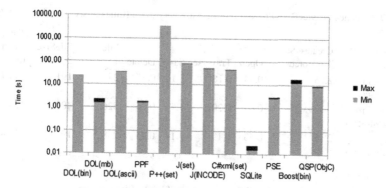

Fig. 7.7 Minimum and maximum times for <u>combined save+open,</u> one million books, without abstracts. Serializations move all the data between the memory and disk on open or save. In technologies based on memory paging, data moving blends with traversing the data

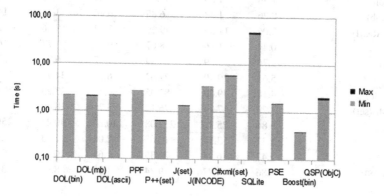

Fig. 7.8 Minimum and maximum of the total (<u>sort+topVoted+traversal</u>), for one million books without abstracts

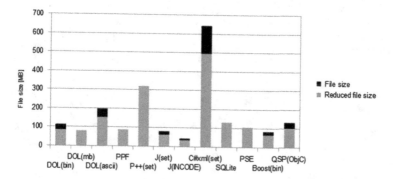

Fig. 7.9 Size of the disk file before and after one quarter of the data has been removed, for one million books, without abstracts. When there is no dark top, there was no file reduction

Table 7.6 Times on MacBookPro and iPhone 5 are very close (times in sec, file sizes in MB)

QSP with SSD 1M books	Create+ Sort+ TopVoted	Open	Traverse	Save	Delete	FileSize 1	FileSize 2	Total mean time
MacBookPro (no abstracts)	2.75	0.43	0.18	3.14	0.25	248	191	9.07
MacBookPro (with abstracts)	3.32	0.63	0.20	4.57	0.26	526	400	12.4
iPhone 5 (no abstracts)	2.75	0.43	0.19	3.14	0.25	248	191	9.34

Table 7.7 Average total times for different number of books (times in sec)

Technology/books count	No abstract			With abstract		
	50 k	250 k	1 M	50 k	250 k	1 M
DOL (bin)	1.36	7.00	31.11	1.83	9.57	46.00
DOL (mb)	0.26	1.38	6.85	0.46	3.37	14.38
DOL (ASCII)	2.06	11.59	49.29	3.02	18.06	72.73
PPF	0.44	1.86	8.67	0.78	3.77	16.21
P++(set)	0.76	3.59	14.89	1.47	6.72	32.98
J (set)	5.61	29.70	127.63	6.74	34.73	157.66
J (InCode)	4.18	19.40	82.05	4.51	23.23	105.57
C# XML(set)	3.23	17.24	76.13	3.25	18.40	80.30
SQLite	3.84	25.33	212.08	10.20	40.41	256.59
PSE Pro	1.37	3.14	10.65	2.06	6.73	28.72
Boost (bin)	1.47	6.97	28.35	1.65	10.64	31.97
ObjC (QSP)	0.86	4.77	19.74	1.30	8.62	30.75

7.9 Improvements

Benchmark rule No.4 was:

When a participant improves his/her system beyond the publically available version, the improved results will be accepted only if the participant reveals the technical details of the improvement.

This chapter provides full stories and the technical details that may improve the performance of your persistence system by the order of magnitude.

7.9.1 Warmup of the Hard Drive Cache (PPF)

This improvement is specific for problems where all the data must be in virtual memory for fast traversal such as, for example, in VLSI CAD systems. Our benchmark also falls into this category.

The IO cache on today's hard disks is 64 MB and it keeps increasing. With RAM well in the GB range, the internal buffers used by the disk drivers may be even larger.

If a persistent system is based on memory paging, and all the data can fit into this combined fast storage, any re-read of the data is lightning fast.[18] But does the order in which the pages warm up (or move to the cache) matter?

This question led Soukup to the following experiment. When running the PPF benchmark,[19] he did the opposite to running the CacheKiller: he traversed the entire disk data in a serial manner, without doing anything with it.

That did not take long, left the disk image in the cache, and made PPF amazingly fast. The total time including the initial warm-up was $12.5\times$ shorter comparing to the run after the CacheKiller, where PPF would slowly warm up by randomly accessing the pages.

Useful Trick No. 5.
Before the run which loads the data from disk to memory, read the entire disk file into a temporary buffer. This can be a short buffer which you keep overwriting until the end-of-file. This moves the entire disk file into the cache, and the subsequent load will be just as fast as if you ran it right after saving the data.

---

[18] This idea is based more on experimental evidence than on the exact knowledge of the HD construction or of the internal design of the disk drive.

[19] This idea is applicable only to persistent systems based on memory paging, because all the other systems read the disk sequentially anyway.

Table 7.8 Initial warm-up or preloading pages serially significantly improves the overall time

Technology	Create (s)	Open (s)	Sort+ TopVoted + Traverse (s)	Save (s)	Delete (s)	FileSize 1 (MB)	FileSize 2 (MB)	Total mean time (s)
PPF orig	7.27	0.01	4.79	1.05	296.4	351.90	351.90	310.30
PPF warm	5.91	3.67	9.46	0.80	3.85	358.18	359.18	24.18
PPF preload	5.88	4.12	3.66	1.90	0.63	359.29	359.29	16.22

Times for one million books with abstracts

This performance improvement is easy to explain. For mechanical hard drives, the repositioning of the head is the main source of the delay, and traversing the disk sequentially minimizes this delay. The performance improvement may not be as significant for solid state drives (SSD).

Soukup added this warm-up to PPF as one of the options, and we invited all the other participants to use the idea if they thought it would improve the performance of their system. Similar additions improved the performance of POST++ and PSE Pro by about the same rate.

The advantage of Useful Trick No. 5 is that it we can apply it to any persistent system without having any information about its internal implementation, size of pages, etc. PSE Pro support group proposed the following improvement, for situations where we have the information about the paging of the particular system.

> **Useful Trick No. 6.**
> Before the run which loads the data from disk to memory, access one pointer for each page, in the order in which the pages are stored on disk. This reads the disk sequentially in the cache and, at the same time, it loads all the pages directly into their memory locations.

This loads the pages to the cache sequentially just as the warmup does it, but it also loads all the pages to memory. Useful Trick No. 5 throws away what it reads, and only later do these pages move from the cache to memory. Table 7.8 shows the effect of using warmup or preloading for PPF.

7.9.2 Problem with Collecting Objects (Boost)

For testing Boost serialization[20] we chose the Boost implementation of the STL library. The first results (see Table 7.9) were a disaster with the worst total time of all tested systems, 30-times slower than DOL mb.

---

[20] We used Ver.1.53.

Table 7.9 Original poor results obtained with BOOST Ver.1.5.3, and improved results by Ramey and Machacek (times in sec, file sizes in MB)

1M books without abstracts	Create	Open	Sort+ TopVoted+ Traverse	Save	Delete	FileSize 1	FileSize 2	Total mean time
(1) Original Machacek	4.28	193.86	0.96	10.34	0.51	84.42	79.99	218.46
(2) New Ramey	9.21	13.7	14.0	8.24	1.30	70.4	53.9	51.3
(3) New Machacek	5.62	7.06	0.40	8.75	0.81	84.4	65.5	28.9

The author of Boost serialization, Robert Ramey, analyzed the problem and found the problem in the algorithm which collects all objects before saving to disk. In the case where STL containers were given pointers, it performed excessive searches.

Situations like that can happen easily, for example, when invoking:

```
class Book { ... };
std::set<Book*> books;
```

and we wondered why, with the world-wide use of Boost, nobody has complained about it.

Our discussion about the internal workings of the algorithm convinced us that even after this fix, the algorithm is still quite inefficient. It moves around objects instead of pointers, thus changing the object address; yet this address is used as a key in the std::set.

If this part of the Boost serialization is re-implemented with the algorithms from Sect. 2.1.6 (Useful Trick No. 4), it would be at least ten-times faster.

It took several weeks of hard negotiations and testing to find the best data structures for the benchmark. We clearly had different views of what would be a "modern and efficient" implementation. The benchmark requires two OneToMany associations and one ManyToMany associations that should be implemented to allow fast removal of objects, and also, in one case (books), sorting. STL does not provide such classes.[21]

Ramey's design (row No. 2 in Table 7.9) involved:

```
std::set<Book> books;
std::string title;
std::string abstract;
std::set<Author> authors;
std::string name;
std::multiset<BookToAuthor, order_dereferenced_pair<
    std::set<Book>::iterator,  std::set<Author>::iterator> authorToBooks;
std::multiset<AuthorToBook, order_dereferenced_pair<
    std::set<Author>::iterator,  std::set<Book>::iterator> bookToAuthors;
```

---

[21] InCode library has them but we did not want to go through the conversion of InCode to Boost. Also, we believe that persistent systems should be tested with their native libraries.

Machacek's design (row No. 3 in Table 7.9) involved:

```
std::set<Book*> books;
std::string title;
std::string abstract;
std::set<Author*> authors;
std::string name;
std::map<Book*, std::set<Author*>> booksToAuthors;
std::map<Author*, std::set<Book*>> authorsToBook;
```

Note that both designs use std::set, which is internally implemented as a binary tree. It is not as fast to remove an object from such a tree as it is from an intrusive linked list,[22] but it is reasonably fast. However, the set of books cannot be sorted by the vote, because the vote count is not unique. Both versions use a temporary array of Book* pointers, and sort this array with *qsort*.

Since our benchmark rules called for the best results to be published, Table 7.4 shows the results of Machacek's implementation. The improved version of Boost, Ver.1.5.4, will be released in June 2013.

Observation.
If you recently noticed a significant performance improvement of Boost serialization (version 1.5.4 or higher), Code Farms PPF library (version 3.5 or higher), or ObjectSTORE (c) PSE Pro, possibly running over ten-times faster on certain types of data, it is likely the result of the intense but friendly competition associated with this benchmark.

---

[22] Such as available from InCode or DOL.

Proposal to Add a Keyword to All OO Languages

8

Jiri Soukup and Martin Soukup

Abstract

Implementation of libraries that can handle bi-directional associations today requires a simple code generator. This code generator could be eliminated if the programming languages supported a new keyword described in this proposal.

Keywords

Object-oriented languages • Syntax • Features • Aspects • Expansion • Proposal

When building library of generic data structures, existing languages allow us to build only uni-directional association—essentially the containers which we have in our standard libraries such as STL or Java Collections. These containers are only a small part of what we need in practice. Every day we need bi-directional association such as Aggregates, ManyToMany associations, various graphs and finite state machines, and we have to custom code them any time we need them.

These bi-directional associations are missing in our standard libraries because they require insertion of members, usually references, to two or more classes, and the existing languages do not have a mechanism for this coordinated insertion and for controlling their access which should be restricted to the dataless class which represents (and manipulates) the data structure.

J. Soukup (✉)
Code Farms Inc., Richmond, ON, Canada
e-mail: jiri@codefarms.com

M. Soukup
Irdeto Canada corp., Ottawa, Canada
e-mail: the.martin.soukup@gmail.com

J. Soukup and P. Macháček, *Serialization and Persistent Objects*,
DOI 10.1007/978-3-642-39323-5_8, © Springer-Verlag Berlin Heidelberg 2014

Being able to store all data structures, including the multi-directional ones, in a library has a major positive effect on code clarity, because it moves all reference members from the application classes to the library, where they can be well tested and guarded. It also improves software reliability and quality. Having all pointers in the library also simplifies the implementation of persistent objects. If all associations are implemented as library classes, conversion back-and-forth between the UML diagram and the code becomes trivial, no special tools are required.

For all these reasons, we propose an addition of two keywords (and of two simple concepts) to the existing object-oriented languages. With their help, we will get all these benefits plus, as a bonus, static aspects will become a part of the language. For two decades, libraries based on this idea have been used in a variety of application with great success.

8.1   The New Keyword

Within the context of class R, keyword *insert* will transparently add a specified member to a given class S. Using Java syntax:

```
class R {
        insert S memberType1 memberName1;
        insert S memberType2 memberName2;
            ...
    }
```

Only R will have access to these members, and it will access them through another keyword *myown*[1]:

```
class R {
        public void xyz(S s){
            s.myown.memberName1=null;
        }
    }
```

The C++ syntax would be

```
public void xyz(S *s){
        s->myown.memberName1=NULL;
    }
```

---

[1] This is only a temporary arrangement; we will show later that we really do not need this keyword.

Keyword *myown* would not trigger any processing. It would only instruct the compiler to create an internal name parameterized by the association and its types. For example, if we have Aggregate

```
class Aggregate<P,C> {
    insert P C head;
    insert C P parent;
    insert C C next;
    ...
    C getNext(C c){return c.myown.next;}
}
```

then invocation

```
Aggregate<Library,Book>  books = new
Aggregate<Library,Book>();
```

may trigger the insertion of the following members into class Book:

```
Library Aggregate_Library_Book_head;
Book Agregate_Library_Book_next;
```

and `myown.next` in function `getNext()` is interpreted as

```
Agregate_Library_Book_next
```

Keyword *myown* is a shortcut to make this easy to implement in the compiler. A smart compiler may automatically insert the expanded identification for both the member and its references within the context of the class with the *insert*, and then only one keyword is required.

8.2 Generic Design Patterns

Structural design patterns are essentially data structures which, in addition to traditional references and arrays, also use inheritance. Examples of patterns Composite or Flywheel coded in this style are shown in Soukup (1995). His implementation with C++ templates automatically inserts references and arrays, but expects that the required inheritance has been arranged by the user.

In order to make this fully automatic and transparent, it would make sense to allow two styles of insertion:

```
insert S memberType memberName;
insert S baseType;
```

With this arrangement, for example, pattern Composite may look like this:

```
class Composite<P,C> {
       insert P C; // implies P inherits from C
       insert P C head;
       insert C P parent;
       insert C C next;
       ...
}
```

8.3　Example of Using the New Features for Generic Data Structures

Let's code a reusable Aggregate class in the style that AspectJ does it. For a smart compiler, simply remove *myown* throughout the code.[2]

```
class Aggregate<Parent,Child,Dummy> {

insert Parent Child head;
insert Child Child next;
insert Child Parent parent;

       // add c in a NULL-ending list
       public static void add(Parent p, Child c) {
              if(p.myown.head) {
                     c.myown.next=p.myown.head;
              }
              else c.myown.next=NULL;
              c.myown.parent=p;
              p.myown.head=c;
       }
       ...
}
```

Depending on the language and whether the static/non-static representation of the data structure is used, using the same data structure with the same participating classes more then once could lead to a conflict. For example, in Java this works fine, because in this case instance based representations must be used.[3]

C++ has a special provision for such situations: templates may have an integer parameter. If you don't use it, it is assumed to be 0:

```
typedef Aggregate<Department,Employee> research;
typedef Aggregate<Department,Employee,1> admin;
typedef Aggregate<Department,Employee,2> manufact;
```

---

[2] Aggregate is another name for OneToMany bi-directional association, one of the most frequently occurring relations. This example shows its implementation based on intrusive linked lists.

[3] With Aggregate, such a situation is hard to imagine; the next three lines would not be the most efficient model.

Using Aggregate in Java:

```
class Department {...} // as if not using any associations
class Employee {...} // as if not using any associations

// declaration of data structures
Aggregate<Company,Department> departments=new Aggregate<Company,Department>();
Aggregate<Department,Employee> employees=new Aggregate<Department,Employee>();
OneToOne<Department,Employee> boss=newOneToOne<Department,Employee> ();

// using the data structures
Department d=new Department();
Employee e1=new Employee();
Employee e2=new Employee();
    ...
employees.add(d,e);
employees.add(d,e2);
boss.add(d,e1);
```

Using Aggregate in C++:

```
public class Department {...}; // as if not using any associations
public class Employee {...} // as if not using any associations

// declaration of data structures
typedef Aggregate<Company,Department,Dummy> departments;
typedef Aggregate<Department,Employee,Dummy> employees;
typedef OneToOne<Department,Employee,Dummy> boss;

// using the data structures
Department *d; Employee *e1,*e2;
    ...
employees::add(d,e1);
employees::add(d,e2);
boss::add(d,e1);
```

8.4 Associations and Existing Class Libraries

We can add such reusable data structures to the existing libraries such as C++ Standard Template Library and Java or .NET Collections without any modifications to the existing classes. Existing classes (uni-directional associations) will be a special case of the new, multi-directional implementation. Iterators for the new associations can be coded in the style already used for the collections—for examples look at PTL (1997) or InCode (2004).

It will be easy and straightforward to derive new complex data structures from the existing simple ones. For example, the bi-directional many-to-many association can be theoretically derived from two Aggregates.[4]

---

[4] This is all Java code; in C++, we can use Java classes multiple inheritance.

```
public class ManyToMany<Source,Link,Target>
    {
        Aggregate<Source,Link> srcRel =
                            new Aggregate<Source,Link>();
        Aggregate<Target,Link> tarRel =
                            new Aggregate<Target,Link>();

        // add a link between the given source and target
        public void add(Source src,Link lnk,Target tar) {
            srcRel.addHead(src,lnk);
            tarRel.addHead(tar,lnk);
        }
        ...
    }
```

Using ManyToMany in an application:

```
// application classes as if not using data structures
static class Student {...}
static class Course {...}
static class Enrolled (
    int mark;
}
// declaration of the data structure(s)
ManyToMany<Student,Enrolled,Course> enrollments =
                new ManyToMany<Student,Enrolled,Course>();
// using the data structure
Student s = new Student();
Enrolled e = new Enrolled();
Course c = new Course();
enrollments.add(s,e,c);
```

The Future

9

Abstract

We believe that the ideas described in this book will lead to a new paradigm of how to design software. In the same way as structured programming eliminated goto statements and removed spaghetti logic, this new paradigm eliminates explicit references (or pointers) from application classes and removes spaghetti data organization. The architecture is controlled by a short block of code—the schema, and the UML class diagram is automatically generated with each compilation as a visual aid for the programmer. All this has been demonstrated in many projects over the past 2 decades, but still requires more work in some areas.

Keywords

Algorithm • Class libraries • Future • Goto • OO languages • Pointerless programming • Programming paradigm • Structured programming • UML. QSP

> This chapter discusses how the ideas and concepts presented in this book may lead to a completely new way of designing software, how they may improve existing languages and products, and what additional work is needed to bring products such as QSP or InCode to a massive everyday use.

9.1 New Programming Paradigm

It is not academics or IT researchers, but programmers who work on real-life projects who are conservative in accepting new ideas. Programming differently means thinking differently, as if the problems they have to handle are not complex and challenging enough! And how many times did they get their fingers burnt by errors in new software or by an interface that makes them swear any time they use it.

J. Soukup and P. Macháček, *Serialization and Persistent Objects*,
DOI 10.1007/978-3-642-39323-5_9, © Springer-Verlag Berlin Heidelberg 2014

On the other hand, progress cannot be stopped. If there is a way to design software several times faster—doesn't matter whether $3\times$ or $10\times$, without any special evaluation clearly much faster while producing programs with fewer errors that are easier to maintain, then it is only a matter of time before we will all be programming in this new style and wondering how we could have programmed so inefficiently for such a long time.

The reason for the general acceptance will be twofold: business owners and managers will grasp it because of the indisputable increase in productivity, and programmers will like it because it will make their work less stressful and more fun.

Based on 2 decades of programming in this new paradigm, we don't just believe—we know that improvements of this magnitude are now at our disposal.

9.1.1 Pointerless Programming

We use this term for the new style of representing data structures as described in Chap. 3, with separation of the control (interface) from the pointers and other data stored in the participating classes. The control classes representing the data structures (associations) have the same visibility as application classes.

Pointerless programming is sorely needed for several reasons:
- It will finally get us out of the corner into which we painted ourselves with the existing container libraries. We need generic libraries with bi-directional associations, not just uni-directional ones.
- It will allow us to expand our libraries with a multitude of pointer-based data structures, which were developed over the past 2 decades and which are mostly unused today.
- In general, we need libraries capable of handling intrusive data structure—truly intrusive ones, not what Boost library calls "intrusive".
- Libraries implemented in this style can remove all explicit pointer members from the application classes, thus preventing many hard-to-find pointer errors.

The term *pointerless* comes <u>from the ban on explicit pointer members in application classes.</u> As shown in Chap. 3, we do allow pointer members, but they must not be loose, explicit pointers. All pointer members must be transparent and controlled as a part of some data structure.

Conceptually, pointerless programming is analogous to structured programming which eliminates *goto* statements, which used to form hard-to-manage networks in program logic. Today, lose pointers can form hard-to-manage networks of objects.

9.1.2 Different Way of Using UML Class Diagram

The reasons for using UML class diagrams are:
- It is a visual help in both the architecture design and in the program maintenance.
- It is the prime input for the code generator which creates the initial code skeleton.
- It is the key communication tool between the architect and the programmer.

Our experience is that the block of *Association* statements (or file *ds.def* in the InCode library) is a better record of the architecture than any diagram could be. These statements are compact and concise, and, because they are an integral part of the code, they cannot be outdated. It is easier to modify them with a text editor than to create, remove and move boxes and connection lines on the screen. The diagram can be generated automatically—always up to date and visually pleasing even after a major modification of the architecture.

The change of paradigm involves a major chane in the role for the UML class diagram. The new approach could be called "*UML inside out*". Instead of the diagram controlling the code, we have code (file ds.def with the Association statements) controlling the diagram.

Note that the programmer cannot misinterpret the architecture. The architect provides ds.def and, if the programmer wants/needs to change it, the architect has to approve the change.

Wait a minute, you may say; isn't architect supposed to design at a higher level, thinking in Associations and not in Hash tables or Collections? In many situations the choice of implementation is part of the architecture; for a more general design, libraries like InCode provide a default for each Association type, usually its simplest, basic implementation.

9.1.3 Automatic Persistence and Databases

There are many small and medium sized projects where persistent objects are a better solution than using a database. The code is simpler and easier to maintain, and the program is more efficient both in speed and size.

There are also important practical problems, for example CAD systems for design of silicon chips, where, in spite of huge data size, using a database is not an option because of the speed requirements.

Then there are problems where multiuser access and data security are the key issues, for example banking systems or online flight reservation, and a true database is the only solution.

Traditionally, a light database such as SQLite was easier to use than clumsy serializations offered by various languages including Boost. With the automatic persistence available now, the situation is reversed, and the programming community should be educated about it.

With 64-bit computer architectures available today, persistent objects can efficiently handle huge data frameworks, and will likely replace traditional databases in many applications.

9.2   What Can Be Improved

There are several areas in which the existing software can be improved:

Persistent C++: It would be easy to add paged-based persistence (such as QSP) to the C++ language. It could be completely transparent and it would give C++ a tremendous edge compared to other OO languages.

C++ class info: It would greatly simplify the implementation of persistent objects if the C++ compiler produced a file with the list of classes and their pointers.[1] That would allow one to add a completely transparent persistent layer, and products like ObjectStore PSE would not need a code generator, or their generator would be much simpler.

Standard libraries: The difficulties with converting existing libraries is the main hindrance to the mass use of automatic persistence. In all languages, no library should be accepted as a standard unless it provided a general support for general persistence, not just for their own serialization.

Boost serialization would be significantly faster in saving data to disk, if the algorithm for collecting objects applied Useful Trick No. 4.

Serializations in Java, C#, and Objective-C (archiving) would remove their limitations if the algorithm for collecting all objects used a ring stack instead of the recursive function.

Proposal to add keyword to OO languages: After the book is published,[2] we plan to submit Chap. 8 to languages committees and compiler designers for C++, Java, and C#.

9.3   Unfinished Business

If you are looking for interesting projects in persistence, consider these:

QSP needs more extensive testing.

QSP automatic pointer detection should be expanded to handle pointers embedded in a struct.

Existing QSP automatic pointer detection assumes that all classes have several methods including *start* and *getMask*. Using recursive [Persist start], this assumption can be relaxed to only classes with allocated instances, and that will help to detect pointers of library classes derived from other library classes.

QSP internal pages: If QSP page could not allocate because of its size, allocate several smaller pages instead.

InCode version for Objective-C needs to convert remaining classes.

---

[1] This would be a primitive, partial reflection, but the compiler already has this information available.

[2] We attempted to contact some of these places already, but for example Microsoft refused to discuss the matter for legal reasons unless it has been published.

PTL with PPF: Experiment with making Pattern Template Library persistent with PPF. The modifications should be similar to InCode with PPF.

Layout: This program needs more testing.

References

Biliris A, Dar S, Gehani NH (1993) Making C++ object persistent: the hidden pointers. Software Pract Exp 23(12):1285–1303

BOOST library serialization (2013) http://www.boost.org/doc/libs/1_52_0/libs/serialization/doc/index.html. Accessed 19 Apr 2013

Borland C++ Version 4.5, Library Reference 1994. Borland, Scotts Vallley

Core Data Framework (2013) http://en.wikipedia.org/wiki/Core_Data. Accessed 29 Apr 2013

Cornell G, Horstmann C (1997) Core Java, 2nd edn. Sun Microsystems, Mountain View, CA

Cornell G, Horstmann C (2011) Core Java I and II. Prentice Hall, Upper Saddle River, NJ (Eight Edition)

Data Object Library (2013) http://www.codefarms.com/dol. Accessed 19 Apr 2013

Dijkstra EW (1976) Discipline of programming. Prentice Hall, Upper Saddle River, NJ

Forward A, Badreddin O, Lethbridge C, Solano J (2011) Model-driven rapid prototyping with Umple. http://obahy.files.wordpress.com/2012/11/softwarepractexpjournal-proto-fromrsp.pdf. Accessed 19 Apr 2013

Gal E, Toledo S (2005) Mapping structures for flash memories: techniques and open problems. In: Proc. of IEEE Int.Conf. on Software (SwSTE'05)

Goldberg A, Robson D (1989) Smalltalk-80, The Language. Addison-Wesley, Reading, MA

Haradhvala SJ, Weinreb DL (1991) Method and apparatus for virtual memory mapping and transaction management in an object-oriented database system. US Patent No: 5,426,747, 22 Mar 1991

Horstmann C (1993) /DOS/C++. C++ Rep 5(5):54–59

Horstmann C, Cornell G (2012) Core Java I and II. Prentice Hall Upper Saddle River, NJ (Ninth Edition) (The section on Java persistence differs significantly in different editions.)

InCode Library (2004) http://www.codefarms.com/incode. Accessed 19 Apr 2013

Javin P (2011) How garbage collection works in Java. http://javarevisited.blogspot.com/2011/04/garbage-collection-in-java.html. Accessed 1 May 2013

Kernighan BW, Ritchie DM (1978) The C programming language. Prentice Hall, Englewood Cliffs, NJ

Knizhnik K (1999) Persistent object storage for C++. www.garret.ru/post_readme.ps.gz. Accessed 11 Dec 2013

Ku A (2011) Investigation: is your SSD more reliable than a hard drive? http://www.tomshardware.com/reviews/ssd-reliability-failure-rate,2923.html. Accessed 19 Apr 2013

Lamb C, Landis G, Orenstein J, Weinreb D (1991) The ObjectStore database system. ComACM 34(10):50–63

Laddad R (2003) Aspect J in action. Manning, Greenwich, CT

Mariott A, Rousseau B (2003) ObjectStore and STL. http://odbms.org/download/026.01%20Marriott%20ObjectStore%20and%20STL%20June%202006.PDF. Accessed 19 Apr 2013

Nelson S, Pearce DJ, Noble J (2007) First-class relationships in object oriented programs. University of Auckland Software Engineering Workshop (SIENZ) 2007

Osterby K (2000) Design of a class library for association relationships. http://lcsd.cs.tamu.edu/2007/final/7/7_Paper.pdf. Accessed 19 Apr 2013

Pattern Template Library (1006) (2013) http://www.codefarms.com/ptl. Accessed 19 Apr 2013

Pearce DJ, Noble J (2006) Relationship aspects. AOSD 06 conference, Bonn, Germany, 20–24 March, 2006

Persistent Pointer Factory (1997) http://www.codefarms.com/ppf. Accessed 19 Apr 2013

Riley D (2012) Write endurance. http://www.tomshardware.com/reviews/ssd-910-benchmark-performance,3226-6.html. Accessed 19 Apr 2013

Saxena M, Shah M, Swift MM, Merchant A (2012) Hathi: durable transactions for memory using flash. In: Proc. of Int. workshop on data management on New Hardware (DaMoN 2012), Scottsdale AZ, 21 May 2012

Shasha N, Toledo S (2007) Storing a persistent transactional object heap on flash memory. In: Proc. of IEEE Int. Conf. on Software (SwSTE'07)

Singhal V, Kakkad SV, Wilson PR (1992) Texas: an efficient portable persistent portable store. In: Proceedings of the 5th international workshop on persistent object system, San Miniato, Italy. Springer

Soukup J (1989) An easy way to program algorithms. Paper presented at southeastern int. conf. on combinatorics, graphs theory, and computing, Boca Raton, Florida, Feb 1989

Soukup J (1992a) Selecting a C++ library. C++ Rep 4(1):1–6

Soukup J (1992b) Memory resident databases. C++ Rep 4(2):11–15

Soukup J (1992) The secret of efficient software design—internal data organization. Paper presented at IEEE electro-internat conf, Boston, May 1992

Soukup J (1992d) Persistent data, part 1. C++ J 2(2):60–65

Soukup J (1992e) Beyond templates, part I. C++ Rep 4(4):27–31

Soukup J (1992f) Beyond templates, part II. C++ Rep 4(5):29–35

Soukup J (1994) Taming C++, pattern classes and persistence for large projects. Addison-Wesley, Reading, MA (Japanese translation ISBN 4-8101-8088-3)

Soukup J (1995) Implementing patterns. In: Coplien JO, Schmidt DC (eds) Pattern languages of program design. Addison-Wesley, Reading, MA, p 395–415

Soukup J (1996) Quality patterns. C++ Rep 8(9):26–29

Soukup J (1997) Implementing patterns. C++ Rep 9(4):49–50

Soukup J (1998a) Intrusive data structures, part I. C++ Rep 10(5):22–27

Soukup J (1998b) Intrusive data structures, part II. C++ Rep 10(7):5–7

Soukup J (1998c) Intrusive data structures, part III. C++ Rep 10(9):28–32

Soukup J (1999) Data structures as objects. DrDobb's J 24(10):21–30

Soukup J (2007) Implementing reusable associations/relationships, 2007 OOPSLA workshop (organized by)

Soukup M, Soukup J (2007a) Reusable associations. DrDobb's J 32(11):51–56

Soukup M, Soukup J (2007b) The inevitable cycle: graphical tools and programming paradigms. IEEE Comput 40(8):24–30

Spinczyk O, Lohmann D (2007) The design and implementation of AspectC++. Knowl Based Syst Spec Issue Tech Prod Intell Secur Softw 20(7):636–651

Stevens A (1993) Object-oriented database management systems. DrDobbs's J 18(4):7–15

Stroustrup B (1991) The C++ programming language. Addison-Wesley, Reading

Urban J, Vaněk J, Soukup J, Štys D (2009) Expertomica metabolite profiling: getting more information from LC-MS using the stochastic systems approach. Bioinformatics 25 (20):2764–2767. doi:10.1093/bioinformatics/b

Urban J, Vaněk J, Štys D (2012) Systems theory in liquid chromatography. In: Mass spectrometry, LAMBERT Academic Publishing, ISBN-13: 978-3-659-29816-5

UMPLE User Manual (2012) http://cruise.eecs.uottawa.ca/umple/GettingStarted.html. Accessed 19 Apr 2013

Vadaparty K (1997) Memory-resident object databases <DOL> JOOP 10(7):63–67

Vadaparty K (1998a) A closer look at DOL. JOOP 10(8):65–68

Vadaparty L (1998b) Relationships and entry points in DOL. JOOP 11(2):6–9

Weinreb D (2007) Dan Weinreb's blog. http://danweinreb.org/blog/category/objectstore. Accessed 19 Apr 2013

White SJ, DeWitt DJ (1995) QuickStore: A high performance mapped object store. VLDB J 4 (4):629–673

Wilson PR (1990) Pointer swizzling at page fault time: efficiently supporting huge address spaces on standard hardware. Tech. Rep. UIC-EECS-90-6, University of Illinois

Zikari RV (2010) TechView product report: objectStore. http://odbms.org/download%5CTechView%20Progress10.pdf. Accessed 19 Apr 2013

Zino DAD (2012) Apple iOS 4 security evaluation. http://media.blackhat.com/bh-us-11/DaiZovi/BH_US_11_DaiZovi_iOS_Security_WP.pdf. Accessed 19 Apr 2013

Index

J. Soukup and P. Macháček, *Serialization and Persistent Objects*,
DOI 10.1007/978-3-642-39323-5, © Springer-Verlag Berlin Heidelberg 2014

Printed in the United States
By Bookmasters